Up in the Treehouse

By:

Joseph Hirsch

Joehirs123@aol.com

www.joeyhirsch.com

Dedication:

This book is dedicated to Jodie Pierce for all her help in getting this book to see daylight!

"And now you are and I am and we're a mystery which will never happen again."

-e.e. Cummings

"The Leprechaun tells me to burn things."

-Ralph Wiggum

Freeport Ohio, 1988

CHAPTER ONE

Charlie Milner and Johnny Cotter met in the fall of that year, shortly after classes started at Freeport Kindergarten. The entire suburban township was a blooming potpourri of pumpkin orange and banana yellow leaves that were shed and now covered the wet ground. The only remaining green was the foliage of the pignut hickories around the schoolhouse, still shielded in a growth of leaves green as malachite and leathery as batwings.

Francine Cotter parked her beige Chrysler minivan in the school's rain soaked parking lot, got out of the car, and opened the back door for her son. He clutched the front seat headrest and winced, afraid of the new school and new people. He wasn't crying yet. She thought there was a good chance to avoid a scene altogether, as long as she didn't try to wrest the blue Faker doll from his right hand. The true test would come after she led him to the classroom and was ready to leave for the day.

"You ready, honey?"

He shook his head but let go of the headrest without her having to pry his fingers loose. Johnny placed his small hand in his mother's soft palm. "Here," she said, and handed him the clear plastic bag filled with the things Ms. Seever instructed her to bring for him.

"If you get wet while you play, there's a change of clothes in there, okay?"

"Yeah …" His voice was faint. He looked at the gray macadam beneath his feet as he walked forward with his mother. The school was only a single brick story topped by a tarpaper roof, but it frightened him all the same. It struck him at the moment as more foreboding than Castle Grayskull. Johnny looked up at his mother, and she down at him. His hair was golden brown, his features warm and even. He was too young to be considered handsome, but the blueprint was there. He had the best features of both mother and father with none of their flaws.

"Hello!"

One of the two glass doors in the front of the building opened. Ms. Seever stood there. Johnny looked up. Those two syllables from her evaporated all of his fear. Her voice was soothing, hoarse, and cracked. She sounded like one of the women whose voices came out of the speakers at home when his mom played old records. She reminded him of Joni Mitchell or Mama Cass, or maybe Janis Joplin.

Francine Cotter's apprehension melted, and she extended her hand. Both women immediately pegged each other as unreconstructed hippies, refugees biding their time through the Me Decade.

"What do you have in the bag?" Ms. Seever asked, and again, both mother and son admired that voice. It was calming, somehow therapeutic, but without the patronizing lilt so common in such voices.

"Stuff you told me to bring." Johnny hefted the sack like a trick-or-treater.

She held the door open for them. "Well, I'm glad you brought it because when it gets wet, you'll need that change of clothes. You're going to want that sleeping mat when you get tired."

"I'm a little tired right now."

"Oh?" Both women laughed, and the teacher patted him on the head. She kept her palm on the mushroom shape of his bowl cut, steering him toward the classroom. "What do you have in your hand? He-Man?"

Johnny held the blue plastic action figure aloft. "He's not He-Man. He's Faker. He tricks He-Man's friend into thinking he's He-Man, so he can do bad stuff for Skeletor."

Francine Cotter lowered her voice so only the teacher could hear it. "Pretty sure being covered in a coat of blue paint and having a computer lodged in your stomach is a dead giveaway." Ms. Seever smiled and she continued. "Who's writing these cartoons? Other kids?"

He sensed they were speaking ill of his toy and lowered it from their view. The teacher opened the door to the classroom where twenty or so children busied themselves. A teacher's assistant, a frumpy elderly woman, moved from station to station, checking on their progress.

The room smelled of leaking Elmer's glue tubes. There was also the scent of woodchips moldering in the base of the class pet's cage, accompanied by the smells of dried macaroni and

Play-Doh. Beneath that was the faint musk of a bathroom accident whose traces were not totally expunged, despite the best efforts of all involved.

"Class!" There was authority in her voice without any threat. They all turned immediately, wide-eyed, first to her. Then they looked at the new little boy standing there with his mother, his action figure, and his bag of stuff.

"This is …well …" She leaned down to him. "Do you want to introduce yourself?"

Fear blossomed in his chest, like a butterfly busily flitting around in his ribcage. He shook his head and faintly said "No" in one cracked syllable that sapped all of his remaining strength. It was raining outside. Raindrops landed in solid plops on the windows and then slid slowly down the glass panes.

Ms. Seever stood back up, respecting his wishes. "Class, this is Johnny Cotter. Does the class comforter want to show him around?" She leaned over to Francine Cotter, said, "We all have our various chores and jobs that we rotate in and out of."

Johnny's mom nodded and the teacher continued. "We have a meteorologist, and a pet caretaker, and a news recorder." She pointed toward a small black girl in a plaid jumper who wore her hair in thick braids that tapered in conch shells. The girl was pouring water from a small, green plastic bucket onto a plant. The girl looked over at them and said, "I'm the botulist."

"Botanist."

"Mrs. Seever?"

She looked down, and Johnny looked at the boy standing in front of him. They were roughly the same height, though they had little else in common. There was something gnomish, not entirely foursquare about the boy's features. He looked as if he narrowly escaped the vagaries of some hereditary birth defect. His complexion was flushed red, as if he was permanently cold. He smiled at Johnny. It was normal for children to be missing a tooth here, and slowly acquiring another one there, but there was something oddly vampire-like about the boy's grin. There was something menacing about the teeth.

Johnny immediately took a liking to him though, despite this. "*Ms.* Seever," the teacher said, her tone a little harsher than it was up to this point.

"Ms. Seever," he said.

"Yes?"

"Can I show him around?"

"Are you the class comforter today?"

He shook his head, and held up the plastic toy in his right hand. "No, but I got the Bashasaurus Masters of the Universe vehicle." The words came out in one long torrent. It sounded to the adults like something from an ad he memorized in order to pester his parents into buying the toy for him.

Both of the adults laughed. Mrs. Cotter shook her head. "You know, Bruce and I did our best not to raise Johnny to be materialistic. In this day and age, I guess we should just face that we're fighting a losing battle."

Ms. Seever grinned sympathetically. Lightning flashed beyond the rain streaked window and brought an appreciative roar of fear mixed with excitement from the children. "Recess is inside today!" Someone shouted.

"You don't like consumer goods?" The teacher asked. "That's Commie talk!" The women laughed. The boys were confused by the exchange, until Charlie resumed brandishing his toy. He demonstrated the levered action of the stone mechanism for Johnny. He slammed the plastic boulder home several times, crushing thin air with the giant rock.

"I've got Bashasaurus and he's got Faker, so we should be together."

"Okay." Ms. Seever nodded. "Make sure to show him the school bus first." The two boys walked off in the direction of a sink, scaled to a child's height, its faucet operated by a foot treadle.

"This is the school bus." The boy pointed to a cheese yellow cardboard bus. Each of the oversized windows in the long vehicle was filled with the form of a little paper doll with a child's name written on it, or of a photograph of a child. Ms. Seever's photo was at the head of the bus, her eyes reddish from poor ambient light in the flash.

"You didn't bring a picture of you, did you?" The boy looked down at the bag in Johnny's hands. Johnny shook his head. "Then you'll have to use one of the kids for now." The boy walked over to a giant particleboard apple with a cartoonish worm peeking out from a rotted spot. The worm sported bifocals and urged onlookers to, "Read a book!"

The apple was covered in little male and female dolls. They were crude and featureless except for short or long black hair and pants or skirts to delineate sex. They were stuck with Velcro patches to the outer surface of the apple. "Some kids only use these little dolls. They never bring in a picture, so if you don't want to, you don't have to."

The boy took the little doll over to a crafts table where several children were writing the letters of the alphabet with scented markers onto the pages of workbooks. "What's your name?"

"Johnny."

"I'm Charlie."

"Okay."

Charlie wrote onto a hexagon-shaped piece of paper. Then he affixed the white sheet to the torso of the little paper doll. Johnny leaned in to inspect his new friend's handiwork.

"You spelled my name right."

"Yeah, I'm pretty good at reading. My brother taught me."

They both walked back over to the bus. "Do you have any brothers or sisters?" Charlie asked.

Johnny shook his head. Charlie reached up toward the bus, but then paused a moment later. He inspected the still empty windows on the long cheese. Something was still not to his liking. "Hold this." He handed Johnny the Bashasaurus. Its plastic weight felt substantial in his hands. He wondered why Charlie trusted him with the toy. Johnny tried not to be jealous with his own toys. He tried to share when he could, but some toys were too important to risk in the hands of others. He decided that either Charlie was really nice, or maybe he owned the toy so long he didn't care about it that much anymore.

The seats of the Bashasaurus were empty. Something about that wasn't right to Johnny. It certainly was a greater sacrilege than whatever petty business Charlie was bothering himself with now with that big bus stretching across the greasy cinderblock wall like a giant sun yellow caterpillar.

Johnny stuffed Faker into the driver's seat of Bashasaurus, and wondered for a moment if he was doing something contra to He-Man lore. Had Faker ever actually entered the good guys' lair on the show? Had he ever managed to commandeer their favorite, prized vehicle? Impossible!

"There," Charlie said, bringing his new friend out of his thoughts. He stood back from his handiwork. Johnny looked up. He saw his newly christened, faceless male doll in a seat on the bus directly behind a doll whose face was a photo taken of Charlie while at Chuck E. Cheese for his birthday. "How's that?" Charlie asked.

"Good."

"Come on," Charlie said. He walked Johnny in the direction of a fogged terrarium. "I got one brother and sister. It's okay, but sometimes my brother shows me horror movies and my mom gets mad." Charlie stopped at the glass tank, and pointed at a pair of slowly slithering snails that were visible through the wet condensation. He tapped the side of the glass tank. He glanced over his shoulder, searching for the teacher. Johnny briefly wondered if he wasn't supposed to tap the glass.

"Do you guys have any bigger animals? Like fury ones?" Johnny tried to hide the disappointment in his voice.

"We did," Charlie said. "Jennifer has allergies, though, and she was a crybaby who cried until Ms. Seever gave away Dexter the Hamster."

"Oh, man. That stinks."

"Yeah." Charlie tapped the glass tank one last time. Then he walked over to a glass jar resting next to an easel covered in a thick, viscous coat of marine paint. Opalescent marbles floated in the bottom of the jar.

"Everybody's got a job, like Mrs. Seever says."

Johnny remembered how she corrected Charlie for calling her "Mrs." He was tempted to remind his new friend, but then thought better of it. Friends didn't take the teacher's side against each other.

"Your job is to put marbles in there?"

Charlie nodded. "One every day, at the beginning of class. We all try to remember how many are in there at the end of the year. We write our guess down on a piece of paper. Whoever gets closest gets some free pizza from Domino's."

"Oh, man ..." Johnny leaned down to the jar, admired the prism of colors shifting in watery, lambent beams as he moved this way and that. "So you watch scary movies with your brother?"

"Yeah," Charlie said, brightening, more excited than before. He even forgot Johnny held Bashasaurus in his hands. Now Johnny was thoroughly convinced he'd owned the toy for a while. Either that or he was the nicest kid in the world.

"Do you know who Stephen King is?" Charlie asked.

Johnny shook his head. He heard the name before. It sounded vaguely familiar, but he wasn't sure and he didn't want to start his new friendship with a lie. He expected to start the day terrified and alone. He also expected the day to end on a slightly sad note, with a knot of something hard and cold like peanut butter in his stomach. Snot would be caked to his face from crying, clogging his nose like dried rubber cement. Charlie saved him from that though.

"Stephen King," Charlie said, "is like this old evil guy who lives in a castle … a really old man."

"Like Castle Grayskull?"

That gave Charlie pause, and he thought about it. "It could be like that, but no Skeletor. Maybe some moats and a trapdoor or two." He waved, as if swatting an errant bee from a picnic. He was glad for the interruption, since it involved a reference to He-Man, but he wanted to get on with the proceedings.

"When a movie is really scary like *Silver Bullet*, you know, about werewolves, they bring it to this evil old man and show it to him. If he thinks it's scary enough, he goes like, 'All right, it's real scary and evil. Put Stephen King on it.' That's why horror movies say 'Stephen King.'"

"Oh," Johnny said. He thought Charlie was smart. Charlie paused, as if anticipating some kind of challenge. Most other kids usually argued with him when he made things up, if only to irritate him in order to get some entertainment out of it. Johnny believed him or at least didn't call him a liar or go,

"Nah-uh," to negate what he just said. Charlie decided he found a new friend and asked, "Do you want to come over after school sometime?"

"Sure," Johnny said. "But I got to ask my mom."

CHAPTER TWO

The edges of Freeport, Ohio consisted of big box stores and amphitheater sized evangelical churches. Their marquees were the size of professional football scoreboards, featuring a lighted array of only the most well-known passages from the New Testament, like John 3:16. Farther toward the town proper were the various craft and outlet malls. Their tackiness was partially muted by village themes and Tudor accents designed to draw the eye away from the windowless faces of the monstrosities. The real pretensions started once the driver made their way to one of the three Corbett Development Projects that ringed the small town.

Most of the pasturage was converted to lawns and golf courses to serve the residents of the houses with starting prices in the low five-hundreds. The land was still pretty enough, emerald especially in the fading light around sunset. The eye could sometimes be tricked by the beauty into spotting the mirage of a farmhouse or a lone cow, instead of another brick behemoth with a cathedral ceiling pitched in ten different directions.

The whole development struck the older, middleclass residents of Freeport as something ugly and offensive, a *nouveau riche* concentration camp with all the intimacy of a public housing project. Each of the streets in the planned community was named after an Ivy League school or a remote shire.

The Milners lived in a little Colonial Revival house that looked as peaceful as a New England bed & breakfast. The front yard was planted with several full-grown willows, their catkins long since plucked by Mrs. Janet Milner. She made use of them in the nursery she tended on the grounds of her husband's business, Freeport Fertilizer.

It was still officially fall, but winter had already descended in all but name. The trees were shed of leaves and frozen. Their rough bark was a mass of hard, shaggy plates, solid as the scales of a petrified dragon. The crowns of several eastern hemlocks loomed behind the house, forming a row of staggered pyramids above the eaves.

Johnny and Charlie were in the backyard now. "Let me show you how I cook waffles." Charlie Milner held a small lighter in his right hand and a bottle of Raid bug spray in his left. Johnny carried the box of Egos in his arms, cradling them close to his chest. He suspected his mom wouldn't let him sleep over here if she didn't get along so well with Mrs. Milner or if she knew they were playing with fire.

He suddenly stopped thinking about his mom, and the waffles, and let out a loud "Whoa!" He pointed in the direction of some old Victorian husbandry implements, balanced against a wainscoted bench in the backyard. There was a birdbath with a cherub perched in its center, and several ceramic glazed frogs stood on mounts. Their mouths were open for flies and their stone bodies were covered in wet fungus.

"What's that?"

Charlie shrugged. "My mom comes out here sometimes to mess around. She's good at gardening, but my dad does the serious stuff like fertilizer. He sells it to golf courses and schools."

"Cool." Johnny turned from the little scene, his mouth still open in awe. He followed Charlie to a spot in the woods. The foliage rustled beneath their feet, and they kicked the crunching dead maple leaves from their path.

"All right," Charlie said. He reached down into the bed of dead leaves and brought out a frying pan. "Gimme the waffles." He tore the box open and pulled the plastic packaging apart. "These ones got apple in them."

"I like the blueberry."

"Me too, but these'll do for now."

Johnny looked back in the direction of the house. They were less than fifty feet from the glass sliding door on the wooden deck, and he could see Charlie's golden retriever skittering around the kitchen, trying to catch a bit of whatever Mrs. Milner was cooking in a steaming pot.

"Are we going to play some videogames or maybe play with He-Man?"

"Yeah, in a sec. Here, watch."

Charlie set two Ego waffles in the frying pan. He stood back, held the lighter out in front of his face, and flicked it so a wavering flame spurted forth. He depressed the trigger of the bug spray bottle with his right hand. A jet that was blue at the fount and orange at the tip spurted forth and covered the waffles.

Johnny jumped back and laughed. "Cool!"

"I know, right? Now we don't have to wait for them to cook in the stupid toaster." He pocketed the lighter and bug spray. He handed a waffle to his friend a moment later. Then he took the other one for himself. Johnny thought it was nice of Charlie to let him get the first waffle.

"All right," Charlie said. "Let's go in the house, and play some He-Man or videogames. Or we can go bug my sister."

They finished their waffles, passed back through the cover of the eastern hemlocks, and headed for the deck. The dog saw them through the glass and assumed sentry at the door. "You don't want to bug your brother?" Johnny asked.

"Yeah, it won't be bugging him, since he won't mind. My sister will mind though, which is what'll make it fun to mess with her." He grinned and opened the glass sliding door. The kitchen smelled of damp macaroni being strained in a colander.

"We can play videogames with my brother, but we can't play He-Man around him." Charlie slid the door closed behind them once they were in the kitchen.

"Lock it," his mother said. He locked it. Johnny looked up at his friend's mother. Her hair was prematurely grey. He got one look Charlie's dad before he headed back to work, and he saw there was a wide age difference between Mr. and Mrs. Milner. That made him wonder if it was possible for

Russell Milner to somehow transfer his agedness to his much younger wife. Then again, the grey hair didn't make her look older, since it contrasted well with the youthful features of her face. Mrs. Milner, like his mother, had the bearing of a perennial teenager, albeit one in late adolescence. He guessed she didn't have much to talk about with her husband. He figured that was why she was so grateful to talk to his mom, keeping her here with talk until Mrs. Cotter got a little bit uncomfortable.

"Why can't we play He-Man around your brother?"

Charlie cast a quick look up at his mother. She was laboring over the stove, and he was unsure if he should proceed in her presence. A sly smile crept across his face. "Robbie says He-Man's gay."

"Charlie …" His mother looked down at him sternly.

His smile widened. "What?"

She pointed the soaking end of a wooden spoon toward him. "You know I don't like you to use that word that way."

"I'm not using it. Robbie's the one who said it."

The dog snuck between their feet, and snuggled up to Johnny. He felt an instantaneous, kneejerk fear he couldn't contain in the presence of something so large, warm, and eager. He relaxed a moment later and started stroking the dog's honeyed coat.

"You're repeating what your brother said, and you're doing it to drive me crazy."

"Okay." Charlie placed a proprietary hand on the rump of his Golden Retriever and waved the dog's rear from side to side. His pet bore it with remarkable forbearance. It was hard for Johnny to be sure with dogs, but he thought the beast was smiling. "How can I use the word gay?"

She sighed and looked down into the steaming pot she stirred. "You're killing me."

He continued to pet the dog and crouched down so that his knees were touching the linoleum tile. "You said I can't use the word that way. What way can I use 'gay?'"

His mother turned from the stove. "You can use it in the happy way. You can say, 'I was in a gay mood today.' Okay?"

"Okay." Charlie turned to Johnny and grinned. "Let's go be gay."

His mother shouted to his retreating form as both boys disappeared through the doorway. "Don't use it in any way when you're at school! I don't trust you to use it the right way and ..."

Her voice disappeared as they made their way farther down the hall. There was a strong cedar musk suggesting a working fireplace in the house that saw regular use. The scent of recently vacuumed carpet lingered beneath that, along with the smell wafting up from freshly laundered clothes. It smelled like Saturday.

"Let's play with toys and then we'll play with videogames and maybe go get Robbie."

"Okay."

They passed a set of carpeted stairs leading to the second story. Johnny could see all the way up the stairwell to the landing, where a bay window looked out onto one of those wintergreen tree crowns sheltering the house from the view of neighboring yards. That was Robbie's room, Charlie told him. There was a bedroom, directly across the hall on the first floor where several stuffed animals reposed on a trundle bed. A Strawberry Shortcake and Rainbow Bright doll sat on the peppermint-striped comforter.

A twelve or thirteen year-old girl sat on the bed, and it felt to Johnny that his heart stopped when he looked at her. She sat reading a juvenile paperback with a baby blue glossy cover. She looked up from the book and he recoiled from her eyes, a primal fear not unlike what he felt when the dog first snouted him.

"Who're you?" she asked.

"That's Elise," Charlie said before Johnny could speak. He wouldn't speak, anyway, even if given ample opportunity. Johnny thought girls pretty before. He thought things interesting about their faces, or their hair or eyes, but some as yet to be wakened part of him stirred slightly when he looked at Elise. There was nothing he could do with her as of now, he knew. There was nothing he could do to channel the weird fever coursing through him aside from at home where he could give a few tentative humps to a pillow or the floor of a bathtub. He already tried that with no results. He wished it was otherwise. He wanted to be her age for a moment to do whatever it was that boys and girls did.

"Come on!"

Charlie jerked his arm, and Johnny was so keen to remain in place that his shoulder socket smoldered for a moment as he felt himself pulled away. He thought he could detect the slightest smile from her for a moment when his mouth was open and he was staring. It was pity. Elise thought he was pathetic, but at least it was a reaction.

"What was she reading?" Johnny asked.

"Stupid stuff," Charlie said, and shrugged. They were in his room now. It was remarkably neat, certainly neater than his room. There was a Nintendo, and two directional pads. There was also the *Duck Hunt* gun. All of the game cords were coiled and wrapped perfectly.

Charlie walked over to his toy chest and said, "I like horror. She reads dumb books about girls that babysit spoiled brats for pizza." A malicious grin spread across his face. "She had this one book. She got mad when I read it, and she took it away from me before I could finish it." He tried to push aside his toy chest, shoving it across the thick, plush cream carpet. "It was about this girl who turns thirteen and her butt starts to bleed or something."

They both laughed. Charlie finally managed to push aside the chest and revealed a toy so amazing that Johnny forgot about Elise, if only for the moment. It was a scale aircraft carrier with a Teflon coated deck. Several die cast metal fighter jets were on the runway. Plastic airmen were frozen in poses, clearing the birds for takeoff. The planes were covered in patriotic star decals.

"Man …" Johnny leaned down on the carpet. The dog entered the room behind them, and Johnny coughed once as a few errant shed hairs snuck into his mouth and nose. He wondered for a moment if the dog was ever in the room when Elise changed clothes.

"What's your dog's name again?" He wasn't sure whether or not he already asked Charlie that question, or if he answered it.

"Bowser." Charlie's back was to his friend, and he dug through another toy chest, throwing action figures this way and that.

"Like the main bad guy in *Mario*?"

"Yep."

Clawful sailed from Charlie's hand onto the carpet. The little anthropomorphic crab monster stared up at Johnny with his beady eyes. He looked at some of the other He-Man action figures now littering the carpet, as Charlie threw them one by one from the toy chest. He briefly wondered why his friend never put any of them in the Bashasaurus vehicle he brought to school. Maybe he was afraid one of the toys would get lost or stolen. He hoped Charlie didn't think he would steal one of his toys.

Nah, he wouldn't have invited him over if he thought there was a risk he would snatch one.

Johnny turned his attention back to the aircraft carrier. He flicked the plastic radar antennae mounted atop the ship. He pivoted, swiveled, and rotated the ballistic missile launchers arrayed on the craft. "I see this whenever I go to the toy store. They always put it on the top shelf. Nobody ever comes in to buy the thing unless their parents are getting divorced or something."

That made his friend laugh. "My mom and dad don't like each other, but they're not getting divorced, I don't think."

Johnny leaned down to the aircraft carrier. He stretched out on the floor, wondering as he lay down if he wouldn't find himself to be as long as the great ship. He held his arms to his sides as if readying himself for a coffin. Next he tucked his chin tightly to his sternum and looked down at his Velcro sneakers. The rubber soles of his shoes stopped short of the end of the battle carrier's deck. *Yep*, the ship was bigger than him.

"Holy mackerel," he said. "I wouldn't mind my mom and dad getting divorced if I could get one of these."

Something made of hard, molded plastic slapped his forehead. "Ow!"

"Sorry."

He picked the toy up from his nose, and inspected it. It was She-Ra, wearing her crown with a red ruby jewel inlaid in the golden center. Her red cape billowed behind her. He bent the plastic knees at the joints and admired her strong, flesh-toned thighs.

"Elise hates all the He-Man toys except for her."

Johnny had forgotten about Elise a moment before, but his friend's mention of his sister brought her back to mind. He thought of her now, and the strong features of her face. She had a masculine nose and jaw, but when he considered those features framed by that glorious black hair, it didn't make her seem like a boy. She looked more like a girl, who, through some magic or authority, couldn't be pushed around by boys. Every other pretty girl he saw made him want to hold their hand. She made him want to fight her and lose.

He looked over at the aircraft carrier, still holding the action figure in his hand. Charlie still had his back turned, which made it easier for him to do what he did now. He looked up at She-Ra, at the powerful shadow cast by her skirt looming above him. He imagined Elise's face on She-Ra's body. He saw himself as any one of the faceless, nameless revenant minions in Skeletor's army on the march against He-Man's twin sister.

She would wield her sword, and exult triumphantly, "I am She-Ra, princess of power!" Then she would slay him and stand on his chest with one of her golden boots pressed into his chest. He let the crotch of the doll rest on the bridge of his nose. "Princess of Power," he whispered.

"What are you doing?"

He sat up, embarrassed. The action figure fell from his face onto the carpet. "Here," Charlie said, and he tugged his shirtsleeve. "Do you have Grayskull at your house?"

"Yeah," Johnny said. They both crawled across the carpet over to the sickly green ramparts. A few Lego men were perched in one of the turrets of the castle. The slimy minarets tapered down into a skull whose saber tooth fangs hovered above the main drawbridge entrance.

"I don't like to keep only He-Man toys in the castle. I bring in toys from other universes."

"Like the Legos?" Johnny grabbed one up in his hands. He noticed the man, a construction worker with a wrench in his fingerless grip, was missing most of his face.

"Yeah, I use Legos. Like, I like to make them fall through the trapdoors and stuff." He opened the castle. There was an armory of plastic battleaxes inside, seated in a rack beneath a coat of arms featuring two crisscrossed swords.

"What'd you do to these Legos' faces?" He inspected all of the little yellow Lego men sequestered in the various nooks and crannies of the castle. He looked at a pirate from the moat and an Indian with plastic feathered headdress from the parapet. Both looked to have endured the same gruesome surgical practice. He figured Charlie hit them with the Raid and lighter, but his friend set him straight.

"My dad has a treadmill in his bedroom and I like to set it on high and hold their faces to it. I watch them burn off."

"Really?" It struck him as messed up. The little figures were inanimate, but he felt a pang of sympathy for the poor plastic toys. He studied the pirate a little closer, and saw that its face retained a half-smile where the fast-moving tread didn't burn the features entirely away.

"Yeah, it's not like you can't play with them after you mess their faces up, so it's not really a big problem."

Charlie dug a white bullhorn and a yachtsman's cap from the toy chest. He placed the hat on his head and ran his pointer finger over the golden rayon lifesavers' emblem sewn into the center of the cap. "Pretty cool, huh?" He leaned down to the aircraft carrier, depressed the horn, and Bowser ran out of the room.

A voice came from the upstairs bedroom. "Stop that, penis breath!" He depressed the bullhorn a couple more times in defiance. Charlie shared a conspiratorial smile with Johnny who wasn't so sure about all this. He didn't have siblings, and he didn't know what kind of line needed to be crossed in order to warrant an ass kicking. He got nervous, though, when he heard the groaning sound of socked feet padding over the carpeted stairs above them. Someone was moving downstairs, toward them.

"Shit." He backed away from the door over toward the bunk beds. Both of the mattresses were covered with Transformer comforters.

"Don't worry." Charlie held his ground, and hit the horn again.

"Were you talking about me?" His brother suddenly appeared in the doorway. "I heard you talking about me to mom. My ears were burning, you little bag of douche." He darted for his younger brother, and flipped him upside down. Charlie's face turned crimson. The hat fell off his head, but he maintained his grip on the bullhorn.

He thrashed in his brother's arms. Robbie tightened his grip around his brother's ankles, and he let him dangle so that his head was almost touching the carpet. "You're lucky I don't give you the Rowdy Roddy Piper treatment, you little homo."

Johnny glanced between his friend's brother's legs, and briefly glimpsed Charlie's face.

Charlie was smiling, so Johnny relaxed a bit. Robbie didn't bother acknowledging him until this moment. He briefly glanced over now, winked once, and then turned his attention back to his brother. Charlie's face was turning purple. Charlie made his hands into fists and pounded his older brother's knees using his forearms and balled hands like hammers.

Robbie simply extended his own arms farther from his body, holding his little brother away from him. Charlie thrashed, but he could no longer reach his brother's legs with his errant punches. "What has this cock gobbler been telling you about me?"

"Stop calling me names!"

"Nothing," Johnny said, shrugging. He felt nervous in the presence of teenagers. They made

him far more uncomfortable than grownups.
Fortunately Robbie lost interest in him, if he ever
had any interest in his little brother's friend in the
first place. He turned his attention back to
tormenting Charlie.

"I told him you were pretty good at
videogames," Charlie said. He unclenched one of his
fists and pointed over to the library of gray
cartridges. They were stacked neatly in a cabinet
beneath the television next to the Nintendo and the
gun used for *Duck Hunt*.

"Yeah, I'm all right, but I don't like
Nintendo anymore. I mainly play computer games."
He made sustained eye contact with Johnny for the
first time. "They're more challenging, you know. I
like puzzles." He set his brother down. Charlie,

breathless, ran over to his friend by the bunk beds.
There was a rope ladder leading from the bottom to
the top. He scaled it as if to attain a higher vantage
in his never ending war against his big brother.

He leaned over the side of the bed after he
was safely situated on the top bunk and said,
"Robbie can beat Ganon in *Zelda*. He can beat
Bowser in *Mario*."

"Holy mackerel," Johnny said. His mouth
was open in awe again, and he looked over at
Robbie. He thought Charlie was the luckiest kid in
the world. His sister was as darkly beautiful as an
evil villainess in a comic book, and his brother could
get to the end bosses in Nintendo games. Johnny
never could get that far in either one of the games
Charlie just mentioned, not without codes at least.

"Yeah," Charlie continued, unaware now that he was starting to make his sleepover guest just the slightest bit jealous. "When he gets to the final bad guy, a lot of the time he hands me the controller and lets me take over and try to play."

"Do you ever win?" Johnny asked.

Charlie shook his head, and then pulled himself back up onto the top bunk. The frame above Johnny rattled, and he feared the top bunk might come down on top of him. He was grateful he didn't have a bunk bed at home. He was perfectly comfortable with his Porsche convertible sleeping arrangement.

"I don't have to play *Zelda* for you," Robbie said. "I saved a game for you so you can just load it whenever you want." He looked back over at

Johnny. "That's another good thing about computer games. You don't have to fucking start over every time. You can save your game, unlike in pretty much every Nintendo game except *Zelda*."

Johnny looked closer at his friend's older brother now. He noticed Robbie Milner was as handsome as his younger brother was ugly. His was an athletic build, but his frame was lithe. His was the body of a fencer or tennis player, rather than the physique of a football player. His hair had a lacy, filigreed quality to it. The golden mop spilled over a strong forehead tapering down to a severe hatchet of a nose. The shape of his face made Johnny think of a bird of prey. He would like to have a brother who looked like that. He bet Robbie could protect a weaker, younger brother in a scrap. There was also enough intelligence lighting his eyes to make it just as likely for him to win a war of insults without having to throw a single punch.

His beauty was the opposite of his sister's in a way. Elise had features which individually were masculine but added up to a powerful feminine whole. Robbie Milner had long, sweeping black eyelashes, soft doe eyes, and full reddish lips. This made him look girlish until one considered the rest of his face and body. His Adam's apple looked to be the size of a golf ball. His hands were large, and sinewy veins cabled down his muscular arms. There was about him the suggestion of a barely contained virility uncommon in a sixteen year-old, even one who hit the full flush of puberty early.

Johnny looked away from him, toward the row of Nintendo games. He saw the golden *Zelda* cartridge sticking out conspicuously among the other gray cartridges. His eyes flitted back over to Robbie and he asked, "Can you get to Mike Tyson in *Punch Out*?"

His heart beat hard in his chest. He was aware this was first time he spoke directly to Robbie. It was the first time actually that he ever spoke to a teenager. Robbie bit his lower lip. He sucked at the tooth that would be gold if he were the pugilist he now prepared to mimic. He spoke in a strange, lilting falsetto, "I can not only get to Mike Tyson, I can beat Mike Tyson."

Johnny laughed. He never heard such a good impression of the champ. Charlie giggled from the top bunk. The dog barked from the other room, and the sound of The Smiths', "There is a Light that never goes out" came from Elise's room. "I beat the Jheri curl juice out Mitch Green's head."

Robbie struck a profile, started shadowboxing against an invisible opponent. He threw the short, stocky jabs and angled uppercuts for which Tyson was famous. He incorporated the perpetual head motion of Cus D'Amato, Manassa mauling an invisible, helpless opponent against an equally imaginary turnbuckle. "It's called fighting in a phone booth. I turned Trevor Berbick's face into ground hamburger." The two younger boys giggled again at his lisping impression of the young heavyweight champ. "I wanted to push his nose bone up into his brainstem, you know?"

Charlie climbed down the rope ladder. He landed on the carpet feet first. "Hey," he said to

Johnny, "Have you ever noticed that when you're fighting in *Punch Out*, if you look out in the crowd, Donkey Kong is watching the fight, too?"

"In which fight?"

Charlie stopped to think about that one. "I'm not sure. I think it's in the one where you fight Bald Bull." He squinted. "Or maybe King Hippo? Or Glass Joe."

"You don't know what you're talking about," Robbie said, throwing haymakers into thin air and working his way back over toward his brother. "Talking out your ath and scared to sthtep into the thsquared thircle wid a real man!" He ducked low, kept his arms as tight to his sides as a tyrannosaurus. Robbie did body work on his little brother, who giggled and blocked. "You don't want to go at it hammers and tongs with me, buddy."

Charlie caught one of his brother's arms as he threw a punch, and held on with both of his hands. Robbie tried to free himself, but his little brother clung on for dear life. Charlie turned back toward Johnny and said, "Robbie says white guys can't fight."

"I never said that," Robbie said, forgoing his Tyson impression in order to argue more seriously for the moment. "I said white guys can't box. It's the harsh truth."

Johnny walked over toward them. He wished he could wrestle and box with Robbie, but somehow sensed it was only okay for these two to fight because they were brothers. "What about Rocky?" Johnny asked.

Robbie finally managed to reclaim his arm from his younger brother. He spun Charlie around, holding him in a bear hug and ready to make him pay penance. He grasped Charlie in a headlock and said, "Which Rocky? Graziano or Marciano?"

Johnny was perplexed and squinted. "From the movie."

That made Robbie laugh so hard he let go of his brother. "That's a movie. Sylvester Stallone is a pussy. Rambo, my balls! The fucking guy hid out at an all-girls school in Switzerland during the 'Nam. He couldn't punch his way out of a wet paper bag. All that steroid muscle is just for show. You could probably kick his ass."

Johnny felt his body warm, and his skin prick with little nettles of pride. He understood Robbie was only saying he could win a fight with Sly to demonstrate how weak Stallone was. Still, Robbie said Johnny could probably win a fight!

Robbie adopted another accent. Johnny wasn't exactly sure who he was mimicking this time when he spoke. "'How come every time we start talking 'bout boxing, a white man got to pull a Rocky Marciano out of his ass?'"

Johnny and Charlie regarded him silently. Their heads were cocked to the side, like dogs encountering a new sound for the first time. "Eddie Murphy," Robbie said. "*Coming to America.*"

"Oh," Johnny said. He knew who Eddie Murphy was. He thought for a moment longer about

Mike Tyson. Then he thought about Mr. T., perhaps because he played a boxer in one of the *Rocky* movies. He briefly wondered why there were so few black people in Freeport. There was Samantha, the botanist in Ms. Seever's kindergarten class, and then there was the janitor at school. Those were the only black people he actually knew of off the top of his head, who weren't famous boxers like Mike Tyson or famous singers like Michael Jackson.

He wondered what would happen if Iron Mike ever went toe to toe with Michael Jackson? MJ would probably use some magical dance moves to stun the boxer and then sic Bubbles the Monkey on him to kill him somehow. Robbie spoke, bringing him out of the haze of his hypothetical. "Mom know you have that?"

He looked at his brother and pointed at the red gun used for the *Duck Hunt* game. "Yeah, she says I can use it for the game. If I unplug it from the Nintendo and walk around the house shooting, she'll take it away from me."

"I will."

Mrs. Milner streaked across the hallway with a basket of laundry in her hands, heading for the basement. "Dinner ready in five." Her voice trailed off, and both Robbie and Charlie's eyes strayed toward the hallway.

"She's angry with you," Charlie said. "She wants you to stop saying He-Man's gay."

Robbie waved away his little brother's concern. "I got news for you," Robbie said, "there's no such thing as He-Man."

Charlie's face twitched, a reflexive little tremor that would be imperceptible to Johnny if he wasn't standing so close. Something Charlie cherished and prized was now perilously close to being destroyed. Robbie sensed he was close to his objective, and pressed forward. A sadistic smile was plastered on his face. It did nothing to mar his perfect, even features. "Yep," he said, pacing, stepping gingerly between the various action figures strewn about on the carpeted floor. He leaned down and picked up the plastic He-Man.

"You know, Mattel made these action figures for the *Conan* movie with Schwarzenegger, but when the final film ended up being too violent …" He twirled the little doll in his hand.

Charlie smoldered. He kept his eyes fixed on the action figure, the strong Nordic god now reduced to a mere plaything in the hands of this spiteful ogre. Johnny sensed the mood darkening. If the brothers rushed toward each other and came into contact again, this time they wouldn't be playing around. This time there might actually be a real fight, and he didn't doubt the outcome.

"It was *Ah-Nuld*," Robbie said, mocking both his little brother's love for He-Man and the Austrian muscleman. His impression was pitch perfect. It wasn't funny though, like his earlier impressions of Tyson or Eddie Murphy.

"Robbie …" His mother's voice defused the tension, and both boys turned to the doorway. Mrs. Milner stood there with the now empty laundry basket. A single sheet of fabric softener floated inside of the plastic berth. "Stop torturing your brother." She looked over at Charlie. "I don't care so much about the gun. I'm telling you right now though, if you guys spend all day inside playing Atari, I'm going to confiscate that machine and I won't give it back until I see some mud on your shoes and some bruises on your knees." Johnny looked at her, trying to discern some of the lineage that led to the creation of Elise. He didn't see the resemblance between mother and daughter. "I think your dad's right about those games being a Japanese conspiracy to make American kids stupid. I'll bet Japanese parents don't even let their kids play those stupid games." Mrs. Milner turned from the door and departed with a final warning. "I mean it."

"Mom!" Robbie shouted after her. "You dropped too much acid in the sixties and your memory's shot. I'm the one who had the Atari. This is a Nintendo."

"Whatever," she said, as her voice was heard faintly from the hall.

Robbie looked back over at his brother. Both of them forgot about the He-Man. He tossed the action figure back onto the ground, next to the She-Ra action figure with which Johnny previously experimented. Fear swirled in Johnny's stomach, and he was fighting against a conspiracy now hatching itself in his mind. He never contemplated stealing a toy from a friend; he'd never even stolen anything in his life. He wanted the She-Ra doll to take home though, and he was too embarrassed to ask Charlie for it. What if he knew why he really wanted it? Then again, he could ask either his mom or dad to buy it for him the next time they went to the toy store. It wasn't like the thing had a big price tag, not like that crazy aircraft carrier. What if his mom or dad got suspicious? He never bought a female action figure before or asked for one. That might make them wonder why he was asking for one now.

"I wish Nintendo was around when I was your guys' age, but mom's probably right. Keep fucking around and you're going to get Nintendonitus so bad you won't even be able to beat off properly when you're my age. Beating off is frankly the only way to release tension in this madhouse." Robbie looked over at Johnny. "You ever play games on a Commodore?"

"No, but my dad's got an Apple computer with a good monster mystery game on it."

"Yeah, well, count your lucky stars. The Commodore's nothing to write home about. I had *Doctor Jay versus Larry Bird, One on One*. That thing sucked donkey dick. They just looked like a couple of stick figures. I think the kids in your kindergarten class could probably do a better job with the artwork."

A voice shouted from the kitchen. It echoed down the hall that was growing dark, as the sun lowered and less light poured through the bay windows of the ground floor. "Boys, Elise, dinner! Spaghetti!"

Robbie placed a hand on top of his brother's head, tousling the hair that was so coarse, so different from his fine mane. He then placed his other hand in the small of Johnny's back. A chill went through the younger boy's body. He desperately wanted Robbie to be his older brother too.

"Alrighty, Rocky Graziano." Robbie looked at his younger brother, and then at his brother's little friend. "You too, Rocky Marciano." He walked forward with them both in tow. "If you want to stand a chance against Tyson, you've got to eat your spaghetti." He looked at Johnny. "Or maybe you want to fight Clubber Lang instead?"

Johnny paused where he stood on the carpet. "Who?"

"Mr. T."

"Oh."

CHAPTER THREE

The playground sundial was made of bronze, and its aquamarine contours were rusted so that it looked like an empty wishing fountain in the dead of winter. To the left of the sundial was the sandbox, which didn't see much action when it was this cold. The kids who pulled wagons or rode on plastic bikes usually spent the first five minutes experimentally rollicking over the gravel or asphalt until finally migrating over to the smoother surface of the mats.

Charlie and Johnny set up a makeshift hermitage for themselves under some redwood cedars giving off a smell as powerful as Eastern Orthodox incense. More and more the boys tended to separate themselves from the other children whenever the opportunity presented itself. That usually meant during recess or naptime. Naptime came directly after recess, and that gave them a substantial block of time together.

Ms. Seever and Mrs. Balmos, the teacher's aide, liked to discourage the boys from isolating. Their attention was elsewhere today though. Mrs. Balmos was inside policing up colorful pegs from a Lite Brite set Martin Little tipped over in a fit of rage. The sheet of black construction paper previously stretched over the sockets was shredded into two pieces, and the electronic lights were scattered across the floor of the classroom.

"It's a postmodern art masterpiece," the graying old matron joked. Ms. Seever laughed indulgently, but none of the kids understood what she was talking about.

It was a bit strange to make the scoliotic woman bend down to pick up the four-hundred or so miniature bulbs. Ms. Seever was much younger, and unlike Mrs. Balmos, she never complained of arthritis. Then again, Ms. Seever was better at monitoring the kids on the playground, corralling them especially when they got too close to the windbreak of pines separating the playground from the fence. The pines faced a four lane road, and there was a hole in the fence large enough for a child to worm their way through.

Earlier, Charlie told Johnny about what his brother did with the Lite Brite set at home. "He took all the yellow letters and spelled out 'piss.' Only he didn't say anything, and then when I turned out the light, I saw it." He giggled. "My mom said it would be cute if he spelled out 'pee,' but piss is a bad word."

"Yeah," Johnny said, admiring Robbie's wit. "Bad words are better. 'Piss' is funnier than 'pee.'"

"They're both pretty funny," Charlie said. He prodded the hard mud of the playground with a gnarled twig on which a caterpillar was frozen solid. "Anyway, he said some kid stuck one of the Lite Brite pegs in his pee hole, and now he can't have kids of his own."

That conversation ran its course, and now Charlie was crying. He hid his red face in the warm woven fabric of his mittens, which featured a design of reindeer clomping through snow.

"Don't worry about her," Johnny said, and patted Charlie on his back. His hand landed dully on the diamond quilted fabric of his friend's winter jacket. "Jessica probably has more cooties than you and me put together."

Jessica Wentworth's dad was a doctor, and she always tried to get her hands on whatever medical toys were lying around Ms. Seever's class. Sometimes she went for the stethoscope, and harmlessly went around listening to the heartbeats of various girls in the classroom. Today however, she grabbed the Fisher-Price booster shot needle, whose body was as large as a turkey baster. She didn't focus her attention on the other girls as she usually did. This time she went from boy to boy, jabbing the hypo into the arms of the various males she passed in her rounds.

She tagged each one of them in their turn, and announced, "I'm giving this to knock-you-late against cooties." The boys bore it with good humor.

A couple of eager patients even lined up and rolled up their sleeves despite the frigid air bearing down on the playground.

She shot Johnny without incident. Then, after giving Charlie his first phantom injection, she doubled back to him and said, "He has more cooties than all the other boys put together, so I have to give him another shot." All of the girls and about half of the boys laughed. Johnny didn't laugh, but he did smile a little. He couldn't help it. The gesture was involuntary.

Now, he felt bad as he patted his friend on the back. Charlie was crying, and Johnny was close to certain his friend saw him smiling earlier.

"What's wrong?" The shadow of an adult loomed over them, and the two boys looked up. Ms.

Seever was there holding a bucket and trowel she took from the sand play area.

"Nothing." He dragged the back of his limp left hand across his face in an attempt to conceal his tears and anger from the teacher. She leaned down, and her floor length denim skirt bunched up around her. Johnny always enjoyed her smell, like spearmint gum that never lost its flavor. He always inhaled deeply when it was faintly on the air. She was close enough to him now that he just breathed normal and still got the full effect of her wintergreen musk. It, along with the scent descending from the trees, made him think of Christmas. He got excited as he realized the holiday wasn't too far away now.

"How about I let you guys go inside before the rest of the class?" Charlie removed his hand from his face and revealed his tear stained eyes. He looked over at Johnny, who nodded eagerly. These little privileges didn't come that often. This would be even better than being message runner for the day.

"Yeah?" Ms. Seever smiled. She held the expression until the contagion caught, and Charlie grinned and nodded. He stood, and Johnny stood with him. Their hands found each other and they walked back into the red brick building with their arms linked together.

Mrs. Balmos cursed lightly under her breath. She glanced up, and her eyes widened, rolled as if she had strabismus. She looked at the clock hung on the far cinderblock wall, above a pull down Rand McNally map left from the days when this was the elementary school. "You guys still have ten minutes left on the playground."

Charlie shook his head. "Nah-uh." He gave a defiant little sneer that curled his face, and Johnny wondered why he didn't just explain Ms. Seever gave them this pass. That would settle things. It was as if he wanted to get into it with the old lady, and she had enough misery on her hands already.

Johnny glanced down at the carpet, saw a few glowing nettles. Mrs. Balmos stepped lightly, as if they were shards of glass. It didn't look like Charlie was going to explain the situation, so Johnny said, "Ms. Seever said we could come in early." He left out the part about how Charlie's tears precipitated her good favor. Charlie looked over, and his sneer melted into a look of gratitude.

"Okay, this is almost done." She shook her head, stooped back down, and they moved in to help her. "'Why don't we get a Lite Brite?' Ms. Seever says. 'It'll be easier to clean up than paints.'" She shook her head again. The boys continued prodding the carpet for errant little plastic lights, and they exchanged an uneasy look. They thought Mrs. Balmos must be pretty angry to mock Ms. Seever in their presence. Sometimes, when the two women disagreed on some point, they would go over to the library nook and stand between the two lime-green beanbags. They sometimes squabbled there for anywhere from five to ten minutes.

"Then, to top it all off, you guys didn't even seem that interested." Johnny wondered why she taught here. She looked tired, like she didn't even want to interact with them. She probably didn't like whatever other kids she dealt with in her personal life, maybe grandkids or something. He decided she was here for money, and he wondered briefly how much kindergarten teachers made. Probably lots, was his conclusion. He jiggled the miniature light bulbs in his hand. They glowed red and green, and he thought of Christmas again.

"Mrs. Balmos," he said tentatively. He didn't really like her all that much, but he decided to try and help her anyway.

"Yes?"

"I think the kids would be more interested if you get one of the refill sets." He walked toward her and deposited the lights into her wizened palm. There were weird, loose blue veins in her arm, not like the cables on Robbie's arms that tightened whenever he was wrestling against Charlie. She also had little brown spots all over her like an overripe banana. He thought she might make a good bad guy in Skeletor's army.

She took the lights in her palm. "Thank you." Charlie sidled up to her and handed her the little plastic shards he found. "Thanks." She looked back over at Johnny. "What are the refills?" She walked the lights back over to the plastic cereal bowl where the other ones were.

"Well, the set comes with pictures, like of a clown and things like that. If you like G.I. Joe, you can order a set of those. Or, if you like some other show, you can get some lights that will make a picture of Scooby or whatever. I think the kids would be more interested in something like that."

He looked over at the glowing set, which was especially radiant now the overhead lights were dimmed in preparation of naptime. He and Charlie would be busy here soon. Charlie was the mat helper for the day while he was the snack assistant. The best thing about helping prepare the snack was that he could always spill a little Kool-Aid and sop up the tangy juice with his palm. That pitcher was pretty heavy for a kid, so no one ever questioned it when he made an accident on purpose.

Mrs. Balmos looked over at the steaming heat lamp. Johnny thought it shouldn't be exposed. It was too naked without the black construction paper and the little thumbtack sized lights. He hated Martin Little or was at least mad at him for wrecking the illusion the glowing little box provided until now. He would never look at a Lite-Brite set the same way again, and he wasn't sure if he would even play with his own set at home after today.

"There's more than the clown that came with the set," the old teacher's aide said. She looked over at the box. "There's an American flag, and a sailboat, and I think there might be a fish too." There was a look of doubt on her old face, and Johnny saw she wasn't convinced by her own words. Mrs. Balmos nodded, acknowledging his suggestion. "I'll talk to Ms. Seever and see if we have any money for the refills or whatever you call them." She glanced through the window, which was smudged gray from the dull, chalky light filtering from the sunless sky above Freeport. "I think we're done with this toy for now."

"Is there anything else we can do?" Charlie asked. He was cheered up at least enough to realize they had the place to themselves, and that this was a prime opportunity that might not come again. When he got double tapped with the cooties needle, it was the first time he ever cried publicly, at least since that first day at Freeport Kindergarten when his mom took him to school and he broke down in the entryway. Almost every kid cried on the first day of school. If there was a way to cry every day in order to get this alone time in the school with just his buddy Johnny and the old teacher, then he would do it every day. Faking tears was like faking being sick. Grownups could only be fooled so many times.

"Check on Herbert and his children," Mrs. Balmos said.

Charlie tapped Johnny on the shoulder and both boys made their way over to the humid terrarium. It was next to the empty cage where Dexter the hamster once reposed in splendor before that real crybaby and her allergies ruined it for the rest of them. It took a special kind of wimp to start crying just because they were sneezing. There was something sad about the cage, its empty confines, and the unused rodent running wheel. The little water feeder was still half-full and brackish from not being changed in all of this time.

Johnny and Charlie leaned down to the cage with the snails in it, and watched the little brown mollusks as they moved their slug bodies over the wilted lettuce. They exuded a trail of slime as they shimmied toward a ceramic diver standing on his mount. Charlie thought the aquanaut and his little treasure chest belonged in the fish tank, whose filter gently hummed on the other side of the room. The bubbling noise soothed him, made his earlier sadness recede even more. Now there was only the slight discomfort of his red cheeks burning from the combination of salty tears and cold wind that blasted the quadrangle of the playground outside.

He tapped the side of the cage, and shouted, "Hey!" even though he knew the land snails were deaf to his words. "That one looks gold." He pressed his pointer finger against the glass, and Johnny's eyes followed to the bronze carapace of the old man who sired the smaller snails.

"They have babies fast!" Johnny said, and looked over at Charlie. "I wish people had babies this fast. Maybe then I'd have a brother or sister."

Charlie shrugged. "Robbie's fun to play with sometimes, but sometimes he's a grade-A butthole."

"Charles ..." There was a note of warning in her voice, and he shrank from the threat in it. He smiled when he looked over at Johnny. "I like that we've got the place to ourselves," he said. "I wish that old skeleton wasn't here, so it could be just you and me."

The wind picked up outside, and the keening of the gale sounded like the howl of a beast that might reach inside and devour them all.

CHAPTER FOUR

This was his first time in a Mercedes.

Everything Johnny knew about cars came from

riding in his mom's minivan or playing with his

toys, but he still knew enough to know this car was

something special. The roadster's seats were heated.

If he leaned forward as far as his seatbelt would

allow, he could see the chrome hood ornament

glowing in the sunlight.

"Not bad, right?" Robbie turned from the

front passenger seat, to look at his brother and

Johnny in the back.

"It's like the Batmobile."

"Ugh," Russell said. His accent was thick,

transatlantic sprinkled with a dash of the Borscht

Belt. Johnny thought he talked like people in old

movies. That made sense, as he was old. "That show

was so dumb. I mean, I know it was supposed to be campy, but it was just awful." He tapped his right hand against the burr wood inlay dash once, and sighed.

The Milner patriarch shifted in his seat, and the leather cringed beneath him. Johnny glanced at him in the rearview at just the moment where the old man was checking the mirror. Their eyes made inadvertent contact. Johnny thought his face contained generations of sadness. He wasn't able to shed the woe from his features as a first-generation American, but at least he was able to give that gift to his sons. Johnny figured World War II probably also had something to do with his face.

"So you were in the war?" he asked. There was no way he could present that question with his mom here, but there were just four males in the

Mercedes now. They were on their way to Freeport Fertilizer to kill some time and play at the family business, while Russell handled some important matter that came up.

Mr. Milner made eye contact with the boy in the rearview mirror. "Yeah, me and pretty much everybody else in these United States. It wasn't like your Vietnam there."

"My dad didn't have to go because he was in college," Johnny said.

Russell shrugged, which drew attention to his neckless body. Johnny thought the old man resembled a turtle without a shell. His natural posture looked painful and impossible to hold for any length of time. Johnny changed his opinion of the man's face, and decided there was some real pain mixed in there with the sadness.

"Your dad's situation is kind of the opposite of mine," Russell said. There was no judgment in his tone, and he didn't seem to begrudge the man his deferment. "I got out of the Army and used the Montgomery GI Bill. I went to Cornell College of Agriculture." He jerked his thumb toward the rear of the Benz, as if the college were directly behind them on the road. "In Ithaca."

"Oh," Johnny said, just to say something. Neither Charlie nor Robbie was interested. The Milner boys stared out the windows at the cutover remnants of farmland being drawn into the orbit of yet another Corbett housing development.

"It's the only Ivy League agriculture school."

"Dad," Robbie said, looking away from the window. "He's in kindergarten."

The old man hunched his shoulders defensively over the neckless region below his chin. "Don't mean nothing." Johnny saw him on the fire escape in the New York of his imagination. He saw Mr. Milner wearing a newsboy's hat and climbing down the stairs to get away from the fuzz. Russell and Johnny resumed eye contact in the rearview, and Russell asked, "You know what an Ivy League school is?"

"I think so." Johnny sat back in his seat, and offered "It's better than the other ones."

"See," Russell said, "he knows what the hell he's talking about."

The stucco arcade fronting the Steeplechase Country Club appeared on the right. The parking lot was flush with cars as expensive as, or even pricier than the one they rode in. Clay tennis courts were

visible to the right of the main arcade. The Olympic
sized swimming pool was closed for the winter,
covered in a green tarp.

Russell glanced over at the country club
with a look of contempt on his face, so intense
Johnny thought he might spit if he was outside and
not in his precious coupe. "More money than sense."

"Yeah, but what do you care?" Robbie said.
"It means more money for you, doesn't it?"

The Benz turned left, away from the
remaining amoeba of greenbelt surrounding the
township, onto a strip where the largest feature was a
car dealership with a mirrored glass front. The
Freeport Center Mall appeared ahead of them. Its
ten-thousand vehicle capacity lot was overflowing
with holiday shoppers here to spend in the interim
between Thanksgiving and Christmas.

"I got news for you. More money for me means more money for you too. The last time I checked, you were living under my roof."

Johnny and Charlie exchanged a look, smiling. They were both used to getting their balls broken by Robbie. Johnny liked him with a fondness verging on love, but it was still fun to see him get pushed around a little, if only in a quick bout of verbal sparring with his dad.

Robbie was unfazed. "Right, so the looser these old millionaires are with their dough, the better it is for us all."

Russell shook his head. "You don't understand. It still hurts when you're a professional to see them behave like morons."

"What are you talking about? I know you're an Ivy Leaguer, but maybe you could break it down in layman's terms."

They drove from genuine countryside to the ersatz version cultivated by the rich. They now pierced into the heart of working-class Freeport. A Veterans of Foreign Wars hall blurred past on their right. A few bikers stumbled out of Freeport Lanes smoking cigarettes and brandishing open containers of Pabst hidden in brown paper bags.

"You know why we're going to my place of employment right now?"

"Yeah," Robbie said. "Charlie and his little friend want to kill some time at mom's nursery, and you've got to meet Gentleman Jim Corbett."

Charlie leaned forward, interlocking his fingers on the contours of his brother's headrest. "Why do you call him that?"

"Gentleman Jim Corbett was a bare knuckle prizefighter, a boxer back about a hundred years ago. That was back when white guys could still sort of box." Robbie turned away from his brother, done with his explanation. He looked back toward his dad. "Right, you're meeting with the grand poobah of the suburbs. Big deal."

His father drew a deep breath, prepared to explain. "Corbett called up last night, said he wants to build a golf course for himself, not another one at the country club." He jerked his thumb back in the direction of Steeplechase. "He wants it on his own property. I quoted him a price last night, and he thinks it's too high. Says he wants to take some of

the soil from his wife's old Palace of Versailles
garden on his property and use some of that to save
money."

"What's wrong with that?" Robbie asked. "I
was there once, for some stupid thing where they
paid us to set up tables for a party. There's more
than enough dirt to go around."

"What's wrong with that?" Russell repeated
his son's words before choosing his own. "You
don't mix heavily-irrigated soil with soil that's been
on a different regimen, especially not on an
ornamental program."

They arrived at the business, and the wheels
of the luxury car crunched over the gravel as they
rolled toward a parking space. They stopped next to
a cream Jaguar. Russell spied Corbett in the other
car, his son Alex sitting in the passenger seat.

Russell lowered his voice, reticent to bash the man too much when he was this close. "He wants nothing but putting quality greens, no drive area." Russell unbuckled his seatbelt. "That's problematic because putting greens are the most high maintenance form of turf."

Johnny and Charlie sat up, looked through the windows of the Benz at Alex. The boy pressed his face against the glass of the Jaguar's window so intently the pressure caused his nostrils to flare. His breath fogged the window.

"I've never seen him at Freeport," Charlie said.

"You never seen him," Russell said, still speaking softly, "because his dad sends him to a magnet school that costs an arm and a leg." Russell looked over at Robby. "Cheap prick doesn't skimp on that, does he?" He glanced over at Corbett Senior, waved, and let a cordial smile wash across his face. He spoke out of the corners of his mouth to his older son, one last time. "Doesn't skimp on transportation either. Looks like this year's model."

They all got out at once, and there was the loud sound of doors slamming shut as each man and boy exited the cars and walked toward one another.

This was Johnny's first look at Jim Corbett, and he was confused. There was a layer of doughy fat on him that melted downward from his breasts. His breasts were slack and more like udders than pectorals. They spilled into a paunch that hung in his baby blue Polo shirt. His gut declined over the belt buckle of his designer khakis. He wore a white visor and designer red-tinted shades with gold frames. He looked rich, but he didn't look as strong or tough as someone with so much power should look.

His son looked like a little princeling, someone quite aware even at his young age of the power his father possessed. His facial expression was sour and contorted, like a baby prematurely wakened from his nap. Johnny immediately didn't like him, and was glad he went to his special school where they played with magnets all day.

"Got something here," Corbett Senior said, and opened a black three-ringed binder. There were several loose-leaf pieces of paper in the book underneath a laminated sheet. The pages were covered with intricate pen scrawls and blue ballpoint chicken scratches. "I've been doing some research, and I decided I want to go with hybrid Bermuda grass." He paused as he flipped through the sheets.

He looked at Russell with eyes that were inscrutable behind the red lenses of his sunglasses. He waited expectantly, and bit his lower lip. Johnny thought it looked like a tic designed to keep him from taking a bite out of Russell. Corbett clearly resented having to depend on anyone or acknowledge their expertise.

"No good," Russell said, and Corbett's teeth bit deeper into the lower lip. Johnny could smell him from here. He gave off a weird ambrosia of aftershave and expensive imported beer. "You got to go with roughstalk or creeping bentgrass, or maybe a solid perennial rye if you want me to supply you your fertilizer."

Corbett released his teeth from his lower lip and hissed while he sanded his molars together as if working his jaws over tough steak. "Huh," he said. Then he glanced backward, ensuring no one besides some dumb kids were here to witness this minor act of defiance he had no choice but to brook. "Okay," he said. Johnny could tell from the elongated pause flowering between the men that it was not okay for either of them.

"Come on," Robbie said, tapping his brother on the shoulder. Then he brushed Johnny lightly along the back. "Let's go check out the nursery and whatnot."

Charlie placed both of his arms around his brother's waist, barely managing with his limited wingspan. Robbie was thin, but Charlie's arms were short. Robbie picked his brother up. He groaned, contemplating whether or not to go through with one of his half-speed Rowdy Roddy Piper moves. He finally set Charlie down in the gravel.

Johnny looked up. The sky was bone-white, threatening snow and making him wonder if it was possible to go blind from looking at something so bright. The sun was invisible in the cloudless, pallid expanse. "Can we play with the proton packs?" Charlie asked.

"Yeah, sure. Dad wants me to check on the plants anyway." Robbie walked over to a Quonset shaped building where there was a sheet of plastic thrown over the aluminum exoskeleton frame. He took a small key from his pocket and stuck it into a padlock, which snapped open. He held the door open for the boys who filtered inside.

The wind made the plastic crinkle. The sheets beat against the metal ribs, causing a loud slapping sound that forced Johnny to flinch a few times until he got used to it.

The plants were arranged in a neat matrix, row after row of hydroponically grown flowers floating in rafts. They lightly bounced in their aerated solutions, making a sloshing sound that was a bit like frogs leaping on Lilly pads.

"What's all this?" Johnny asked.

Robbie was on the other side of the room, messing with something Johnny couldn't see. He was making a loud sound though, whatever he was up to. Charlie ran over to be with his brother. "Not even dad knows what this stuff is," Robbie said. "The kids at the local diploma mill are doing some research here, and they pay for the space."

Robbie appeared from a batch of plants at the far left side of the Quonset hut, near where a black timer rested. He held a misting tank with a steel hose attachment coiled to its multi-gallon berth by a snaking PVC line. "Dad thinks they're growing weed. He's an old man so he calls it pot." He held the green canvas backpack straps of the mister out to Johnny. "Here, give me your arms." Then he did a spot-on impression of his dad. He spoke in the elongated, whiny tone of a Catskills comic begging for laughs that weren't forthcoming. "You damn beatniks need to quit smoking that reefer."

Johnny settled comfortably into the pack, enjoying its weight. He held the sprayer across his chest at the position of port arms. He had his rucksack and his machinegun, and now he was ready to shoot some Japs. Charlie came toward him, his own pack on his back. Johnny asked Robbie, "Does your dad ever talk about the war?"

He suspected his mom's lessons on good manners might not just be her way of trying to spoil his fun, and that maybe he did a bad thing by asking Mr. Milner about the war back when they were in the car. "Yeah," Robbie said, sweeping some of his blond hair from his forehead. "He'll talk about it if you ask him. He's not afraid to or anything."

Robbie walked toward the door and held it open for the two boys. "He gave me a couple books to read about it. I'll give one of them to Charlie when he's older." He secured the padlock to the door, and turned the key. "*The Naked and the Dead* is about the most boring piece of shit I've ever read in my life, so I want to spare my brother that agony." He pocketed the key. "*The Thin Red Line*'s about the best book ever written, about war or anything else, and I want Charlie to read it when he's old enough."

"What's old enough?" Johnny asked.

"My age. Sixteen."

Charlie contradicted Johnny's fantasy, slapping his own spray nozzle against his friend's in a gesture that meant there was about to be a sword fight. Johnny would rather think of himself as a World War II soldier than an Arthurian knight, and he was glad when Robbie accidentally turned the game back in the direction he wanted it to go.

"Hey, those things are expensive. You can squirt each other, but you can't beat each other's brains out."

The nursery was up ahead of them. "This is where your mom works?" Johnny asked Charlie the question, but Robbie answered him.

"Less and less these days," Robbie said. "Dad is doing well enough to hire employees. I think she's losing interest."

"Maybe she's pregnant," Johnny offered. "That's why she doesn't want to work anymore."

The smile that broke across Robbie's face surprised even him. "I think her tubes are tied. Charlie was the last straw, the demon seed."

Charlie removed his hand from the mister's pistol grip long enough to flip his brother the bird.

Robbie ignored him, and walked around to the back of the cedar building. The nursery was shrouded in shagbark hickories standing vigil, and Johnny walked past the trees carefully. They looked like the kinds of trees haunting the misty moors of fairytales. Their bark was coarse and dark as pumpernickel loaf. Johnny finally worked up the courage to touch the trunk of one, and he thought the mossy plates armoring the tree looked and felt like the hair of a haggard old witch. These were the kind of trees that might come to life, the hollow where an owl nested assuming the form of a mouth and warning him to leave this place.

He shivered and picked up his pace, until he caught up with Charlie and Robbie. They were in back of the nursery. Charlie uncapped the plastic berth of his misting system, and now held the hole over a metal tap. The water issuing forth smelled rusty, like it came from a stagnant well.

Robbie shivered slightly, but Johnny knew he was trembling from the cold and not from fear of the trees. "It's damn cold for you guys to be squirting each other like this." He looked over at Johnny. "If you catch a cold, don't sic your mom on me. I might need you to sign a permission slip actually."

"Hey," Charlie said. "I got an idea."

"What?" Johnny leaned down to him.

"Instead of taking all this time to let both proton packs fill up with slime, why don't one of us play the monster, and the other one tries to zap him?"

"Okay," Johnny said. "I'm the monster first. You got to find me." He ran across the gravel, and Robbie shouted to his retreating form. "Don't go too far, Slimer." Robbie absently tugged at some of his mother's prized Sphagnum, which was as lacy and golden as mythical fleece. He stroked it. "Rapunzel, Rapunzel, let down your golden hair."

Charlie looked up at him. The tank was almost filled with cold water. "I know who Rapunzel is. Ms. Seever read us a story about her."

"Good for you." Robbie tugged the peat moss, and the blondish fiber responded with spongey give. The hanging basket from which it dripped spun in a series of blurring convolutions.

"We didn't get to hear the whole story, 'cause Lawrence Baker wouldn't sit still and he was being disruptive."

Robbie laced his fingers into the fine silken moss. Now he wasn't just absently thinking of a fairytale princess. His mind was set on a particular girl at school, Sarah Fineman. She had frizzy hair that corkscrewed in a way that reminded him of the texture now spilling through his knuckles. He briefly wished someone his own age was here with whom he might share his theory. He would broach the subject with Adam tomorrow at Freeport, during lunch. He already knew how his friend would react when he explained it to him, though.

There was truth in his idea, he was convinced, and he would remain convinced no matter how hard his friend laughed tomorrow. The bottom line was that if he liked a girl, fantasized about her too much, and then tried to talk to her, he became painfully shy and awkward. He felt as adolescent as he actually was in those moments. His voice would crack, and a hormonal sweat would break out across his body and every pore of his skin would become clammy. He'd already lost track of the number of times he beat off thinking about the dark-eyed Jewish girl with the kinky hair, and he was yet to say so much as, "Hi" to her. If he approached her, he would immediately feel both creepy and guilty. It would be as if he was spying on her all this time, and feeling like that wasn't conducive to talking to a girl or asking her out on a date.

Robbie looked over at his little brother, pausing as he struggled to think of a way to impart at least some of this knowledge in an age-appropriate manner. "Charlie," he said. "If you like a girl …" He paused again. "Just talk to her. Don't spend all day thinking about her." There, that would do. He turned from his brother and shouted toward the chained succession of ironwoods into whose midst Johnny disappeared. "Don't go too far, dummy!" A few snowflakes, insubstantial as communion wafers, landed on the hand not gripping the Sphagnum. They dissolved just as quickly as they landed.

"It's snowing," Charlie said.

"I know, and you dumbasses are going to shoot each other with cold water." He swayed his head from side to side, amazed by their stupidity.

Robbie's voice came to Johnny faintly, carried on the cold air. Johnny stumbled into another one of Mrs. Milner's little mystery alcoves in his effort to escape the rays of the proton pack. She might no longer have much interest in the nursery, as Robbie said, but that clearly wasn't the case at one point. He crouched down, hidden between the walls formed by four trellises facing each other.

There was a good chance the wilting layer of perennials might protect him from the Ghostbuster now hot on his trail. He wasn't going to respond to Robbie's voice, either. He was sure that was a trap.

Johnny gazed quickly around, searching for the form of his friend, looking for him and his hose filled with cold water. Johnny liked the trees around here a lot more than those bordering the nursery. They weren't as creepy. The hornbeams had large weeping fronds blurring like watercolors when the wind was this strong. He felt safe and wished he could stay here. He wished there was no school, no homes, and no world beside this one.

***

The subject of treehouses came up at dinner that night. Johnny didn't know why he didn't think of it earlier. Hiding behind the nursery made him realize he and Charlie needed their own space, somewhere to hide out a little bit closer to home.

They ate at a Perkins situated like a redoubt between the lonely office parks and the four-lane highway. There was an endless sea of detached houses on the other side of the highway. The kitschy clones were platted far off into the distance, muted now in the year's first heavy snowfall.

Johnny asked Mr. Milner if he would help them build a treehouse. Russell massaged his scalp, which shined with a high varnish now, after decades of baldness. "Building a treehouse should be easy enough to do. I'm handy as all get-out, and I've got reciprocity with all the lumber and nursery suppliers around here."

Robbie took one last lingering look at the swaying ass of the waitress who just served them their drinks before prodding the effervescent surface of his Dr. Pepper with a straw. "I got an A in shop class. I can keep you knuckleheads from cutting your fingers off if you're serious about this." He took a sip from his drink and looked at his little brother. "You've got to help."

"I will."

Johnny squinted, chewing on the big word Russell used. He could already read at a third grade level, but "reciprocity" was a bit too much. "You have what with the suppliers?"

Russell opened a creamer over his mug of coffee. "Reciprocity," he said. "It means I give them stuff, and they give me stuff."

"Did you learn how to grow plants in the war, Mr. Milner?"

Russell stirred the coffee with a stainless steel spoon. "They had hydro plants in the Pacific, believe it or not, but not where I was."

"Where were you in the war?" Johnny's eyes briefly darted over to Robbie. He knew Charlie's older brother said it was okay to ask Mr. Milner about the war, but he still had doubts. He saw he didn't need to worry about Robbie. His own gaze was fastened on the kitchen. He was waiting for the waitress to return with their food and her butt.

Russell laughed hoarsely. He'd been stressed and a little crabby on the drive away from Freeport, muttering bitterly under his breath about "that cheap prick" Corbett and his wife. "To be honest Son, we were never sure where we were over there. Mostly the Ardennes."

"The Hardens?"

He nodded. "That's close enough. Sometimes we thought we were in France, sometimes Germany."

"Didn't you guys have maps?"

"We were I and R, intelligence, but we weren't always smart."

The talk of war and its details got Robbie's attention. He looked away from the kitchen for a moment, and leaned forward on the Formica table. A lamp with a chartreuse casing hung above them and threw buttery light across the vinyl booths. "The Germans were out of good soldiers at that point, mostly babies and old codgers were what they were left with. Our chances of running into some real Wehrmacht tough guys were getting lower and lower in those days. If we'd been that careless in the beginning of the war I'm pretty sure I wouldn't be talking to you now."

"You never hear about the war from the other side," Robbie said.

"You mean from the German side?" his father asked.

"Yeah." Robbie drummed his fingers on the table, doing paradiddles with the crawling spiders he made of his digits. "You know any good books from the other side?"

Russell pushed his cup away from him as if the question was so stupid it made him lose his thirst. "What, you mean like *Mein Kampf*?"

"No, like a German soldier's account."

Russell reached out for his coffee. He retrieved it and even took a sip, now that his son's question was clarified and no longer struck him as so dumb. "Yeah, *The Forgotten Soldier* by Guy …" He squinted. "Guy something or other."

"Here we are."

The waitress leaned over the table with their trays. Her massive bust heaved above Johnny's head as she set the plates down. Charlie touched the beer-battered exterior of one of his chicken fingers, and pulled his finger away when the hot grease burnt him slightly.

"Gotta wait for it to cool off first," Robbie said.

Russell took a fork from where it lay on his paper napkin and speared a watery piece of broccoli garnishing the edge of his early bird special hotplate.

Johnny took the plastic ketchup bottle from the display, where it rested between several packs of sweetener and jelly. He squirted the condiment out on his plate, as much to cool down the food as for the flavor. "Lawrence Baker has a treehouse in his backyard."

Charlie laughed from the sound of the half-empty ketchup bottle as it protested in Johnny's grip. It sounded like either a really coarse belch or a watery fart. Charlie blew on one of his golden fries and said, "I was telling Robbie about Lawrence Booger Eater Baker earlier today."

Russell held up both of his hands in a pleading gesture. "Hey, people are trying to eat."

"Sorry, Dad." He looked back over at Johnny. "I told him he always interrupts story time."

"Not just story time," Johnny said, and thought about Larry to himself now. He would like to talk about him with Charlie, since he was a mutual enemy. He didn't trust himself to speak though, because he would refer to him as Booger Eater Baker. The nickname was part of the fun of hating him, and he didn't want to spoil Mr. Milner's meal. Charlie's dad was really nice to them. He took them to the nursery and was now even thinking of building them a treehouse.

That booger eater ruined News of the Day and sing-alongs, too, not just reading time. Someone would talk about how they watched a movie and ate pizza, or how their mom went away to Texas on a business trip, and they missed her. Then Baker would stand up and run in a circle. He'd act if it was duck, duck, goose time at recess, and he was it. Sometimes Ms. Seever might break out *American Folk Songs for Kids*, and sing in a way that matched her Joni Mitchell face.

Ms. Seever even went out of her way to change the lyrics for the kids in the room. If one of the songs in the book said, "The handyman does handy work, handy work," she might say, "Charlie Milner has a red shirt, red shirt." Nothing ever calmed Booger Eater down, not even when she incorporated his name into a song. He didn't appreciate what she tried to do with that book Johnny grew to love so much. It smelled like glue and weathered binding fraying into dust, like all the Newberry Award winners molting in the reading nook next to the beanbag chairs.

Johnny looked over at Charlie and whispered, "I hate Booger Eater Baker." His friend understood him, and he giggled. Charlie kicked Johnny's legs underneath the table. His friend responded by kicking him back, and they both started laughing loudly. Their hands met in the space above the Formica table while their war below the table raged on. Their fingers interlocked, and they thumb wrestled for supremacy. Their roughhousing threatened to knock their drinks over. They ignored their food, even though it was finally cool enough to eat.

Russell's brow furrowed. "Are you two boys queer or something?"

"People don't say 'queer' anymore, dad," Robbie said. "It's 'gay.'"

His father shifted in the booth and sliced his turf with a dull steak knife. "Jerry Vale says gay. That means happy."

"That's what mom says," Charlie said, still trying to wrestle his friend's thumb down and pin it for the count.

"Who?" Robbie said. "That some old singer?"

"Genaro Louis Vitaliano was his real name. He grew up in Yonkers."

"Yonkahs," Charlie said. Johnny struggled not to laugh at his friend's joke at his father's expense, but he broke down a moment later. He only hoped Russell thought his laughter was caused merely by the wrestling match, not his funny New York accent.

"Don't worry about it," Russell said around a mouthful of tough beefsteak. "It's not your Metallica, so what do you know from real music?" He turned his attention back to the two younger boys. "So, you two kids really want a treehouse or what?"

CHAPTER FIVE

There was an argument about where and how to build the treehouse, and Russell won. Robbie was convinced he was right, but the old man was arranging for the delivery of supplies, so he was forced to let his father have his way.

That didn't mean he still couldn't bitch however. "I'm telling you," he said to Charlie and Johnny because his father refused to listen. "You look for a tree shaped like three fingers," he splayed the digits from ring to pointer, "with two big branches to the left and right, and the trunk in the middle." He lowered the outer fingers, leaving the middle one, which represented the trunk upraised. He used the finger to flip his father the bird.

Russell's back was to his son, as he was busy getting specs on the tree he selected.

Robbie walked over to the tree he wanted to use. He regarded it with forlorn pride, patted the pleats of its warty outer bark. "Pops needs to stop treating me like a baby," he said to Johnny. "If he wants me to take over the business someday, he needs to let me have more responsibility."

"What's wrong with this oak tree?" Johnny asked. He liked Russell, but he wanted to let Robbie know he was on his side. It made more sense to side with the younger man, since he spent a hell of a lot more time around him. He only saw Robbie really get angry once, and it was a scary sight.

"It's not an oak," Robbie said in a peeved tone, as Johnny shrank from him. Robbie noted the boy flinching, and his tone softened. "It's an

American beech." He gazed up. The last snowfall was a meager show of flurries, a soft watery spurt from the sky that didn't stick or accumulate for the most part. There was, however, a shimmering coat of frost on the branches of the tree above them. The sun was setting and it made the snow glow with a virginal brilliance. Johnny thought it would taste like sugar if he were to climb the tree and eat some of the frost for himself.

Robbie looked up, and Johnny noticed how large his Adam's apple was again. He didn't know why, but he was jealous of the feature. He always focused on the strangest things, like with Elise. He thought her large boy's nose made her somehow powerful in a way that a word like "pretty" couldn't contain. Most guys focused on boobs or butts, like Robbie back at the Perkins admiring the waitress's derriere, and he wondered if maybe there was something wrong or weird about him.

"I was going to let the one beam cantilever out past the other two." Robbie made a gesture with his hands as if he was the foreman and the two boys were his pint-sized construction crew. "I already checked the bark, and she ain't rotting." Robbie pointed to the side of the tree at a spot where the outer skin was rubbed off to reveal a chestnut layer of living wood.

"Would you quit your bellyaching!" Russell shouted. He grounded his heavy winter coat, and was stripped down to a ribbed white jersey already slicked with sweat. His chest and back hair were both white, reminding Johnny of Santa's beard. He was twisting a manual post hole digger into the cold ground, and Johnny was astonished that someone with such poor posture could work so hard.

Robbie gave up on his sentry beneath the beech and walked over to his father. Various tools and supplies were scattered on the ground beneath the old man. "I don't doubt you know what you're doing," Russell said, his breath fogging in the cold air as he spoke. "If we do things your way though, it's more dangerous for you and me."

Robbie reached down for a hammer and gathered up a handful of galvanized nails from a toolbox laid at his father's feet. "The hell you talking about, old man?"

"I'm talking about your tree over there." Russell pointed, and then rested both of his gloved hands on the grip of the auger planted in the hole beneath him. His chest was heaving and sweat collected in the bevel of his throat, moistening the tufts of white hair. "You got to suspend your beam you wanted to cantilever, and that means one of us has got to lower it. Then the other one has got to wait to catch it. While the one of us is holding it, the other one's got to hold the level out, and make sure the damn thing's plumb."

Russell shook his head as he imagined the agony of the task his son set for them. "It's cold, it's wet, and it's slippery. Accidents happen under the best of conditions." He resumed his task with the post hole digger, gritted his teeth, and spoke as he exerted himself, sweating. "See why we're doing things my way?"

"Cool!" Charlie leaned down and grabbed a drill. He held it up to Johnny, who stuck his hands in the air and pretended he was on the receiving end of a stickup. Charlie zipped his jacket up and concealed the lower half of his face in the silky down coat.

"Gimme your money, punk!"

Robbie snatched the drill from his brother. Russell said, "You know your mom doesn't like you to play guns. She wanted me to take away your little Nintendo gun, but I went to bat for you, you little hellion."

"Besides that," Robbie said, "the torque will spin your ass around."

"Then what can we do?"

High beams split through the trees behind the Milner homestead, blinding them all for the moment. Robbie said, "There's the rest of the stuff for the treehouse arriving in that truck. We don't need it now, but you can drag it into the garage."

"Cool!"

Charlie ran off toward the truck from Freeport Nursery. Johnny stayed in place for the time being. Russell Milner wasn't a big shot like Gentleman Jim Corbett, but he must have some clout to make one call and get the truck to show up within a matter of hours. The arrival of the pickup got the attention of someone in the house. Johnny wasn't sure who it was until Elise finally ran outside. She brought two friends in tow who came over for a sleepover.

"Damn it," she said. "I thought it was the pizza man." She ran back in the house to watch *Labyrinth* for the thousandth time and pine for David Bowie once more.

Johnny looked away from Elise, back at Russell and Robbie. He was proud the panic didn't start in his stomach this time. Fear filled him when he usually saw her. Then again, she was twenty feet or so away from him, and she didn't see him. That made it somehow easier to remain cool. The true test would come later tonight.

"One other thing," Russell said. "Your way would take a few weeks. I can have this puppy knocked out in two, three days tops."

"You're shitting me?"

"I shit you not." Russell shook his head. "If it wasn't getting dark, it'd all be over except for the crying by close of business tomorrow. I'm a man of my word, so believe me when I tell you that, boy. You can set your watch to my word."

Mr. Milner jerked his head in the direction of the garage and spoke to Robbie. "Start bringing me the stuff I need for now." He released his grip from the digging tool, and removed his gloves from his sweating hands. He wiped the newly-formed blisters on the sore padding of his palms. "I want some of that plywood, and the Sakrete. The wood's cut by the running foot and should be easy as pie to carry. The only two-man gig we got coming involves that telephone pole we're gonna put here. The Sakrete's a bitch and a half without the wheel barrow, so use that unless you feel like going to the ER with a hernia. You're a bit young for a worker's comp claim, so I don't advise trying to lug it over here."

"You don't need any help with the hole?" Robbie walked cautiously to the edge of the breach his father made in the ground. He gazed inside with a look of wonder on his face, as if for a moment he thought the old wives' tale about digging to China might have some truth to it.

"Work smarter, not harder," Russell said. "I got a sixth sense about these things." He resituated the leather gloves over his raw hands. "I can smell when there are too many rocks under the ground and I don't aim to use an iron pick." He glanced over at Johnny, a little surprised to still see him here after Charlie scurried off. "I can still swing an axe with the best of them, but why waste the energy?"

Russell leaned down toward the wet ground, where dead pine needles made a soft bed. He found a hammer after a moment's search and hefted it in his hand. "Look here, Johnny Boy."

No one ever called him that before, but Johnny liked it. The old man asked, "You know how to hold a hammer?"

Johnny shook his head. Russell's gloved hand choked up on the hammer, gripped it near the metal head. "You hold it close to the head when you start out." He let his grip on the hammer slip and clutched it tightly near the end of the handle. "Then, once you've got your nail started, you move down. That way you got more power in your stroke."

"Okay." Johnny nodded.

"Good, you learned something today. You listen, unlike my boys. When you listen, you learn."

"Mr. Milner?"

"What?"

"Which one of these trees are we going to build the treehouse in?"

Johnny looked up. Night crept up on them while they were busy, but the stars and moon threw enough light over them to make work possible for a while longer. Now the only real enemy was the cold.

"We're not building the treehouse in either tree," Russell said. He pointed at the two sugar maples bookending the crater he dug in the snowy ground. The leaves of the trees were a prismatic explosion of gold and red during daylight. They were colorless in the dark. They joined the shadows blending into the larger forest snaking down the hill toward a foul smelling creek.

"We're going to stick a telephone pole into this hole I dug and we're going to stretch a plank across the two trees on top of that. *Capisce*?"

He never before heard that word Mr. Milner just used, but the lilt of his voice let him know it was a question. He looked up at the empty space between the two sugar maples, and imagined a house balanced on a pole between them. What he saw in his mind was something like Baba Yaga's shack, propped on a giant chicken's leg.

"You're going to balance the treehouse between the two trees, sort of like a hammock?"

Russell tousled his hair. "Smart kid." He pointed toward the garage. "Go help your little friend. You," he said, to his elder son, "go help yourself. Get cracking."

Johnny rushed toward the warmth of the garage. Charlie was setting down some sheets of readymade thatch. They rustled as he struggled to make them all sit in one pile, next to a synthetic Christmas tree and a Tupperware container overstuffed with ornaments and shimmering tinsel.

The employee from the nursery struggled with a rack of expandable bamboo fencing. It sprang loose and now flexed and contracted like an accordion in the hands of a novice. "Whoa, little help?" The man struggled to see around the latticework. Johnny thought it looked sort of like those baby gates parents set up between rooms to confine toddlers and keep them safe.

Johnny slipped his fingers through the bamboo and guided the worker toward the accumulating pile, where Charlie deposited his last batch of thatch before heading to the bed of the truck to grab more stuff. The deliveryman asked, "You guys building a Tiki bar where you can knock back a couple after work?"

"Treehouse," Johnny said very seriously.

"Ah, my mistake." Charlie cleared the berth of the truck and it was empty now except for some loose strands of thatching that were jarred free. "Well, you guys stay warm up there this winter."

The man closed the back of his truck and got in on the driver's side.

Robbie walked around him into the garage. He looked over at his brother, and grabbed the red wheelbarrow by its wooden handles. "Elise and her girlfriends still playing Truth or Dare?"

"Nah, Girl Talk."

"Same shit, different pamper. Who cares? What kind of stuff they making each other do?" Johnny noticed Robbie now donned his dad's gloves. Robbie leaned down, bowed his legs, and hefted a bag of Sakrete into the wheelbarrow.

Johnny said, "I saw her make Ashley put an ice cube under her armpit, and Rachel had to eat a whole lemon, even with the outside part."

"The rind." Robbie grunted, leaned down for another bag.

"What?"

"The outside part of the lemon is called the rind."

"Oh."

Bowser barked from inside the house, and Mrs. Milner laughed at something she saw on TV. Robbie rotated the wheelbarrow and prepared to push it out into the cold. "I wish Elise would dare Ashley to …never mind."

Johnny stared at him blankly. Robbie misinterpreted the look, hunched defensively, and said, "Hey, Elise is twelve, but Ashley's fourteen. There's only two years between us. I'm only human." He pushed the barrow out into the cold, disappearing into the dark, except for his voice. "I hope you two douchebags appreciate what me and dad are doing for you."

"We do!" Charlie said. There wasn't as much as a hint of sarcasm in his voice, which was rare in any interaction with his brother. He smiled at Johnny, who smiled back. "We're going to have a treehouse soon!"

They both jumped up and down. They slap-boxed each other silly until a stray blow from Johnny cuffed Charlie on his earlobe, which was already stinging from the cold. "Ow, franks and beans."

"Sorry, man."

"It's okay." Charlie shrugged it off. "Come on, let's go out there. There's nothing left to do now."

Robbie got a head start on them, but the burden of the Sakrete slowed him considerably, and they were alongside him in very little time. "You two knuckleheads are going to help me set up a railing around the treehouse after we get done with the basic construction. That way you won't fall off and break your legs."

"If I break my leg," Charlie said, "I don't have to go to school for a month or so."

"Yeah, well, then how about you'll break your neck?"

"If I break my neck, I'll never have to go school again."

His older brother stopped pushing the wheelbarrow for a moment, and contemplated saying something. Robbie eyed Charlie, scrutinizing him to see if his brother was serious. "Don't talk like that," he said, and pushed his wheelbarrow again.

"It was only a joke."

"Then don't joke like that."

They were almost to Russell. Johnny asked, "How come sometimes you call us douchebags and other times you call us knuckleheads?"

"Because sometimes you act like douchebags and sometimes you act like knuckleheads."

Johnny thought about that. It made sense. Robbie parked the Sakrete next to the treehouse. "All right, pay attention, you douchebag knuckleheads."

"There should be a rule," Charlie said. "You can only call us one or the other."

Robbie removed the gloves and tossed them back to his dad. "Charlie, you could screw up a wet dream, which is why I'm not letting you touch so much as a Tenpenny nail. Even you can't mess this up. Okay?"

"Yeah."

"Good, we're taking five for the night. I want you and lover boy awake at the ass-crack of dawn. You need to come out here and jitterbug this Sakrete while I pour it."

"Jitterbug?"

Robbie leaned down to the cold earth, took a stick, and handed it to his brother. "Yeah, either you or *you*," he pointed at Johnny, "poke the Sakrete, while the other one pours water on. I'll be here to help you some, but this is an all-day thing you've got to keep an eye on. It's like a campfire, so you know what that means?"

Robbie couldn't see his brother shaking his head in the dark, but assumed correctly Charlie didn't know. "That means no snuggling up to Brave Heart tomorrow morning and watching your cartoons, and no videogames. Nothing but keeping watch on the cement while it dries around the pole."

"I put a rock down there," Russell said. "I boarded it up too, so they don't have to worry about the pole falling over after you and me set her in place."

"Good deal," Robbie said.

Another set of headlights burrowed through the dark, splashing their way through the trees. All three of them squinted like rodents caught rummaging through trash.

"Pizza's here," Robbie said.

"Good," his dad replied. "Let's go inside and eat with the womenfolk."

Johnny thought of Elise and gulped.

CHAPTER SIX

It was as Mr. Milner promised. The treehouse was built, and it was all over now except for the crying. It took three weeks rather than two days to see the project through to completion.

Most of the remaining work fell to Robbie after Russell's initial flush of enthusiasm spent itself, the hole was dug, and the telephone pole planted. The boys stood on the ground below and watched as Robbie affixed weathered cedar shingles to the roof, and then nailed shiplap to the sides of the plywood body of their new fortress. Charlie thought it looked like a ship. He decided to play pirate and got Johnny to join him once they were able to ascend and survey their mostly completed treehouse.

"Argh, matey, get me my debuts!"

Robbie snorted, struggling to corral and then lasso the orange extension cord attached to the jigsaw he used to cut the last pocket hole in the plywood. "Doubloons, dummy. Don't jump around until we have the guiderails in place." He unplugged the saw.

"I'll put those posts in, and you and Dill Weed can string the nylon ropes through them. Then you can run around out here to your heart's content. In the meantime, go inside with your friend."

Charlie went into the treehouse, which reeked of new wood, and Robbie switched to a finer blade. "What's up?" Charlie asked.

"Not a lot, but check out what I found." Johnny hopped off the overinflated blue air mattress and walked to the center of the treehouse. The place was big enough for an adult to stand comfortably. There was more than enough room for two six-year olds to feel like they had the run of their own loft apartment.

"I put the cooler here to hide this secret spot from any bad guy swash buckles who might want to come up here and kill us and take our treasure."

"Swashbucklers," Robbie said, over the metallic whine of his saw.

"That's what I said."

Johnny pushed the cooler aside. The thing was filled with snacks Mrs. Milner made for them. This was going to be their first overnight in the treehouse. They had a bunch of comic books and a flashlight sitting in the hammock strung between two hooks on the other side of the room in addition to the food.

There was a wooden panel painted a conspicuously different color from the sheets adjacent to it below the space where the cooler was a moment before. An imperceptibly small bit of string- no larger than a shoelace- peeked from the panel. Johnny snuck his pointer finger into the little bit of rope and pulled up.

The panel came free. There was a rope ladder coiled on the other side. Johnny undid the ladder, allowing the nylon lashings to spill to the snow covered ground below them. "Cool!" Charlie turned back toward Robbie who stopped using the saw for the time being. "Did you do that?"

"That I did."

Johnny resealed the secret hatch and stood up. "We'll pull the rope ladder back up in a little bit. Bad pirates will definitely try to use it to mess us up and steal our treasure."

Robbie appeared before them in the doorway. "You guys really want to be pirates?"

"Yeah!"

"I've got some extra dowels that I won't be using as posts here." He nodded in the direction of the treehouse's still vulnerable perimeter. "I'll cut you guys up some debuts, and I'll hit them with that spray paint. That way you can have your gold coins. What do you say?"

They didn't have to say anything. Their response was written on their faces. "This is like

Indoor in *Star Wars*," Charlie said, spinning 360 degrees to marvel at his enchanted forest palace.

"Endor," Robbie said.

"Nah-uh," Johnny said. "It's more like the Sixteen Chapel."

Robbie drew a breath, about to correct him, but let it go. "Come on," he said. "I've got the debuts taken care of. You guys go get the treasure chest from mom."

Robbie descended the log ladder, taking the wooden posts two at a time, and jumping to the forest floor when he was halfway down. His little brother and Johnny slowly made their way down to the ground after him.

They went into the house where Mrs. Milner was sipping Czech liqueur and chiding Bowser for lapping up a bit she spilled on the kitchen floor.

"Ma," Robbie said, "where's that old chest of yours?"

"No, you don't." Johnny noticed a restless cast to her face, a rapid blink combined with a twitch of the lip. He didn't know how to interpret it, but she was pining to have her first cigarette in sixteen years. The alcohol always made her want to have one, even though it was light drink. Earlier she seriously contemplated going to the convenience store, and staying there long enough to smoke a whole pack of Pall Malls.

"Me and dad have been busting our humps out there!" Robbie pointed toward the treehouse. "I shed about ten pounds in sweat equity and now you've got to contribute."

"Yeah!" Charlie said. "We want our treasure chest."

She sighed. She simply didn't have the energy to tolerate the migraine her younger son's pleading would induce. It would be better, she decided, to part with the heirloom now, rather than to cave after being pestered for an hour or so. "All right, it's in the guest room closet."

Elise breezed into the room wearing her headphones. The caterwauling coming from the yellow cassette player clipped to her hip sounded like Steven Tyler. "Hope you losers don't want anything from me."

Johnny wasn't sure whether or not he was included in that insult, but hoped so. He looked down at the floor and saw the bottoms of her white socks were stained brown from walking around the house without shoes.

"No, we know better than that," Robbie said. "You're as useless as they come."

She ignored the insult, opened the fridge, and extracted a carton of orange juice. Her mother watched her. "I hope you're not planning on drinking straight from the carton."

"Actually, mom, I was planning on pouring it into the dog's bowl."

Johnny wondered how she could hear her mother with the music playing as loud as it was. She left the kitchen the way she came, disappearing back into the warm mystery of her bedroom. The walls in there crawled with a collage of boys from TV shows that bored Johnny to death, except for when he considered that Elise liked them. He was born too late, he decided, and wished he was twelve now.

"You two jokers get the chest. I'll start on the doubloons."

"Come on."

Johnny followed behind Charlie, down the hall. Bowser trailed behind them, his butterscotch tail curling into a furry scythe shape. The walls of the guest room were painted harvest gold, and there was an intangible coldness to the room that let Johnny know no one slept there. He doubted anyone even walked into the untenanted space for quite some time.

Charlie opened the closet door, which was the only thing in the room painted white. Johnny noticed there were massive holes in the walls on either side of the closet's interior, where wire hangers but no clothes were strung across a rod. "What happened to the walls?" Johnny coughed, and something fine as asbestos made his nose burn and his eyes water.

"I used to come in here sometimes and punch holes in the walls when I was angry."

"Oh, why?"

Charlie shrugged. "Bored, I guess." He crouched down to the hardwood floor and dragged the chest out.

"Whoa!"

"Yeah, it's cool."

The chest was stained walnut, covered in gold decorative strap hinges that rattled as Charlie pulled the chest free. The front of the container featured a hasp and padlock attached to a brassy Masonite plate.

"You grab half and I'll grab half."

Johnny took a handle in his grip. It felt cold and reminded him of the brass knockers on the front doors of rich people's houses, the ones that usually featured a scary mascot, like a lion with the facial features of a Greek god.

Elise breezed past them as they lugged the chest out into the hall. The box slapped Johnny's legs as he walked with it, making his thighs sting where the hard corners bumped him. His shoulders also burned in their sockets from the pain of having to keep the chest from hitting the floor, as they walked with it held between them.

They set the chest down when they came to the kitchen. Elise, who passed them a moment before, emerged from the kitchen pantry with a brown paper grocery bag in her hands. "Screw Robbie. I wasn't going to help you guys, but if he tells me not to do something, I have to do it."

"No foul language." Mrs. Milner refilled her little glass with more of the sweet liqueur.

"I said 'screw' not 'fuck.'"

"Now you're just trying to give your poor mother conniptions."

"Conniptions" was a new word for Johnny, but "fuck" was familiar. It was a big and bad word, and a kind of exalted feeling transported him when Elise said it. *Fuck*. Elise set the brown paper bag down on the kitchen table and furiously rubbed it with her hands.

"They taught us this in art class." The bag rustled from the pressure she applied. She gritted her teeth as she worked, messing up her shiny dark hair as she rubbed the brown paper in her hands. "This will be your treasure map."

"Cool." Charlie walked closer to his sister to observe.

The aerosol scent of spray paint poured from the garage, and she made a face. "Ugh, what is he doing in there?"

"Painting our double-oohs."

Elise frowned. "I frankly don't even want to know what that means."

David Bowie's voice oscillated through four octaves from the black foam of her headphones, and she sneered at her handiwork. She held out the rough brown pelt to inspect it. "There."

She handed it to Charlie, and then patted him once on the head. It was an affectionless tap that was more like counting coup. "Put your 'X' on there."

"Huh?"

"'X' marks the spot where you put the treasure, genius."

"Oh."

She left the kitchen again, satisfied to prove her older brother wrong. Mrs. Milner stood up from the kitchen table, wobbled slightly, and walked over to one of a series of drawers across from the vulcanized kitchen range. "Here you go." She handed her son a marker and then sat back down at the table with her bottle of Czech carob.

Charlie held the marker like a knife poised in an overhand grip, and jabbed the felt tip at an arbitrary point on the brown bag. He made an 'X', as his sister instructed. He looked over at Johnny. "Let's go outside."

Johnny opened the face of the chest, and Charlie dropped the map inside. "No," his mom said, shaking her head. "You keep the map to tell you where the treasure chest is. You don't bury the map with the treasure, boys."

"Sorry."

Johnny opened the face of the treasure chest and allowed his friend to extract the distressed piece of brown paper. Charlie, after considering his mom's words, discarded her suggestion and threw the paper bag back into the box. "Let's go."

They each took one of the handles, and headed outside. Mrs. Milner shook her head one last time, watching them as they went. "That was my grandmother's."

"Yeah," Robbie said. He came to stand in the doorway, grabbing the trunk from the boys and unburdening them. "It's ours now. Just be happy I'm not painting a skull and crossbones on the thing, because I'm seriously tempted to."

He gripped the trunk in his strong arms. "Play your cards right and you might get the damn thing back in a condition I would describe as fair or better, in a month or two."

"I'm not holding my breath."

"Let's go, douchebags."

They followed behind him. Robbie was in just a T-shirt, not wanting to get the gold paint on his winter coat. Johnny noticed Robbie's back formed a perfect "V," the rhomboids like sharp meat cleavers and the fascia at the base of his spine a perfect diamond.

"Call them debuts or doubloons, but they're ready." His hands sparkled with the dry, gold paint. "Reach in my pockets and get them." Johnny and Charlie each reached into a pocket of Robbie's stonewashed jeans with the shredded knees. They knew the coins were really just wood cut from the dowels, but they sparkled like the real thing.

The boys opened the box and sanded the coins into the chest. The doubloons clinked as they tumbled to the base of the walnut container. Robbie walked the chest all the way to the bank of the sulfurous creek, and dropped the antique at the water's edge. Then he grabbed a spade sitting next to the auger his father toiled over when they began their project a few weeks ago.

Robbie turned to Johnny. "You spending the night?"

It sounded like Robby wanted him to sleep over. He wasn't sure who he liked more, Elise or him. "Yeah, my mom says I behave better and that I'm calmer after I spend a night over here. I think Ms. Seever says I'm more concentrate after I spend the night here, too."

"Are you orange juice?"

"What?"

"Nothing." Robbie braced the spade's wooden handle between his shoulder blades. He stared up at the sky, which was positively Siberian, as they stood around. "It's gonna be a two-dog night," he said.

"That means it'll be cold?" Johnny said.

"You're quite the sharp tack. It's not a problem," he said. "If we get enough snow, I'll take you guys into town tomorrow and we can have some fun."

Robbie looked toward the cloaca-smelling water, stagnant in the creek. The coarse twigs of devils walkingstick sprouted out from the water's edge, bullying the much prettier mountain laurel growing alongside it. The laurel held on for dear life against the walkingstick, and the evergreen leaves refused to bow to the brown thickets of decay.

"Well," Robbie said, "'fifteen men on a dead man's chest' and all that." He unlocked the wooden spade handle from where it was laced between his shoulders. Robbie chucked the shovel toward the ground, where it speared through the leaves and sliced into the soil.

"Let's bury this sucker."

CHAPTER SEVEN

There was no way the old man was going to let Robbie take the Benz down to the village square, especially not with a sheet of plywood in the backseat stretched across two already snow covered kids. His mom was a bit nicer, or at least she was tired enough to give in.

"You know if the cops pull you over when you just have that learner's permit, it'll be the same as if you were riding without a license."

Robbie stood in the center of the kitchen zipping up his bubbly ski jacket. Johnny and Charlie hung behind him, waiting sheepishly in the entryway. "I know."

"Then you'll have to wait until you're eighteen to drive." Mrs. Milner was sipping black coffee from a white porcelain mug featuring Schultz's Peanuts gang running around the cup's perimeter. "Okay, if you think it's worth it."

"Worth nothing," he said, turning to head out into the snow covered world. "I'm not going to get pulled over."

"If you do, you have to say you took the car without my permission."

He ignored her, and pulled his brother's silk hood over his head. "Come on." He veered right to the mudroom, and snatched his mother's keychain from the pegboard where it hung next to a clock shaped like a Siamese cat. The cat's tail and eyes moved at one point. The battery died a long time ago, and no one bothered to replace it. The hands of the clock still moved, however.

The harsh winds were passed. Earlier they caused ground blizzards to form in the already fallen snow, creating drifts and the kinds of temporary whiteouts that caused car accidents. Robbie would take it especially slow, at least on the backstreets.

"Get in."

His mom's Volvo station wagon was covered in a thick coat of off-white slush. "Did mom drive the car this morning while I was asleep?"

Charlie shrugged, and climbed across the backseat. Johnny got in after him. "All right." Robbie carefully slid a plywood board across their legs.

"What's this for?" Johnny thought all of the wood was used on the treehouse.

"You'll see when we get down there." Robbie grabbed a shovel and ran around to the driver's side. Then he opened the door and hopped in, throwing the spade onto the passenger seat. He started the car and rubbed his gloved hands together, turned on the radio, and lucked into some new wave. "Hopefully they're still cool this year, but Gentleman Jim can be a dick and likes to throw his weight around."

He glanced over his shoulder and pulled out. "Ah, piece a cake." Wet accumulation slushed beneath the Volvo's tires as he drove onto the side street. The leaves the trees shed in early fall now drowned in puddles of frozen water, going quickly from dark red and bright yellow to mottled brown. "Dad can say what he wants about these rich fucks, but they pay the taxes that keep the army of snow plows moving."

Robbie pointed out the window, at the white driven piles lining either side of the road. They were the size of ice cornices at ski resorts that proved so perilous.

"You guys keep your eyes out for the Yeti while I drive."

"Yeti?"

"Abominable Snow Man." A lighter appeared in Robbie's hand, the same one Charlie used to cook waffles with bug spray the first time

Johnny came over. "Tell mom I'm smoking and I'll beat the living shit out of you."

"I won't say anything," Johnny said.

The scent of a stale cigarette that he'd stolen long ago and saved for some time filtered into the cabin of the Volvo. "I know you won't," Robbie said. "You're cool."

"Can I have a drag?" Charlie leaned forward and reached his mitten for the cigarette. Robbie slapped his hand away.

"Get the hell away! Come see me when you're twelve and then maybe."

He took another drag and turned right, singing along with a morose latter-day Wilde on the radio who bitched about materialism in L.A. "Shit, I wish I was in L.A. right now." Robbie turned the knob on the radio down, blowing out a cloud of smoke. "Shh, listen."

"What?" Charlie leaned back, realizing he wasn't going to get a puff on the cigarette. He didn't really want one, anyway. He merely wanted to piss off his brother, and the mission was accomplished.

"I hear it," Johnny said.

The solstice carillon bells were ringing from the town square, a cacophony that rattled through each of them. "It's beautiful," Robbie said, and Johnny was almost frightened by his lack of cynicism. He waited for the punchline, for him to undermine his own words, with a fart perhaps. Nothing followed, however.

Robbie smoked his cigarette and steered. The village square loomed before them. It was like a living snow globe that someone furiously shook, the perfect white snow borrowed from some Currier & Ives or Norman Rockwell dream. There were horse-drawn carriage rides offered, and genuine gaslight lamps lined the streets. It was a warm and soft vision, suspended in a mosaic of falling snow like a paperweight laid down to keep the whole of the village beneath it from blowing away.

"You know, they still got a town crier here." Robbie cupped his cigarette in his hand. He smoked furtively now, afraid to be seen by someone who knew his mom and would only be too happy to report him. This town was crawling with gossipy old biddies. His mood soured, as his mind turned from the place's beauty, and toward the people who owned it all.

"This place reeks of money, not just money, but old fucking money."

"Mom and dad aren't poor," Charlie said.

Robbie's eyes scanned for a parking space. "No, but we ain't rich like this."

Across the street were an inn and a series of boutique retail shops. There was also a theater that saw continuous service since before talkies and the Great Depression. The inn once hosted Mark Twain and Ulysses S. Grant, who now had suites on the top floor named in their honor to commemorate their stays.

"I'd like to stay there," Robbie said, gazing up at the dormers of the timber-framed hotel. The flying buttresses looked sharp enough to impale a man.

"Are we getting out soon?" Charlie writhed restlessly in his seat. It was cold outside, but the Volvo got hot superfast. Now he was sweating uncomfortably.

"Almost, Dill Weed. Looks like a lot of other people had the same idea as us." Charlie looked out of the window and could see kids pelting each other with snowballs. They ambushed each other behind gazebos and darted behind statues and park benches. The mixed Tudor and Norman sanctuaries made Johnny feel as if he stepped into another time.

Robbie was yet to shake his growing insecurity. "Mayflower money," he said. "Even if I got rich I couldn't be one of these people."

"Ah ha!"

There were a generous number of parking spaces in a lot serving a series of walking trails and unpaved arteries that led to bird and wildlife sanctuaries seated on Freeport's endless acreage.

"No one's stupid enough to try to go for a long walk on the trails in this weather. That'd be a doomed expedition."

He parked and got out. Then he went around to the side of the vehicle and grabbed his shovel. The boys slowly got out of the car. "I wonder how Freeport got started?" Charlie said. He slid the plywood across the backseat of the Volvo, scraping the leather padding as he did so. There was no way his dad would let them pull this stunt in his Benz.

"Pioneers," Robbie said, and motioned Johnny with the hand not holding the shovel. "Help your boy."

Johnny turned around and carried the front half of the plywood on his arms stretched out behind him like a litter bearer bringing wounded from the field of battle. They followed after Robbie, who continued his answer to Charlie's question. "They came here on flatboats and did battle with the Shawnees, 'til they scared the red man out of these parts of Ohio."

"Is the town crier around here?" Johnny asked.

"He might be. He wears a tri-corner hat and he has a bell in his hand. The guy does a lot of shouting, too. He's kind of hard to miss."

They waited at the miniature sierra of snow piled at the curb. A jeep sped past them, hitting an icy puddle that sent a spray toward them. "Shit on whole wheat toast," Robbie said. He trembled from the jet of cold water that got inside his jacket and crawled down his shirt, making him shiver as if someone stuck an ice cube against his spine. He was otherwise undeterred.

"Come on, men."

He crossed the street and they followed. There was a stillness to the land, something behind the kind of silence a heavy snow imposes. It was as if this was a land apart from the rest of the world, a dream that could forever withstand the scrutiny of waking life. Johnny thought the people who lived in this historical portion of Freeport could only die of natural causes. They couldn't have died in World War II or Vietnam, and they couldn't get cancer. There wasn't even any chance of dying in a natural disaster, because there was some kind of force field around this village square protecting it from tornadoes and earthquakes. Time was marked only by holidays, the harvest of Halloween and Christmas followed by the bright green renewal of Easter.

A cemetery ahead of them caught his eye, where all of the headstones were crumbling, and the names and dates were hidden by phosphorescent moss and lichen. "Who's buried there?" Johnny asked.

Robbie turned, looking a little annoyed with the barrage of questions. "A bunch of Jamesons and a bunch of Archibalds."

Charlie looked up at his brother. "Just two people?"

"Just two clans."

The cemetery was small enough that they were already past it. "Those pioneers who came here were just two big families, and there wasn't anyone around to marry but each other, so that's what they did."

"I want to marry Elise when I get older." Johnny's words shocked him, and Charlie.

Robbie was unfazed. He walked over to an igloo-sized mound of snow and said, "Yeah, well, I don't want to spoil your fun, but something tells me she's a dyke. Here," he said, and pointed, "put your board on top. After you do that, I'll get to work building your fort. All I've got to do is dig out the inside and put all that snow on top of the board, and you guys will have your little fortress of solitude where no girls can enter." He grinned at Johnny. "Sorry, no girls but Elise, but good luck getting that snotty bitch inside your little ice hut."

They laid the wood over the top of the plowed mound of snow. "What do you want us to do?"

Robbie pierced the sharp point of the spade into the hard white pile. "I saw some kids over by the gazebo throwing snowballs. Go play with them until I'm done."

"Good deal." Charlie lightly grazed Johnny's hand with his itchy wool mitten and they headed off in the direction of the gazebo. *Rain Man* and *Die Hard* were playing at the theater. Bulbs illuminated the movie poster on which Dustin Hoffman and Tom Cruise walked down a street with sunglasses on, and the other poster on which Bruce Willis bled slightly, superimposed over a skyscraper with a gun in his hand.

"Can't see either one of those," Charlie said.

"Yep, both rated R."

"Once they're out, my brother will let me watch them with him when my parents aren't around."

The kids on the gazebo were throwing hard enough to be little league forkball pitchers. Two of them were brandishing garbage can lids like miniature gladiators. A stray snowball whizzed past Charlie and Johnny as they walked toward the pavilion, and Johnny was sure the missile was nothing but ice lightly coated with a dusty outer layer of snow.

"Hey," Charlie said, "it's Alex Corbett."

The boy was center stage in the gazebo, king of the hill. He was accompanied by one other boy. They were both furiously making new snowballs, one after another on an improvised assembly line. They worked beneath the eaves where bluish icicles dangled like stalagmites.

Alex winged a breaking screwball at a boy on the lower steps who aimed to kill the king, and got a wad of ice to the node of his hipbone for his attempt. The boy lay on the ground, expressing an intensity of pain that was usually reserved for older boys taking a direct hit to the testes.

"Man," Johnny said. "He looks like a dickhead."

"Yeah, let's not go over there."

They turned from the gazebo before Alex Corbett spotted them. Johnny cast a final sidelong glance at the façade of the art deco theater across the icy, slick street. The popcorn machines were rumbling at full blast behind the glass of the concession stand, visible through the window. The smell wafted all the way to the frozen park where he and Charlie now trudged, leaving deep footprints in the snow.

"Why do you want to keep letting Robbie show you R-rated movies? You said they give you nightmares, right?"

Charlie shook his head emphatically. "No, just the horror movies. Regular R action movies don't scare me much at all."

"Ah, that makes sense."

Robbie was puffing from exertion when they reached him. He'd shed his winter jacket and laid it on the ground. The rippling veins of his forearms bulged like fatted earthworms. "Why didn't you knuckleheads go over to the gazebo and play for a spell? I'm nowhere near close to being done."

He wiped sweat from his brow, and coughed once, rasping. "Shit, I'm gonna be sick. This is how you get pneumonia, sweating and freezing your ass off at the same time."

"We can't play over there," Charlie said.

Robbie stopped excavating snow from the main body of the pile, and used the backside of his spade to tamp down the ice atop the plywood that was now invisible, buried underneath the white layers he laid on top of it. "Why not?"

"Alex Corbett's over there being a jerk."

"Yeah, well, at least you don't have to go to school with him."

"Not this year," Charlie said. "He's still at the magnet school. Ms. Seever says that most of the magnet kids will go to Freeport Elementary next year. They go to special, gifted classes."

"Maybe you won't see him," Robbie said, and continued shoveling.

"Maybe" Charlie said, but he wasn't so sure. He looked over at Johnny, who was also worried.

Freeport, Ohio 1994

CHAPTER ONE

Everyone saw what they wanted in clouds. Johnny's specific vision was of a giant squid, tumbling over the saucer of the sky. The charcoal wisps emanating from its center were the underwater monster's poisonous ink squirting out over the suburbs.

A voice from behind the vinyl seat where they sat brought his mind away from the dark sky visible through the bus window. "Cat Piss!" someone shouted.

Charlie Milner lowered his head. His long, greasy hair spilled over his face. The hair hid his eyes, but still didn't offer enough protection.

"How'd they find out so quick?" His voice was barely audible. The bus's noises, the shouting and loud thudding of feet on the floor, made it hard to concentrate on anything. The permanent scent of carbon monoxide pouring in through the windows of the bus didn't help much.

"I don't know. Crowes only started that shit yesterday."

Apparently Mike Crowes was Alex Corbett's teammate both on and off the field. They were in the cafeteria during second period lunch yesterday, when the regular volley of Skittles and Reese's Pieces was chucked in their direction. Alex Corbett and Mike Crowes sauntered away from their popular table, after the usual projectile attack. They left the rest of their clique to sit and marinate in their spirit colors, the cheerleaders in their silk warmers with the vertical stripes running up the legs and arms, the boys in their crimson and gold bombers.

Johnny had to hand it to Corbett for exhibiting as much diplomatic tact as he had. True, he was a quarterback, but it took a special kind of pinpoint precision to sidearm Skittles over the Asian and Jew Crew tables to make well placed direct hits on Charlie's jawline. Today apparently, target practice wasn't going to be enough.

"I can smell you from over there," Corbett said, and came to stand at the end of the large cafeteria table. "Don't you ever empty the litter box at home?"

"I don't have a cat," Charlie said weakly.

"What?"

"Cat Piss," Crowes said, "you smell like cat piss."

Charlie turned to him. He knew he should remain silent, but said, "Isn't that a little bit redundant?"

Crowes squinted. "Huh? What the fuck did you call me, faggot?"

He shoved Charlie hard on the shoulder. The bullied boy stared down at his brownbag lunch and remained silent. "Cat Piss, after school you need to go home and launder your clothes, and put on some deodorant. Understood?"

Charlie remained frozen. Johnny could tell he was balking, and had an insult at the ready. His friend was definitely smarter than Crowes. He was probably even more intelligent than Corbett, despite his placement in AP classes. The threat of another shove, or maybe even a punch, finally caused him to give an obeisant little nod. He reminded Johnny of a housewife who feared her husband's fist.

"Good," Crowes said. Johnny studied the bully's face. He wondered if it was at all possible that Alex Corbett selected his right-hand man solely for his ugliness. There was any number of men from the eleven on the line of scrimmage, from whose ranks he could select his personal partner in crime.

Crowes' face was a whitlow mass of pimples, blackheads, and craters. They looked like the scars from an explosion burned permanently into his ruined skin. He couldn't smile, and when he tried, there wasn't any pleasure in his eyes. There was just the pained expression of an extremely constipated man alone with his misery. He was muscular, but the form of his body was uneven. It was as if he trained on his own with no expertise, and as a consequence overdeveloped certain muscles and let others wither. His biceps looked like the skulls of human infants, and his chest looked like the breastplate of a knight's armor.

Alex Corbett looked like a Roman emperor with the fine chiseled nose and Caesar haircut to complete the impression. Snippets of hair snuck away from the coif from time to time and plastered themselves to his forehead matted from sweat after a practice, or a shower after a game. He possessed the permanent, unpierced confidence of someone who was never contradicted and never really lost. His was a bearing he and Crowes permanently took away from Charlie.

"See you later, Cat Piss," Corbett said, walking away with Crowes behind him. Charlie looked down at his shoes. They gave him a nickname and he knew nicknames stuck regardless of the facts. Virgins had the permanent stigma of sluts when the rumor mill churned, and if he washed himself in bleach tonight, he would forever remain Cat Piss through his tenure at Freeport Junior High. His handle would probably follow him to college if he didn't put enough miles between himself and this shithole town when the time came.

"You know it's bad," he said, looking over his shoulder toward the back of the bus, "when they've stopped screwing with Billy Wilhelm."

Johnny laughed, caught off-guard. He was relieved to see Charlie retain this much of his sense of humor. He hated to see him like this, this ritual performed every day. It was some sort of prepubescent Cinderella act. Charlie came to life each day when they got home from school. He loved videogames, books, theater, and music. He was full of wit and knowledge, a miniature adult encased in a twelve year-old frame. He was as light on his toes as a seasoned comic performing crowd work outside of school. His days in school were one long, agonizing display of flop sweat, like a presentation given before a silent classroom by a nervous wreck of a boy who feared public speaking more than death.

Charlie was right, though. If they prioritized calling him Cat Piss over heckling Wilhelm like they usually did, then their own stock among the Populars was rapidly plummeting. Billy Wilhelm was the same person who walked to the chalk drawing of the female reproductive system in Mr. Young's health class and confidently wrote "Ethiopian Tubes" above the thin, hornlike protuberances emanating from the uterus. One time they were in Ms. Lander's social studies class, and Billy raised his hand when the subject of the campaign of extermination waged against the Native Americans came up.

"Yes, Billy?" Ms. Lander said. Every boy in the school was infatuated with her, and for Johnny each interaction with her was a secret way to amass more ammo for the spank bank.

"How did the white man exterminate the buffalos?" Billy asked. "Why didn't the buffalos just fly away?"

Ms. Lander squinted. An explanation of his imponderable question finally materialized about five minutes later. Billy worked part-time as a busboy at the Wild Buffalo Wings location in town, and somehow got it into his head that the partially eaten bones slathered in hot sauce, which he cleaned from tables, once belonged to buffalos.

Ms. Lander wasn't a sadist. She didn't let the jocks humiliate their enemies in class, unlike most of the teachers, especially the males. Even she was forced to suppress her smile, as she explained, "The hot wings are a special invented in Buffalo, New York, Billy. They didn't come from buffalos."

"Oh."

That marked the end of Billy Wilhelm's chances of commanding any respect at Freeport

Junior High. There was a shot to survive the furor caused by his "Ethiopian" mistake, but there was no way to weather this storm, no way, at least, until the coinage of Cat Piss.

"Bus ride's almost over," Johnny said, lightly tapping his friend on the shoulder. He stared out the window again. He was looking for his big dark cloud, but it was gone from the slate canvas of the sky.

"Somebody get Cat Piss some kitty litter."

"Ugh." Charlie sighed, hid his face again in his long hair. "Be honest," he said, quietly. "Do I smell like cat piss?"

"No." Johnny felt stupid even dignifying the question with an answer. "Don't let them get to you."

"Easy for you to say. They're not bothering you."

That was true now that Johnny thought of it. The bus hissed to a stop. It halted at the terminus of the dedicated loop feeding around the carpool where the luckier and wealthier kids were driven to school by their parents. Some of the girls from the cheerleading team got out of a Land Rover behind them. They wore ribbon bows in their hair that featured an alternating lattice of crimson and gold, the colors of the Freeport Spartans. They also carried tote bags that said, "Corbett Construction: Building Homes and Leaders for the Future." Gentleman Jim was a major booster for all of the sports and extracurricular activities (except theater). His surname was everywhere, from trophy cases to scoreboards.

"I can wrap myself into a pretzel," Jen Lazarro said. She had warm, Mediteranean features with a splash of reddish freckles that made Johnny imagine her mother as Italian and her father as Irish. The contrast heightened her beauty, and he thought the mix worked.

Jill Brentwood was the last one out of the car. The rest of the girls waited for her to catch up to them. Jen spoke to Jill. "I'm telling you, you need to learn the rules of football. It'll be more fun to watch if you do. Otherwise, you're gonna keep on getting bored silly."

Charlie sighed as they walked away from the bus. He and Johnny followed behind the pack of cheerleaders, catching the scent of shampoo on wet hair, tortured by it. "I want to hate her, but I can't, man."

"I know," Johnny said. "She's actually kind of nice, and she doesn't really seem to see him when he does it."

Jill Brentwood and Alex Corbett were steadies. That didn't mean much more than that they talked a lot on the phone, from what Johnny could tell. They also sat together when their schedules permitted, and held hands when they walked together in the hall. He heard that some guys already got blowjobs. He personally thought his chances of winning the Congressional Medal of Honor were better.

Jill Brentwood was now at the front of the pack of cheerleaders. She turned back to say something to one of the girls behind her, a chipper blonde with birdlike features whose gold-spangled bloomers rode up her bare midriff. It was cold out and she had a ridge of gooseflesh running around her waist.

Jill Brentwood had a heart-shaped face, given its form by the dark brown widow's peak bisecting her otherwise golden hair. She was a little thickset for someone so young. Her ass had a powerful rhythm to it that could make Johnny follow it through the halls until he forgot he had a class to attend if he let himself fall under its spell. He barely knew the rudiments of cheer. What little he knew was forced on him, when he was in homeroom or study hall and couldn't escape the girls talking shop. He figured that a girl as powerfully built as her should be the base of the pyramid, and not a flyer. Her build didn't keep her from alighting from the hands of her fellow cheerleaders with the grace and speed of an acrobat on the trapeze.

Jen Lazarro blew a bubble of her purple Bubble Tape until it exploded, and her tongue darted out to bring the goo back into her mouthful of braces. The spaghetti straps of her swimsuit were crosshatched with the threads of her tank top, and she pulled at the complicated mess.

The brick hexagon of the West Wing loomed ahead of them, tinted glass sashes fixed in its face. Johnny imagined there was some good reason the windows were so dark, but a paranoid part of him thought it was done just so the outside world could never know the cruel little games played behind the walls of the junior high school.

He found his cloud up in the sky again just before they went into the school. It loomed over the football field, where the sprinklers were doing their machinegun staccatos over the greens sodded with help from Russell Milner's supplies and his expertise. Johnny thought it should do something for Charlie, that his dad's wares were used by everyone in Freeport in one way or another. It should give them both some sort of claim on this structure, but it didn't. They were aliens and they didn't belong. They were required to be here through a glitch in the law, but they weren't wanted.

Those sprinklers, he thought, mind still wandering, *aren't watering the field*. He imagined them performing a baptismal rite over the land where these pagans worship every Friday night. There were other sports besides football at Freeport. Soccer was becoming more popular. An ever-growing number of kids got out of their parents' cars wearing cleats and shin guards, goalie gloves, and red silk shirts. There was no doubt about the hierarchy of sports at school, though. Those soccer goals over there were Kwik Goals. They were on wheels and could be pulled aside with as little as a vaudeville hook. Ditto for the Pro Gear hurdles. The Fast Pitch dugout over by the baseball diamond was built to last, but something about the two goals planted at either end zone up on that football field looked to have the permanence of Stonehenge. The leather of the dummy sleds might eventually tear, and the drill cones might blow over in a stiff wind, but the football field would live longer than all of them. Nothing though, would live as long as the eternal memory of Corbett and Crowes, the "Dream and the Nightmare" as they were dubbed by Coach Vanhauser.

One of the lesser cheerleaders in the pecking order held the door open for her sisterhood who entered the school one at a time. The girl stood there with the poise of a ballet dancer, refined by gymnastics, (a double threat) and with the pedigree to potentially be a future Miss America candidate. She briefly brushed back her shoulder-length chestnut hair that was as poufy as a show dog's from a morning blow drying.

Johnny grabbed the door at just the moment that she let go, and he held it open for Charlie. "Got to stop at my locker," Charlie said.

"No shit," Johnny said, patting the underside of his friend's backpack. It bulged with heavy texts and something sharp, like maybe a protractor or compass. They were blessed to have their lockers situated so close together, and so far from the nerve center of "Varsity Row." That was where the athletes and cheerleaders tended to cluster between classes. Sometimes they even hung out there during class when the teacher wrote them passes.

This bank of lockers was between the special ed wing and the industries wing, the latter of which housed meeting space for the Future Farmers of America. They were "hicks" in the parlance of the

Populars. Woodworking and home ec were also down here. The smell of overcooked chocolate baking powder comingled with glue and sawdust in the air.

Charlie started on the combination to his lock, and Johnny stood aside while he worked on it. "Be honest man, do I smell?"

"Jesus, I just said no." Johnny reflexively rubbed his upper lip searching the frenulum for the first hints of his moustache. He hoped it would soon form from the little peach fuzz that already sprouted. He checked under his armpits and saw his first black hairs sprouting the other day, shortly after an especially intense masturbation session. He was convinced that working his crankshaft precipitated the growth, but there was only one way to find out.

He would get home today after school, play some videogames, and feed the dog. Then he'd beat off again, after which he would check the mirror for more hair. He didn't need an excuse, but if there was some correlation between jerking it and reaching manhood, he had no problem with pleasuring himself into the full werewolf boom of virility.

Charlie's voice brought him out of his daydreams. "Just smell me."

"Smell you?" This was a world where any sort of friendly intimacy could get one pegged as a "fag," and Charlie just definitely crossed some kind of red line.

"My shirt," Charlie said, and held out the black material of his *Master of Puppets* ringer. Johnny looked up and down the hall, making sure no one was around. He leaned his nose toward his friend's shirt and inhaled deeply. He smelled nothing but the strong scent of Mrs. Milner's detergent. "Nothing, man. It smells like clean clothes."

"Well, smell the rest of my clothes next time you come over."

Johnny shook his head. "Weird request, but will do."

Charlie set his backpack down, unzipped it, and set the cumbersome texts inside his locker. The walls were graced with a collage of rock stars. The cast rotated somewhat since the last time Johnny peeked in here. Kurt Cobain was still cool, and was likely to remain so. Eddie Vedder somehow now struck both of them as almost as silly as Bono from U2.

Charlie nodded in the direction of the special ed wing. Two handicap ramps buttressed the vinyl composite tile patterned like a chessboard, which stretched across the floor as far as the eye could see. "It's a good thing those assholes never come down here."

Johnny didn't know exactly what his friend was getting at. "What are you talking about?"

"Crowes and Corbett," Charlie said. There was an impatient edge to his voice, as if it should be obvious. They loomed over his life like an eclipse, more imposing than his parents or his future plans to attend UCLA. "I bet they'd screw with those kids mercilessly, calling them retards and whatnot."

Johnny thought about it. "I doubt it, man, at least not Corbett. I could see Crowes doing it." Alex

Corbett was a little too high on the totem pole to prey on someone with autism or a serious debilitation. The cheerleaders might cream their boy cut bloomers for a fight in which their knight in shoulder pads crushed the opposition, but even they might think twice about swapping spit with someone who picked on the kids in special ed. Crowes, however, was a definite maybe in that department.

Johnny Cotter had his own private relationship with this remote wing of the school. He sometimes snuck over here for walks for two reasons. One good reason to come here was that the place was immune to the pressure of the junior high. It was a world apart, where the judgment ceased and there was a stillness to the air.

The more basic reason had to do with his fear of taking shits in the stalls in the main wings of the junior high. That constant marauding pack of preadolescents in the hall could spill at any moment into the bathroom. He and Charlie were always vulnerable, but there was something terrifying about being trapped in the bathroom with his sphincter muscles puckering. He saw himself praying silently, despite his uncertainty in a God, as he hoped the squeaking feet passed by the stall. He could imagine the sound of hands drumming on the cinderblock walls. Then the owner of the hands would peek their head over the side of the stall walls and announce, "Hey everyone, this guy's taking a shit! In school!"

It didn't happen yet, but it was a contingency he was hoping to avoid. There was cruelty in the halls, in the cafeteria, on the bus, and in the gym, but the bathrooms were a true blind spot hidden from an already indifferent authority. Bad things could happen in the bathroom, he was convinced, but he was equally convinced that no evil could befall him in the special ed bathrooms. The stalls were spaced a leisurely distance from one another, and there was even a changing station and shower stall. The tiled suite was too commodious for him to enjoy anything less than a peaceful shit. The only problem was it sometimes might be too peaceful. He might find himself ten minutes or so late to homeroom. He would be tardy, but in perfect harmony with the world and enjoying a stomach free of cramps for the rest of the day.

He felt his bowels shift on him, a consequence of the two high fructose squeeze boxes he downed this morning followed by two packs of

Handi Snacks, whose processed cheese spread didn't exactly go over like gangbusters with his stomach. He gripped the contours of his belly and headed off quickly down toward the handicap ramps. He strode across the black and white checkered spaces beneath him two at a time, even though such moves were not officially open to a pawn. The fluorescent light fixtures glinted off the paraffin wax shellacked across the floor. That janitor was one overzealous son of a bitch, who aimed to make this entire school shine like the savage edge of a samurai blade.

"Hey," Charlie said. "Where you going?"

"Water fountain," he lied.

"Meet me in the auditorium after eighth?"

"Sure. What's up?"

Charlie usually didn't ask him to check out his work on school productions until at least dress rehearsal time.

"You'll see," Charlie said, and slammed the face of his locker shut.

Johnny walked down the hall, toward his private bathroom. He felt bad for lying to Charlie. Sometimes it was necessary to keep secrets, even from your best friend. He suspected Charlie probably even kept a few secrets of his own.

***

The auditorium was off in a building by itself, housed in a fortress built from acoustical concrete masonry that made it look more like a bomb shelter than a place where creative spirits might soar. It was sanctuary for Charlie, though. Drama did nothing for Johnny, but seeing what it did for Charlie Milner was more than enough reason to stay after school.

The library exit was separated from the outdoor quad by a steel and glass vestibule. It caught a blinding amount of sunlight and reminded Johnny of an old-fashioned phone booth. He squinted as he pushed his way outside. He spotted Michael Gottlieb walking to the auditorium. He knew Mike was a drama geek (a "drama fag" in the parlance of the meaner and more numerous students), and he also knew Gottlieb caught hell when someone discovered his father taught origami nights on a public access TV channel.

The only girl with a better (or at least bigger) ass than Jill Brentwood walked alongside Mike toward the concrete colossus. Ashley Marks had the kind of body that made men slow their cars in traffic, gawk in admiration, and then cringe in shame when they saw the young face that went with the overdeveloped frame. It was sheer pleasure for Johnny, as long as he stayed behind her. If he got ahead of her or tried to talk with her, it could expose him to all kinds of humiliations. His voice might crack, he might extend his sweat slicked palm to introduce himself, and his wet hand might overshoot and slap a nearby locker.

He drank in the contours of Ashley's teardrop shaped butt as it swayed, each gluteus speaking sign language to him, a brainwashing pattern that dwindled his own mental vocabulary to a series of grunts and clicks. She walked into the theater without noticing him or holding the door, for which he was thankful. Johnny entered the auditorium a few moments after her.

"It's an acoustical dead spot right here!" someone shouted from the fourth row and stood up on one of the red upholstered stadium seats. Charlie was on the stage apron, some sort of massive contraption laid across the floor.

"Thank you for pointing that out!" Charlie shouted. "Now get off that chair!"

There was no one else visible aside from those two, and the two who Johnny had followed in. He heard voices from backstage and from the wings off to the side of the proscenium arch.

The boy standing on the seat ignored Charlie's order and said, "Make a note that the stage manager needs to tell his players to project!"

"Got it. Now get down, please!"

"You think you run the joint, but you're just tech and stagecraft."

"Your mother is tech and stagecraft."

The boy hopped down from the seat and walked slowly toward the stage. "My mother's dead."

"Oh," Charlie said. "How'd she die?"

The boy pointed up at the tableau curtain arrangement hanging from a single batten above them. "Someone pulled the wrong rigging and a sandbag fell on her head." The building was new, but the velour curtains gave off a charming musk. Their claret color made Johnny think of an old Shakespearean theater or maybe the hall where Abraham Lincoln got shot in the back of his head. He could see why Charlie liked it here. This was his very own giant special ed bathroom.

Johnny mounted the stage. "What did you want me to see?"

"This," Charlie said. Johnny looked down and inspected his friend's handiwork. He stood beside the boy who found the dead spot out among the chairs, where the audience would sit and watch their family members perform a few weeks from now.

There was a latticework of soft wood, which looked like it once was a pallet from Freeport

Fertilizer. It was attached to a squirrel cage fan.

Billowing sheets of satiny parachute silk, in shades

of red and yellow, were weaved through both the

centrifugal fan and the former pallet. Mrs. Milner

gave up on the nursery portion of Freeport Fertilizer

after the divorce and opened her own arts and crafts

supply store. It failed less than a year after opening,

much to her chagrin and her husband's delight. One

of the few good consequences of the failure,

however, was a surplus of neat little knickknacks

and curios accumulating around the old house she

kept in the divorce. Johnny figured that was where

his friend got the varicolored silks.

"What's this for?" Johnny asked.

"For Prometheus."

"What?"

"Don't you ever read the school bulletin?"

"Never."

"We're staging a production of Prometheus," the boy next to Charlie said. Johnny didn't know his name.

"*The Legend of Prometheus*," Charlie said, and reached his hand down between the shadowed spaces of the wooden panels. Johnny noticed him tinkering with the ends of red LEDs housed in casings that made them look like little police sirens. "He stole fire from Mount Olympus and gave it to man, which pleased Zeus none too much."

"Yeah," the other boy said. "He was pissed."

"Now, I've got to make the fire."

"You've done this before?" Johnny didn't know why he was worried. It was clearly all illusion, nothing pyrotechnic about it. Still, he feared his friend might somehow set them all on fire. He glanced up again at the red curtain hanging above him, breathed in that dank, wine cellar mustiness soaked into the velour.

"I've done Franklin stoves and fireplaces before, but this is my first real fire. This has to look like it comes from the gods." He turned on the lights and cued the fan. Immediately there was a whirring as his jerry-rigged monstrosity came to life.

The long parachute silk strands soared and billowed, dancing like the serpentine locks on the head of the great gorgon Medusa herself. The cued LEDs backlit the display. A brimstone glow lit all of their faces, but Charlie's more than the others. The ersatz flames danced against the ivory of his teeth, all of which he bared in his pleased, ear-to-ear smile.

"Not bad," he said, "but on opening night, we're going to use a dry ice machine."

"Yeah," his friend said, "but the machine will either make everything look more believable, or it could screw everything up. Those things are hard to control." The boy looked toward the stone-scalloped proscenium. "I don't know if there are smoke alarms in this building. If there are, the dry ice machine might set them off."

"Let me worry about the smoke alarms." Charlie stood up, and walked toward backstage. Johnny noticed he was limping slightly and his right shoe was missing. Charlie clopped across the wooden stage apron and Johnny followed.

"Hey man, isn't there a Greek tragedy about a guy with one shoe?"

Charlie shrugged. "I saw it in *Jason and the Argonauts*, that movie with the stop-motion skeletons. That movie isn't exactly historically accurate, you know."

"What happened?" Johnny nodded toward the socked foot.

Charlie groaned, and Johnny regretted asking, knowing he didn't want to know the answer. "We were playing soccer today in gym class. I kicked the hell out of the ball, and I guess my right shoe wasn't tied and it came off." He pointed at the white sock where before there was a gray Nike.

Charlie turned to the left. Several actors played with pancake makeup, eyeliner pencils, and props, like plastic Viking helmets and a pitchfork. "You didn't think about getting your shoe back?" Johnny asked.

"I couldn't," Charlie said and stomped his feet. He was queasy and he hated his friend for the moment, for bringing the outside world into a holy place like this. "Fucking Crowes got it and took it away. I went and told Mr. Gorleck about how that cock-gobbling Neanderthal bum rushed me." He winced, lifted his shirt, and exposed a bruised purple mass expanding across his ribcage and hip.

"Jesus."

"Yeah, it's fucking soccer, man. Even in hockey that would get him penalty box time. I went up to Gorleck and I said, 'Hey, if you're not going to do something about the shoe, can you at least do something about the violent-ass collision that just took place?' I'm pretty sure I've got grounds for a lawsuit. Gorleck said that 'if it ain't bleeding, don't bring it to me.'"

"'Grounds for a lawsuit'. My, we are precocious." Johnny glanced behind Charlie and saw Alice Berryman. She wore a flapper hat pulled over her head and a feathered boa draped over her shoulders. She clenched a long-stemmed cigarette holder in her jaws. "Don't let them get to you, *dahling*. I have always depended upon the kindness of strangers, but I've also always depended on such primitive displays from the likes of Mike Crowes."

She removed the cigarette holder from her mouth and handed it to Johnny. He immediately clamped it in his mouth. He chewed, tasting the wetness where she left the impression of her lips and the inside of her cheek. Her spit was in his mouth! There was no warning in the moment before it happened, and his erection rose like the growth cycle of a flower witnessed in a time elapse photograph.

"To the devil with Crowes and his muscles!" Alice stretched her boa until it was as tensile as a whip. She continued her monologue as if this was a real audition that might lead to her big break. "I like my men *refined*." She added a southern gothic emphasis to the last word, the accent of someone who sipped mint juleps and called car horns klaxons.

She disappeared from their midst just as suddenly as she came and retreated farther backstage to study her reflection in one of the bulb-ringed oval mirrors. Johnny shook his head and tried to think about something boring. He imagined Mr. Milner explaining the numerical designations for various grades of fertilizer and ratios of phosphate to nitrogen. He needed to get this hard-on to wilt, so he could walk without embarrassing himself. Nothing was working yet. He removed the cigarette holder from his mouth, deciding that was a good first step in getting limp.

Charlie turned back toward the actors busying themselves behind him backstage. "All right, my work, though largely unappreciated, is done for the day."

Alice called to him without taking her eyes from the mirror. "We wouldn't draw flies in our the-ay-ter without you, dah-ling!" If she was one of the cheerleaders, her staring in the mirror would be an act of vanity. As it was, however, her self-love had more to do with her sense of humor than her beauty, which everyone thought in abundance. Johnny noticed Alice's name rarely came up in locker room bull sessions, when guys bragged about what they did or would do with various girls. It was a show-stopper on those rare occasions when her name did come up. Alex Corbett and Mike Crowes might viciously describe how they'd like to tag team Veronica Tobin and make a rotisserie of her behind the bleachers after practice one day. Then someone might ask, "What about Alice? She's pretty hot."

"Berryman?" Crowes or Corbett would say.

"Yeah."

"She's really ...pretty."

An awkward silence would follow. It would expand over the transgressor and envelope him, letting him know he made a mistake in throwing her name into the mix.

Charlie and Johnny turned away from the backstage area and walked across the apron. The wooden stage was murky, since someone just adjusted the dimmers on the house lights. One of the AV kids was fiddling with an engineer's board composed of thousands of knobs, glowing like the console in a planetarium. A spotlight arced out toward them and spilled across the stage.

Charlie looked over at Johnny. They both hopped directly off the stage, not bothering with the stairs. "Think this school has enough funding?"

"I know. It's more like a college."

"Christ, some colleges don't even have it this good." Charlie looked over at the shadowy head of the AV boy playing maestro with his various light cues in the dark. "Don't let anybody play with my fire," Charlie said.

"I have only one burning desire."

They walked up the rising grade from the pit toward the back of the theater, leaving through a set of double doors below the balcony above them. The bright light of day was harsh, and they both had to squint and shield their eyes. "The sun," Charlie said,

"is the biggest goddamn bully of them all."

CHAPTER TWO

Freeport Lanes was a bowling alley, bar, and arcade, but the game of bowling held little appeal for the kids from the local junior high and high school. The lanes were usually glutted with league bowlers anyway, and the bar was off-limits for unaccompanied minors.

The arcade was in its own wing of the building, though not completely isolated from the lanes or the bar. The foamy scent of flat beer and the fungal smell of processed nacho cheese wafted into the game room. The league play occasionally got heated enough for someone to shout, and for their voice to carry into the arcade when they either got a strike or missed all of the Brunswick pins. The kids had the place to themselves though, aside from these minor intrusions. They could get away with everything from smoking the occasional joint to jimmying open a cabinet's front with a Philip's head, to get unlimited free plays.

Adults only came in here rarely. They tended to play the older models, the Atari games like *Ms. Pac Man* or *Missile Command*. It was only after depositing their quarter into the latter machine however, that the hapless grownup discovered DJ (the kid who always wore the sweat-stained Raiders cap) lifted the trackball and added it to the balls on the green felt of the pool table. The player was forced at this point to stand helplessly and watch in frustration as each one of their silos was nuked and the screen grew pallid. The words, "The End" would then superimpose themselves over the radioactive holocaust.

The adults had things like families and jobs to keep them from ever even really trying what the kids considered the real games. It would be a waste of quarters to make the attempt. Playing against Charlie Milner was pointless for the other kids, too. He somehow managed to reign supreme at all of the games arrayed in the dank room. It was even more amazing to think he did all of this while maintaining a B average at Freeport.

He only lost when he wanted to, like on *Terminator 2*, where the temptation proved too great. The game featured a PVC sub-machinegun with a ball-bearing rattling around in its casing to simulate the *rat-a-tat* of a magazine being expended. DJ put his mind and his screwdriver to the task of getting that little steel ball out, but so far failed.

The object of *T2* was to provide cover fire for the dwindling number of human rebels battling against a superior number of machines, who were bent on enslaving the frail species. The problem for Charlie was that the player was allowed to shoot their allies. If the player allowed their field of fire to stray into the back of a hapless rebel, the soldier first protested the bullet in the back, and then died.

Everyone laughed at the morbid show of friendly fire, but it was less funny when one considered the rules of the game, which stated a player also lost one of their three lives whenever they killed one of their fellow soldiers. Charlie tended to run out of lives pretty quickly. That was a serious matter considering he only made ten dollars a week in allowance. He got a fiver on top of that for every hour he helped his dad at Freeport or did yard work for his mom.

Mortal Kombat was a different story. He could survive on a single quarter for upward of six hours and ruin the day of any comers foolish enough to challenge him. The smarter kids stood off to the side of him and just watched the dexterous, little ergonomic flurries and nimble darts he did with his fingers here and there. He was the suburban equal of any city dweller who fleeced marks at three card Monty.

He was a little distracted today, however, and got a less than flawless victory against the God of Thunder under Chuck Billingworth's control. Charlie still managed to pull off his fatality move, though. All of the kids gathered around to watch his character, a gangster with half his face shrouded in a metal plate, slam his fist into the Thunder God's chest and extract his still-beating heart.

"How'd you do it?" Luke Beerman asked from his left. Beerman was the kind of kid whose asthma could be intuited long before he went for his nebulizer. He just looked he had asthma.

"Screw you, asshole," Chuck said, and Charlie basked in his insult as if it were applause.

"Next."

"There is no next," DJ said, and then looked at Chuck as he adjusted his Hawaiian shirt over his fanny pack. "Don't let Bill see you with that."

"I know. That's why I'm covering it up."

Chuck always carried several things in his fanny pack, chief among them his hacky sack that smelled of British Columbian weed. He also kept several sticks of gum and a little container of Visine. He brought some sticky green slime into the arcade two weeks ago and threw the gelatinous wad at the walls. Bill, the manager, usually let the kids have the run of the place. The exception was that one time when the kids requested his help to bounce that creepy old dude, who said his van in the parking lot was filled with puppies he wanted to show them. The ammonia and rotten milk smell of the new and improved silly putty brought him into the arcade this particular day. He was horrified to discover Chuckie already spilled some of the stuff onto the carpet.

Bill gave Chuckie the boot and a lifetime ban. Bill had a pretty bad case of wet brain from a lifetime of heavy drinking, but there was the irrevocable stain to remind him of the kid every time he went into the arcade to vacuum. The stupid fanny pack provided an additional refresher, if his memory of faces failed him.

"I'll be your next victim," Johnny said, though he was really just using the game as an excuse to rap with his friend. He shared Mr. Palagoni's disdain for the game, and always laughed when the teacher said the stupid thing was responsible for teaching a generation of kids how to misspell the word "combat."

"Your game's off today," Johnny said. "You let Chuckie drain your health bar a little. What's up?" Johnny selected the Bruce Lee-looking martial artist who could glide through the air and do the flying bicycle kick onto the solar plexus of his opponent.

DJ was doing his tired-ass Schwarzenegger impression behind them, mostly "I'm the pahty-poopah" and the line about the tumor. "A few things," Charlie said.

"Like what?"

"Oh, the pit."

"Shit," Johnny said. It was a foregone conclusion that Charlie would uppercut Johnny high up into the air, since they were fighting at the pit. He would then plummet down into the bed of spikes, where his lifeless body would be impaled and jets of blood would squirt skyward.

"My dad," Charlie said, and the metal-faced gangster walked forward.

Johnny's only goal was to get in a few licks, to steal some green from that life bar and leave some red there. All was not lost as long as his friend didn't get a flawless victory. He got in a few tepid punches that did about as much damage as a slap, and Charlie countered the love taps with a punishing head butt that sent the Bruce Lee- lookalike sprawling backward.

"He's like two decades older than everyone else's dad. You've got like twenty or thirty years until your pops croaks, but I've probably got to start getting prepared like when I go off to college."

The gangster backed up on the stone catwalk and Johnny knew what was coming. He blocked but old Metal Face curled into a ball and striated through the night sky and broke Johnny's guard. Charlie sent Johnny's character to the ground. He followed up with a sweep to the leg that sent Johnny sprawling again.

"Jesus, Butt Munch, give me a chance."

Red light gleamed from their peripheral vision, DJ's sneakers sending out a blinking sequence of seizure-inducing strobes in the dark of the arcade. "Your dad's in good health, man," Johnny said. "The dude's like an ox. You've seen the way he lifts those bags of fertilizer."

"Yeah, you might be right."

"Finish him!" An unseen sensei commanded.

"Hate to do this to you."

"Yeah, whatever, Dickhead."

The gangster stroked the Kung-Fu master under the chin and the limp fighter embarked on his journey up toward the white moon, which ended with him plummeting downward and crucified on the bed of rusted spears below.

"Free game!" Charlie said, and walked away from the console.

"What now," Johnny said.

"Cigarette."

Charlie walked to the glass doors and pushed. The parking lot was mostly empty. There was an endless sea of cars ripping through space and making a sonic whooshing noise as they shot in bleary lines, above the grass embankment that muted their view of the highway. The smell of cooking grease wafted over from the nearby Arby's, and the much nearer smell of burning cigarettes drew them to the side of the building.

"Square," Charlie said.

DJ held a mostly smoked butt in his hand, said, "My last one," and leaned down to put the cherry out against the traction on the rubber soles of his light-up sneakers. Sparks and bits of glowing coal flew out and the sickly yellowing fiberglass came free of the paper.

"You lying sack of shit."

DJ grinned, reached into the pocket of his baggy jeans, and handed Charlie a cigarette. "You better be ready to dive if Carson comes in here later."

"I know it."

Charlie pulled his father's D-Day commemorative zippo from his pocket and struck flint, holding the butane flame over the Camel Light.

"Who's Carson?" Johnny asked.

"My older brother," DJ said. "He's a beast. He can bench like four-hundred and could probably squat both of your punk asses without blinking an eye."

Charlie only nodded as he sucked the cigarette. He blew out a cloud of white smoke just above the heads of his two friends. "It's true. How should I put this?" He paused. He was free of the spell that Corbett and Crowes cast over him, and thus regained his vocabulary. "My skillset rapidly diminishes whenever I find myself in the presence of Carson Broward."

"Smart," DJ said, and reached for the cigarette. Charlie shook his head. "Hey, I thought this was mine now."

He relinquished the smoke to DJ, but said, "Just let me get the short."

"So you let him win?" Johnny asked. No one offered him the cigarette yet, and he didn't know what he would say if they handed it to him. It was a little late for that, though. Both DJ and Charlie were past the experimental stage in their habit, and were now genuinely nick-fitting.

"Tis nobler to get one's ass kicked in the realm of pixels than in this real world."

"Oh, I almost forgot." DJ extended the cig back to his friend. "Speaking of brothers and whatnot. Robbie drive a red Cherokee?"

The cigarette almost fell from Charlie's grip just as he took it from DJ. "Why?"

"I just saw him cruising up near Lander Street before I came up here. I was skating in the park and …"

Charlie flicked the still-burning cigarette into the bed of mulch running alongside the bowling alley. DJ called after him. "Hey, Cock Smoker, you can start a fire like that and there were still a few puffs left in that mother!"

Both Johnny and Charlie were too excited at this point, however, to give a shit about anything else DJ said. "He's back from Benning?" Johnny asked. They walked up the grass defilade to the crosswalk.

Charlie pressed the button and they waited, breathing in carbon monoxide from the endless procession of SUVs and sedans ripping past them. "Yeah, if your leave keeps piling up and you don't take time off, they take it from you. I think it's called use it or lose it."

The little red stick figure on the crosswalk sign turned from red to white and they ran. The thing never gave them enough time to walk comfortably across the intersection. Heaven help the odd elderly man with a walker, or woman with child in tow, who took the idea of a crosswalk literally and tried for a leisurely saunter. He or she would meet with an army of angry car horns.

They made it safely across the street. Charlie's mom's house was about twenty minutes from the Lanes. Their route took them across various office parks, four-lane streets, and through several detours into hostile backyards and private grass parcels with clearly posted "No Trespassing" signs.

They walked alongside a wooden fence wrapped around a gated community of condos, where entry was granted by a security guard with a clipboard who manned a post. The barely discernible outlines of the clubhouse and swimming pool were on the other side of the guard post.

"What was the other one?" Johnny asked, shivering.

It was getting colder. Sunset was still a couple of hours off, but the sun was gone. The sky was stippled with gray clouds, an unfurling cover of oyster and iron that looked like smoke rising from a battlefield.

"The other what?"

Johnny sighed. "You said there were a couple of things bothering you. Your dad getting older is one. What's the other one?"

"Oh, yeah." Charlie stopped walking and held his socked foot aloft.

"Oh shit," Johnny said. He forgot Charlie lost the shoe earlier. He was sure the ground was cold as hell right now, too.

"I looked for one of those elf slippers left from last year's Christmas production backstage earlier today, but I didn't find jack." He sniffled, and Johnny thought he was probably going to catch cold.

"Yeah, I guess losing a shoe will fuck up your day."

"It's not the shoe." Charlie shook his head. "I mean, it was the soccer game. It's sports."

"You're no good? Who gives a shit? Neither am I."

They came to a construction site where several giant backhoes recently dug up the brown muddy earth. There was a staked sign planted on the cold ground that said, "A Future Corbett Homes Development."

"Jesus," Charlie said. "There's no fucking escape."

Johnny looked up at the backhoe, its bucket reaching for him like the claw on that stupid game in the bar part of Freeport Lanes. The thing gave him the willies. He stood beneath it. He felt as he imagined a caveman might, after happening on the form of a mammoth he felled with his crude spear, a mammoth he wasn't entirely sure was dead.

"It's not that I suck at sports. It's that ..." Charlie paused, and flung his arms outward, exasperated and momentarily inarticulate. Charlie rarely resorted to speaking with his hands, Johnny noticed, so what he needed to say must be especially hard to get his head around. "It's that we're talking about whether or not we suck at sports. Sports were … *fun* last year. Foursquare, tetherball."

Johnny nodded. "I get what you're saying, man." He slapped Charlie on the shoulder. "I wouldn't sweat it, though."

"Why not? Sports are the center of the universe here." *Here*. Johnny thought about that word as they walked. Charlie meant at Freeport Junior High, but his words were not a mistake or slip of the tongue. Junior high was wherever they were. It wasn't *there*. Afterschool time was a reprieve from the nightmare, but relief was never total. There was always school the next day.

"Look," Johnny said, and his pace quickened. The words he said now were not just reassurance meant for a friend. They were what he believed to be true. "Alice Berryman likes you more than she likes Corbett or Crowes, right?"

"She's got a boyfriend, man."

"I didn't mean that," Johnny said, although he felt his heart momentarily plummet. His tongue reflexively darted for the cold stain where Alice's spit and the impression of the cigarette holder still lingered in his mouth. "I mean that she thinks you're a better person than they are. Alice, the prettiest girl in the school, would rather spend time with you than them."

"Yeah ..." Charlie's voice floated away from him, trailed off as he stared toward the gray horizon where the tract houses were arrayed. He sighed deeply. He was certain for the moment that junior high would eventually end. High school was on the horizon, and was bound to be an even bigger nightmare. High school would eventually come to a close, though. Maybe in college he would trade the title "drama fag" for "theater major." *Maybe*, he thought, if he lived that long.

Johnny sighed, too, relieved to help Charlie. He didn't once resort to guidance counsellor bullshit, either. Alice was definitely the prettiest girl in school. There were sexier girls, but sexy was somehow kind of scary. Those girls' features were hard. Everything about them was perfect, symmetrical, and tanned, but their eyes were the same color as dishwater. Their fine lips were always in tight smiles that made them look like vicious piranhas. Sex with them would probably be the single greatest moment of his life, Johnny was sure. He imagined, though, that when a man jumped off a cliff, or a gnat wandered into the jaws of a Venus flytrap, they experienced a weird momentary bliss before death.

"Well," Charlie said, "we've talked about what I'm thinking, but what the hell are you thinking about?"

Johnny turned toward his friend and answered him. "I honestly don't know how to put it into words."

CHAPTER THREE

The driveway was full when they got home.
Elise's yellow hatchback with the psychedelic
bumper stickers was parked to the side of the cherry
Jeep. Mr. Milner's late model Benz was parallel to
both cars belonging to his kids.

"What gives?" Johnny peered through the
bay window. Mrs. Milner was setting places at the
dinner table and several candles were glowing atop
the centerpiece.

"Who knows?" Charlie shrugged. "Hey." He
turned to the wooded area behind the house where
each of the trees was faintly outlined in the twilight.
Charlie cupped his mouth with his hands and said,
"That's poor light discipline, soldier!"

"Belay that shit, new guy."

They both double-timed it toward the sound of Robbie's voice, and the sight of his cigarette's glowing cherry. Charlie's older brother was in the shadow of a massive chestnut oak. The tree recently shed all of its acorns. The cups of the little shiny bowls crunched underneath Robbie's feet when they shifted in their desert-camo boots.

"What's up, knuckleheads?"

"Chilling." Charlie shook his head and hugged his brother below the armpits. Robbie did his best to embrace his younger brother with the hand not holding the cigarette. He was wearing a Gore-Tex field jacket, and the coat featured the chocolate chip design used for desert campaigning. There was a unit insignia sewn onto one of the arms. Johnny didn't know if it was the insignia of the unit he deployed with from Germany, or if it was the patch of his current unit in Benning.

"Give me that." Charlie snatched the half-smoked cigarette from his brother's fingers.

"Since when do you smoke?"

"Life has gone on without you." Charlie took a couple of puffs and then handed the smoke to Johnny, who accepted it.

"That's the truth." Robbie stretched until his field jacket rose up and revealed the rock hard musculature of his abdominals and obliques. "I sure as hell wouldn't call what I'm doing right now living."

"What do they got you doing?"

Johnny smoked, coughed, and stared at Robbie. He was still in awe of him after all these years. His facial hair was a light stippling the last time Johnny saw him, loose and fine like the bristles on a toothbrush that saw too much service. Now his face was covered in the rough, greenish stubble of a full-grown man. Johnny reflexively checked his meager peach fuzz again.

"I'm range cadre for a basic training regimen." Robbie shook his head. "That means I get to stand up in a tower all day and beat my meat. 'Ready on the left? Ready on the right?'" He shook his head, and snatched his Marlboro from Johnny. "It's no life for a battle-hardened infantryman."

"You see a lot of battle in Iraq?" Johnny asked.

"About as much action as a hunter when he goes out on a turkey shoot." He dredged a goober of spit from deep in his throat, and hawked it into the blackness enveloping the woods. "No, it was pathetic."

"What do you mean?" It wasn't what Johnny wanted to hear. He remembered sitting in the Milner living room years ago, eating on TV trays and watching the tube. It was a rare breach in protocol for Mrs. Milner, but she let the boys get away with eating in the living room because there was news coming in about the war. It was a war Robbie had no inkling would come to pass when he signed on the recruiter's dotted line, while still in high school. He enlisted under the Delayed Entry Program against his father's reservations and his mother's more strenuous objections.

Johnny recalled spearing a string bean wading in A-1-slathered potatoes on his plate. He bit down and watched in horrified fascination as the remnants of a bomb shelter were shown on CNN.

"Military Intelligence," Mr. Milner said, shaking his head. He and Charlie's mom were still together at that point. He hunkered down in his checkered recliner patterned like a used car salesman's jacket. The legs of his chair were fully protracted and slippers were on his feet, their tassels gnawed by the recently deceased Bowser.

"What did I tell you boys about military intelligence," Mr. Milner said. Mrs. Milner winced, as she always did when her husband spoke these days. "You watch," he continued, even though he could feel his wife's hatred coursing over toward him in waves. The kids' eyes were glued to the screen. "America'll take ten to twenty thousand casualties in this pointless, horseshit war for oil."

"Boys, don't look." Mrs. Milner went for the remote, changed the channel to *America's Funniest Home Videos*. The collapse of a balcony punctuated by the laugh track did nothing to alter Mr. Milner's course. "Economic sanctions should be given more time. All right, Saddam's an asshole, but if Bush pushes to Bagdad and kills him, it'll create new problems. That tin pot Stalin's the devil we know, about as dangerous as Gadhafi." Mr. Milner grabbed a book of crosswords from the end table and donned his specs.

"You watch," he said again, before taking up his pen and turning his mind to the crosswords.

Now Robbie dug his pack of Marlboros out of his pocket. He opened them and took one out.

"Chain smoker," Charlie said.

Robbie ignored him and said to Johnny, "Our technology was so much better than theirs that it wasn't any fun."

"War's not supposed to be fun, I thought," Johnny said.

"This one was embarrassing." Robbie lit his smoke with a match from a book. "We had thermal gun sights that were a hell of a lot better than what the republican guard was packing. So when there was a sandstorm and they were at zero visibility, it was about as hard as a game of *Duck Hunt*."

Charlie smiled, remembering the innocent days of his Nintendo console, before Sega Genesis and bloody videogames made the old games obsolete. His brother's words made him want to go upstairs to Robbie's old room and dust the game system off, and bring the Nintendo down for one last round.

"I mean, if my guns have a range of two miles, and yours have a range of practically one-hundred feet in a sandstorm, where's the glory in that?" He stared at Johnny and smoked.

Johnny felt Robbie's anger. He knew it was for someone else, some crack team of researchers at MIT or some manufacturers at Raytheon, but the emotion was so real and powerful he felt afraid of Robbie for the moment. It was dark enough for

Robbie's face to look like a pale mask in the moonlight.

"Where's the honor in that?" Robbie shook his head, and looked down at the ground.

Charlie gave his brother a reassuring pat on the shoulder. The Gore-Tex material of his jacket whispered from the touch. "So how much leave you got?"

"About a month." Robbie looked away from them, deeper into the woods. His eyes fastened on something only he could see, as if he were a huntsman discerning the points of a buck's antlers where the less expert eye saw only gnarled wood.

"I'm thinking of getting a hotel."

"What?" Charlie squinted, tried to grab his brother's cigarette. Robbie jerked his hand away and his little brother was left clutching only air. He might be depressed, Johnny thought, but his reflexes were sharp. They were probably battle-tested, too, despite his humble show. That's what it was, Johnny decided. He was just being humble to put on a show.

Robbie pulled the pack back out of his pocket and threw it to his brother. "Thanks!" Charlie's eyes widened. His brother's gesture was a great gift, since they were still too young to buy smokes, even with the best fake ID.

"Yeah," Robbie said. "Don't take the shit personal, but I didn't know Elise was going to be back from UC. Cincinnati's close, but I was hoping she'd stay cooped up in her dorm room."

"Since when do you two not get along?"

Robbie grinned. "Since I became a war machine and she became a piece monger. I might as well be Lieutenant Calley mowing down innocent Vietnamese villagers."

Johnny blanked on the reference. His dad was at Williams College with a deferment during the Vietnam War. "Son of a bitch," Robbie said. Johnny and Charlie realized what was holding his gaze when he next spoke. "That treehouse still standing?"

He walked toward the structure in the sky, still rising on the stilt-like telephone pole. "I still think my idea was better." He held up the three fingers of his right hand, and glanced in the direction of the dark beeches where he contemplated erecting their treehouse. "I'll be damned if Dad didn't know what the hell he was doing, though."

Johnny coughed. It wasn't the side stream smoke from the cigarette that made him cough. It was the septic scent from the stream where the devil's walkingstick finally overpowered the prettier shrubs. That dank odor was part of the reason they stopped having overnights in the treehouse after the novelty of having their very own clubhouse wore off.

"It's holding up," Charlie allowed. He contemplated using the ladder to climb up, just for old time's sake. For some reason he held off. The place held its own memories, and while there were some thoughts he couldn't escape, it didn't necessarily make sense to run toward the pain, either.

"Yeah," Robbie said, and looked down at his jump boots. He pulled the hood of his field jacket over his high-and-tight haircut. Johnny thought he looked like the marine from the TV commercials. "I think I'm going to be leaving for a while soon."

"You just got here!" Charlie was genuinely pissed. Robbie caught his little brother's neck in the crook of his elbow and administered a noogie with the knuckles of his other hand. The beaded chain of his dog tags jingled against his naked chest.

"Well, before I go, it's my duty as a full-grown man to give you young bucks a heart-to-heart on the fairer sex. Dad's from the old school, so he's not going to give it to you, and mom's nuts."

Johnny thought it was a little harsh for Robbie to say that about Mrs. Milner, but he was also pretty sure Robbie was right. These days her eyes held a look both distant and terrified. Janet Milner's gaze would fasten just to the side of Johnny's shoulder whenever he tried to make eye contact with her. It was as if she was perpetually witnessing a terrifying car accident going on directly behind him.

"How about Elise?" Johnny asked. "She could help." He just wanted an excuse to talk to her and see her.

"I haven't been keeping close tabs on her, but I'm pretty sure she's a dyke."

"So?" Charlie said. "Who knows more about girls?"

That drew the first real laugh of the night from Robbie. He glanced at his brother sidelong, surprised by his burgeoning wit. "You might have something there." Then his voice took on a serious, instructional tone, as if he were explaining proper weapon safety to the privates on his range at Fort Benning.

"Look, you guys won't have much of a chance in high school because most of the really hot girls will be attracted to dirt bags in college or even older dudes in their twenties. They'll have little compunction about banging cheerleaders, even though the law says that's a no-go."

He snapped his fingers, and Charlie removed a smoke from the pack his brother just gave him. He complained as he passed his older brother a cigarette. "Fucking Indian giver."

"Kick rocks, psycho," Robbie said and then resumed with his speech. "You can level the playing field by remembering what I'm telling you now, okay?"

Both boys nodded. "Okay?" They nodded again. "This shit is serious, so listen up." He leaned into them, and they into him. He spoke quietly, like a quarterback getting ready to reveal the outlines of a secret plan. "Don't be macho about sex. You know Napoleon?"

"Bonaparte?"

"Yeah, that one." He scowled at the stupid question, and resumed. "He ruled the world and rose from humble beginnings as a Corsican nobody to become arguably the greatest military genius of all time."

"If he isn't the best, then who is?" Johnny asked. He was eager to hear the chestnut Robbie wanted to impart, but this tangent was equally valuable, he thought.

Robbie waved the question away but still addressed it. "Grant, Frederick the Great, Erwin Rommel, and Patton all have their apologists as well, but that's not what I'm talking about."

"What are you talking about?" Charlie asked.

"I'm talking about cunnilingus."

Neither was familiar with the word, and they looked at Robbie as if he just landed in a spaceship. Robbie sighed. "Eating pussy."

"Oh." Charlie and Johnny made sour faces.

"Look, I knew some dumbass jock back when I was at Freeport, the guy was like all-state wrestling champ and he said, 'Eating pussy is almost as bad as sucking dick.' Bullshit!"

Robbie took out the book of matches, struck one, and held the glowing head to the end of the cigarette he just stole from his brother. The smell of sulfur filled the air. "Napoleon, when he wasn't on the field of battle, kept his face planted in Josephine's snatch. If you want to be ten steps ahead of the rest of the kids in your school, you've got to put your face in it."

"Yeah," Charlie said, "but …" he paused. "You can't just fucking head butt it, like you just said, 'put your face in it.' There has to be some technique, right?" A girl's pussy, he thought, was not an opponent in *Mortal Kombat* he could just slam his metal faceplate against.

"You want technique?" Robbie sucked his cigarette until his right eye closed for a moment. "You know what a clitoris is?"

"We've had health class," Johnny said. "There's a picture of a pussy on the wall in Mr. Young's room." Someone even went in and completed the diagram with a black Sharpie marker, writing "Ethiopian tubes" on the laminated display.

The same comedian smeared their sinful graffiti over the anti-rape poster, which featured an image of a boy and girl enjoying a shared basket of fries at an outdoor table beneath an umbrella at a burger joint. The girl on the poster looked toward the kids in the classroom and smiled, and in white cursive letters beneath the couple enjoying their date were the words, "Just because he paid for dinner doesn't mean I owe him anything." Someone wrote below that, in black Sharpie: "I pay for the date. I get me some rape."

"Well, let me learn you like they haven't learned you in school," Robbie said. He made devil's horns with his pinky and pointer finger, aimed them at Johnny and Charlie. "Your dicks have about four-thousand nerve endings on them. A clit has about eight-thousand. The pussy," Robbie said, "is not where the action is. The little button is the star of the show, except for the cervix, where you can apply some pressure. The pussy is just where you rest your chin while you dot that 'I' on the clit." He took one last drag on his smoke, and ground it out against the warty hide of the nearest tree. Then he field stripped it, as he probably learned to do in the service.

"Every girl's body is different, but for the most part, my advice should work. Remember what I told you here tonight, and you won't need to letter in some stupid sport or drive a muscle car." He walked back in the direction of the house. The other Milners were visible through the bay window, silently eating with their heads aimed downward at their plates.

"Hopefully I've been of some help?" He glanced back at Johnny.

"Well, I can't just dive headfirst for some girl's vagina without even talking to her. My problem is talking to girls. I get scared, you know? My hands start sweating and I get nervous."

"Uncle Robbie's got the cure for that, too."

Johnny ran to catch up with him, and listened at his side like a faithful understudy. "Here's what I want you to do the next time you talk to a girl you like, okay?"

Johnny nodded. "Talk to her exactly as you would to a guy. If she's above average intelligence, then just talk to her like you would a boy. Not flirting is the best way to flirt with a girl. She's probably so used to flirting that the less you do it, the more curious she'll be about you." He shook his head, qualified what he just said with, "Not just curious. She'll be relieved because girls your age get dick thrown at them five bajillion times a day."

They halted before the garage under the canopy of winking stars. "Tell me a little about this girl you like."

Johnny had two choices. He could either mention Alice or Elise. No good could come of mentioning his crush on Elise in front of her two brothers. It wasn't that they were defensive of her. Quite the opposite was true. They would ruthlessly mock and ride him for having the courage to admit his crush on their sister.

"Alice Berryman."

"Does Alice have any hobbies?"

Johnny nodded. "Theater."

"There you go," Robbie said, as if it was all so obvious. "Talk to her about that, and nothing else for a while. Forget she's a girl and just listen to the words coming out of her mouth."

"Easier said than done."

"It can be done." Robbie walked into the garage, which smelled of oilskin cloths soaked in motor oil. "If you guys are necking one night, and she tries to go down on you, here's what you do. Shake your head and say, 'You first.'" Robbie gripped the handle of the door leading into the mudroom. "Then bury your face in Josephine's snatch, Napoleon."

He opened the door to the kitchen. Johnny prepared to step onto the straw mat with the mallards in flight on it. Charlie grabbed him by the arm, pulled him back into the garage. Robbie halted in the entryway between garage and mudroom, waiting for them. "We're coming," Charlie said. His brother took the hint and went inside, closing the door as he did so to give them some privacy.

"I need you to go into the basement," Charlie whispered.

"Why?" It was an unfinished and uninspired space. There was only the washer and dryer as well as boxes of old Christmas and Halloween decorations down there.

Charlie kept his voice pitched low. "I need you to smell my clothes, make sure they don't smell like cat piss."

Johnny shook his head. "I can't believe you're playing their stupid game. Fuck them."

"Just fucking do it, man, okay? Please?"

Johnny shook his head. "Goddamn." He opened the door and stepped inside.

"You're a true friend."

"I know. That's the problem."

Once they were inside the house, Johnny opened the door to the basement and looked down the staircase. The basement was lit by a single unshielded bulb dangling from the ceiling. He walked down the creaking steps to the bottom, and turned left past a bookcase filled with dusty Encyclopedia Britannica volumes and Milton Bradley games.

The washer was rattling, an ancient Maytag job that looked like it was around since the suburb of Freeport sprung up in a frenzy of postwar optimism. He guessed Mrs. Milner preferred changing motors on the thing to actually buying a new one, a slight quirk she had against throwing things away or giving up on malfunctioning appliances.

There were two piles of laundry. The first one was a damp swirl of familiar band T-shirts belonging to Charlie, along with some of Mrs. Milner's sweatshirts and sweatpants.

The other pile was filled with items of a more recent vintage. The clothes were composed of brighter colors than he was used to seeing either Mrs. Milner or Charlie wear. They sprouted from a hamper on the side of which was an "I Voted Today" sticker.

Johnny walked toward it, saw a sunflower dress, a paisley vest, and even a skirt made out of neckties like the one the star wore on that TV show *Blossom*. There were also several pairs of underwear sprouting from the hamper. He approached it as if it were a holy ark that might unleash a lightning bolt on him if he were deemed unworthy. He looked back up toward the staircase, but was reassured when he heard the faint clatter of stainless steel on ceramic plates.

The outermost pair of panties was made of floral lace. There was a muslin-fine bit of thread near the back, like a miniature corset for Elise's vestigial tail. Johnny picked the low rise pair of panties up and held them in front of his face. He felt weak, feverish, drained of strength. He fell down onto the cold stone floor of the unfinished basement, hitting the ground knees first.

The thought that he shouldn't be doing this went through his head. It made him want to do it more. He knew he shouldn't be doing it because it was unfair to Elise. It was disrespectful. This wasn't why Charlie sent him down here. His friend trusted him, and now he was doing this.

He flipped the underwear inside-out and inspected them, his face and nose moving closer. His stomach felt as if he swallowed a whole tray of ice cubes without chewing once. The inside of the panties was as red as the outside. He thought he could faintly detect one spot in the taffeta-like fabric

slightly darker than the others, and he pressed his
pointer finger here.

I won't go as far as Stevie Wentworth
bragged about going, he thought. He said he jerked
off on a girl's panties. He would never do that to
Elise. He somehow talked himself into viewing this
as slightly chivalrous, this grace he was granting her.
His nose moved closer to the red cloth. He detected
a light musk, somewhat like faint underarm odor,
coupled with something new and heavier in its
pungency. His muscles slackened and he fell face
first into the panties.

It felt good to give up, after the fearful,
tentative little motions he made leaning in with his
face slowly. He wallowed in her smell and breathed
as if out of breath. He licked stained spot, ringed

with the salted alkaline aftereffects of sweat. Then he grabbed the fully wakened erection pressing hard against his boxers, straining as if it wanted to break through the barrier of his jeans. He rubbed himself and thought about Elise, going far back into a deep trance, a place he first visited in early childhood. It was a private paradise where the weakness Robbie talked about was a secret strength. The more of a slave he became, the more power he held over the imaginary women he conjured in his mind. Elise was his Josephine and he her secret Napoleon, lost in the forest between her legs.

She-Ra, he thought, jerked off, and panted. *Elise, princess of power*. He stroked once for each word as he imagined those words falling from his mind in a cascading torrent, like the blocks in *Tetris*. *Princess. Of. Power*. He thought of her slightly annoyed, indifferent voice. He heard her sarcastic quips punctuated by pops of her fruity gum, as she blew bubbles and broke them. Her voice echoed in his head, reverberated.

The Elise in his mind sat on a throne, holding a length of chain streaming from her right hand and dangling down to a manacle around his throat. She grinned at him, and, as he came harder than ever before, he heard her say, "Lick me and be my slave forever, Johnny Cotter." He licked the panties, knowing the moment the orgasm was over he would feel guilt. It was going to be hard as hell to eat Salisbury steak and chopped carrots while seated across from Elise Milner at the dinner table tonight. Then again, she was going to college and he figured they probably learned more about human sexuality there than what Mr. Young taught at Freeport High.

He snatched Elise's panties up in his hand, wadded them into a ball, and hid them in his boxers. The theft was accomplished before he realized what he was doing.

He didn't plan to totally betray Charlie either. He was done secretly worshipping Elise, and he would take this time to walk over to the less interesting pile of clothes. He'd cast aside Mrs. Milner's gray cotton underwear (the word "panties" didn't seem appropriate for them the way it did for Elise), and he would smell the Metallica and AC/DC shirts to see if they smelled like cat piss. He guessed they didn't, figuring the odor was all in Charlie's mind, and in the hearts of Alex Corbett and Michael Crowes.

CHAPTER FOUR

The news came while they were at Freeport Fertilizer screwing around behind the nursery. It had been a few years since the last time they were here. Maybe this nostalgic trip was caused by their recent night under the shadow of the treehouse, that moment itself a consequence of Robbie's return home from Fort Benning, on leave. Russell asked them at dinner that night if they wanted to ride along the next time he went to work, and Charlie shrugged and Johnny said, "Sure."

Certain things were different about the place, those changes clearest around the nursery. Mrs. Milner wasn't willing to put in even the most cursory appearance at Freeport Fertilizer after the divorce, and now two younger women did the work that she once performed. They were only on the clock though, and it wasn't much a labor of love. Her shrine area to the rear of the nursery was in disrepair as a consequence. The various tools around there, like the rickshaw and plow, now looked as rusted as Civil War cannons.

Witch hazel also overtook all of the prettier plants, and snaked through the wooden trellises like a mass of rotted dandelions. It depressed Johnny to look over there, and he was happy when Charlie steered him back in the direction of the wooden barn. Mr. Milner kept large stockpiles of coconut coir, rock wool, and pumice there.

"Where are we going?" Johnny asked.

"You'll see."

Mr. Milner pushed a wheelbarrow filled with fertilizer bags. He spoke to Charlie. "Hey, you gonna check those meters?"

"Will do. I'm on it right now."

"Bullshit."

"The grass wouldn't grow without bullshit, and you'd be out of business."

"Check those meters. Don't make me hurt you."

"I said I would." Charlie threw an idle kick at the head of one of the meters poking out of the ground. The glass covering the face of the meter trembled slightly. Johnny felt much better seeing his friend in shoes. That sock on his right foot was an eyesore that bothered him on the whole long walk home the other day.

"We shouldn't still be doing this manually." Charlie went down the rows, glancing at the tensometers. "They've got remote loggers that can do this, nowadays."

Charlie looked back over his right shoulder. Johnny knew he was looking to see if they were far enough away from Russell for him to have a smoke. It didn't necessarily matter whether or not the old man saw them smoke. Russell might be getting older, but his nostrils worked fine, and the scent of recently smoked cigarettes would stand out on the car ride home.

"Why doesn't your dad just buy those remote loggers?"

Charlie stood behind a tree and lit one of the Marlboros his brother gave him. "He says 'cause mom bled him dry in the divorce."

Johnny shrugged. It wasn't his business. "Well, she did get the house, and your dad's paying for Elise's school."

"Yeah," Charlie said, and smoked. "He just bought a new Benz, too. Guy's full of it."

Johnny held out his hand for the cigarette. He didn't start smoking until recently. He wasn't sure if he was past fascination and entering the addiction stage, but that cigarette was calling his name. Charlie handed it to him and exhaled a mouthful of smoke into the cold air. Johnny asked, "Robbie can pay for his own college, right? The Army pays for it?"

"The G.I. Bill," Charlie said. "Something tells me Robbie might not go to college, though."

Charlie lowered his eyes and walked over to a long stick of bamboo braced against a tree. "Why?" Johnny asked. "Why don't you think he'll go to college?"

His friend ignored him and said, "Watch this."

"What?"

Charlie waved the bamboo stick like a magician summoning a dragon with his spell. He slapped the dirt and the ground beneath them erupted in a reddish cloud that brought a loud report and made Johnny fall backwards on his ass. Charlie looked down at him, laughed, and extended his hand to help his friend up.

"What the hell, man!"

"Relax."

The sooty vapor flowed downwind, but Charlie wafted the air toward him and his supine friend. "Ah," Johnny said. "That stuff smells. Why are you waving it over us?"

"For just that reason. If my dad smells smoke when we're in the car, at least it'll be the smoke from one of my little experiments."

"Speaking of smokes …" Johnny looked at the mildewed grass to the left and right of where he lay. The cigarette flew from his hand when he fell. He spotted the smoke on the ground to the side of his lightly-scratched and ashen right elbow. It was still lit. He picked the cigarette up and stood, a cramp forming in his lower back.

He puffed. "Good thinking, I guess." Then he asked, "Where'd you get the stuff for that?" The last of the wizard's plume was rising from the ground, and his heartbeat was steadying somewhat.

"I have my wiles and ways." Charlie smiled cryptically. "I jacked some iodine crystals from Mr. Brackman's class."

It would be easy enough to steal from him. He cared a lot less about science than about arbitrarily handing out detentions to kids who left trash underneath their benches in lab. Most of the science the kids actually learned was gleaned from watching episodes of *Bill Nye* at home.

"The ammonium hydroxide I got from the pharmacy. Easy peasy."

He walked away from the recent explosion back in the direction of the nursery.

"Where are you going?"

"I've got something I want to show you. Another experiment." That didn't sound good, but Johnny followed all the same.

"Fire!" Charlie giggled a berserk little laugh, doing his best Beavis impression. He looked back at Johnny. "You know Robbie said the Iraqi soldiers set oil fields on fire, thousands of gallons of black stuff just …burning!" He gasped and shivered like a drunk relieving himself at the urinal. "Jesus Christ, man, I would love to see that."

"I don't know," Johnny said, thinking about how Robbie looked and sounded the last time he saw him. "It didn't look like he liked a lot of what he saw over there."

Johnny saw the dark shadows of two forms moving about in the nursery laboring over poinsettias. "What are they doing?"

"Defying nature and God," Charlie said, only half-joking. "They're forcing those poinsettias to artificially flower for Christmas." He rapped the glass fixed in the sash of the nursery's window, and the two women looked up. "See, dad put storm windows in so the place could retain heat. It ain't *au natural,* like it was when mama was running things."

Russell was behind the nursery, inspecting sacks for tears on the ball and burlap plants lain out on the gravel. Johnny looked around for the weeping forms of the sphagnum, but they were no more. He missed them.

"You check those levels?"

"Indeed, I did."

"You yanking my chain?"

"Indeed, I am not."

Russell nodded. "I guess I got no choice but to trust you."

Charlie played mock-offended, slapped his breastbone. "You doubt me, your own son?"

"Yeah, you and Robbie are two apples that fell way the hell away from the tree." He turned back in the direction of the front office, where he spent a good part of the day fending off salesmen and trying to help Gentleman Jim and his wife realize their Arcadian delusions. "You boys want to head to the Lanes, play some games when we get done here?"

Johnny couldn't contain his surprise, but Charlie was unfazed. "Sounds like a plan," Charlie said. "Just don't head next door and try the nacho cheese unless you want to be gripping that porcelain 'til the cows come home."

The phone rang from inside the front office, and Russell quickened his pace, adding as he went, "Try C-rations. Or better yet, ask your brother about them."

"Come on," Charlie whispered, and now that his father's back was to him, he knelt down in front of one of the ball and burlap jobs. "That was close."

"What was close?" Johnny asked. "Hey, and since when does your dad want to go the arcade? He's too old to play those games, even the Atari ones." Johnny's own dad played *Tetris*, but he was a Baby Boomer, not a veteran of the Big One.

Charlie lifted a two-liter from between the large plants and slid it under his shirt. The way he cradled it reminded Johnny of the girls in the "At-Risk" program at school, who were forced to carry around eggs and pretend they were newborn children.

"Dad's gotten into playing games since *Golden Tee* came out. He likes to play the golf game just to look at the greens on the holes. He likes to stare at the crabgrass and the fairway turfs."

They did a beeline toward the trees behind Freeport Fertilizer. They passed the old Quonset hut where the college students once conducted their research. Maybe they even grew a few sativa plants if Mr. Milner wasn't being paranoid in suspecting they were potheads.

Johnny looked through the glass fogged with condensation. He remembered there used to be a sheet of plastic draped over a metal-ribbed exoskeleton. He also didn't see the hydroponic setup from all those years ago. Now there were a bunch of tubes that looked like the nozzles dentists used to squirt water into the mouths of their patients. The tubes hovered over beds of red plants.

"It's a drip irrigation system," Charlie said, and continued walking with his friend following behind him. They crossed from the Freeport Fertilizer property line into a no-man's land Corbett Senior was yet to develop or perhaps even discover. The cold air turned the formerly green grass to an ugly verdigris tapestry that was aquamarine, like a decaying penny. Johnny thought the grass the color of death.

Charlie set the two-liter down on the ground. He took the D-Day Zippo from his pocket, and lit one of the cigarettes from his pack.

"You'd better slow down, man. Robbie's not going to be around to just keep buying you packs forever. His leave'll be up soon."

"You know," Charlie said. Johnny knew from his tone that Charlie didn't hear a word he said. The more his words sounded like advice, Johnny noticed, the less Charlie tended to care what he was saying. "Crowes and Corbett call me faggot all the time. I let it upset me, but I shouldn't."

Charlie puffed his cigarette. "Cat Piss hurts, I'll admit."

"I smelled your clothes, man. They don't smell like cat piss." Johnny left out the part about Elise. He failed to make eye contact with her once during dinner the other night.

"'Faggot' is actually a word that just meant 'burning stick' or something like that, originally."

Johnny looked down at the two-liter bottle in his friend's hands. He noticed a thin white strand, a wick improvised from a lace previously gracing the one shoe Crowes didn't get on the soccer field that day. Johnny didn't see the lace peeking from the bottle a moment before because this cold grey day made everything white, and camouflaged the little string. It smelled like kerosene.

"They used faggots to burn witches," Charlie said. He held the cigarette in his right hand between the clawed pincers he formed with his thumb and forefinger. Johnny thought Charlie was offering him the square. He reached out for it, trying to snatch the cigarette. Charlie pulled it away, however, just as Johnny went for it. Charlie leaned down to the two-liter and laid the cigarette at the tip of the kerosene-drenched shoelace.

"A cigarette," Charlie said, "isn't exactly the most foolproof way to light a fuse." He grinned a horrible smile. That smile made Johnny suspect Charlie's face was just a wax disguise his friend might someday peel off to expose the real one beneath the mask. "A shoelace isn't the most reliable fuse."

Charlie stood and walked backward, away from the smoldering lace. White smoke crawled up in a sinuous spirochete. "What I'm trying to say is I don't know if we have ten seconds or ten minutes. I'm still new at this."

Charlie ran back in the direction of Freeport Fertilizer, away from the smoldering two-liter on the ground. Johnny ran with him. His lungs were scorching, a white vapor trail exploding in front of his face as he sucked in cold air and his cheeks reddened. "You fucking asshole! What's in that two-liter?"

His friend ran and laughed until he was out of breath and could run no more. He stopped with his hands on his knees. He leaned over, spent from the exertion and also from the thrill of what he just did. Smacking iodine crystals with a bamboo cane was one thing, but this was a real incendiary device he'd just lit.

"Some denatured alcohol, a bit of diesel fuel." He mimed measuring out a pinch with his right hand, like his mother subtracting a dash of oregano from the bottle on the spice rack. "With just a smidgen of methyl alco-"

A fulminating inferno rose from the dead grass plane and danced up above, forming a reddish face with an evil flaming smile. It was sort of like the form discerned in the white outlines of a cottony cloud, only this one was a burning orange and yellow monster Charlie summoned from hell. The conjuration was a sight worse than the squid Johnny saw in the form of that cloud the other day at school.

Johnny looked at Charlie, the fire reflected in his friend's eyes that were moist, as if he was ready to cry. He briefly wondered how far Charlie was willing to go, and if he was willing to go there with him. He wanted to be angry, but had to admit this infusion of adrenaline was for him like water to the plants arrayed in the nursery behind them. He smoked weed once before, and had his first cigarette recently. They both took tentative sips from the liquor cabinet's store of Jamaican rum when they spent the night at Charlie's dad's condo. This was different, though, and a hell of a lot better.

No one was hurt. He looked back out at that gray-green expanse. A bit of PVC pipe shot out after the initial explosion, and the plastic two-liter was melted to the ground, but there wasn't much besides the smell remaining. A few wisps of smoke were the only remnants of the explosion. The loud salvo, the *boom*, didn't draw much attention.

They walked back toward the two-liter, cautiously, as if a secondary explosion might be triggered at any moment. Little licking flames, like spurts from candles on a birthday cake, winked from the lawn. Charlie stepped on the little orange licking fires, and they ceased, surrendering in small clouds of smoke.

Johnny kicked the melted contours of the warped PVC pipe previously attached to the mouth of the two-liter. Strands of Teflon tape were shredded around the length of pipe. "Hey," he said. "Is that the handle from the machine gun on *Terminator Two*, from the arcade?"

"Yeah, DJ jimmied that sucker free. I've got the actual gun at home."

"He let you keep it?"

"He just wanted that ball bearing for himself."

"Oh." DJ was obsessed with shiny metal, and "chromies" were his greatest passion.

"Chromies" was his name for the little valve stem caps he stole from the tires of any cars he found parked in the lot at Arby's or the convenience store. That was as far from his headquarters at the Lanes as he was willing to venture to steal.

Johnny shook his head. "You guys keep it up and Bill's going to put your name on the shit list with Chuckie. We'll all probably get a lifetime ban."

"Maybe."

Charlie already pulled another cigarette from his pack and lit it without Johnny even noticing him go through the ritual. Johnny became aware Charlie was smoking only after blue vapor snaked his way and made his eyes water. Charlie did have a magician's hands.

They walked back in the direction of the nursery, away from the steaming pile behind them. It slowly settled into dormancy, like an untended campfire when it was no more than a bed of cinders and ashen logs.

"Shit." Charlie threw his cigarette to the ground after only one puff, and ground it out. A look of fear washed across his face. Russell was jogging, and then flat out running toward them. A look of what Johnny thought was rage turned his face a bright scarlet.

Johnny's heart started its drumroll again, punching as if it wanted to beat its way out of his breathless body. He never saw Russell hit his son before, but there was a first time for everything. There was also a chance, he felt, as the man ran toward him, that he might catch a blow to the side of his own head.

He remembered either Robbie or Charlie telling him Russell boxed Golden Gloves. He crossed paths as a young man with many up and comers from the Lower East Side, who eventually went pro. Russell's opponents racked up losses to the likes of Sugar Ray Robinson and Jake Lamotta, but a man who fought those who lost to the best wouldn't have trouble beating the living snot out of two suburban punks who spent their lives playing videogames.

Russell was less than ten feet from them, and they both stopped walking toward him, wanting to delay the inevitable. Freeport was Russell's life and livelihood, and they just lit a dangerous bomb behind his business. *We?* Johnny thought about it. *Was I part of it, or did I just watch it? If I just watched it, does that mean I was part of it?*

"Dad, listen, I …"

"Robbie's been hurt, bad."

"What?"

Johnny was ashamed of the relief he felt at not being in trouble, and his pulse calmed again. He realized Mr. Milner wasn't angry. The man was scared or maybe shocked was more like it. His eyes now looked the way his wife's eyes did for the last few years.

"What happened?" Charlie's mouth was open and his eyes were wide.

"An accident." Mr. Milner turned back around. He headed diagonally across the gravel, stone, and grass. He ran in the direction of the parking lot where his new Benz was parked. The wooden arches, where in the spring the perennials hung, were empty and looked like gallows. The recently planted beds bulged with soil that was dark brown, the sod soaked with moisture. Johnny couldn't shake the thought as it came to him unbidden that Robbie was already buried under the mulched ground there.

"An accident," Charlie said. The tone in his voice was pathetic, bargaining, as if he thought that if he could get his father to amend his answer, then it might change the reality. "What kind of accident? Car accident?"

"He shot himself." Russell winced, realizing he let the barrier between adult and child drop, and that he shouldn't let it fall like that. He was human though, and it was hard to bullshit his son while his other son was lying in a coma or dead.

Charlie gulped, and there was no stopping the question as it formed in his mind. He asked it before he realized he didn't want the answer. "Did he do it on purpose or …?"

Russell paused, hit the automatic alarm on his Benz. The car chirped once as its taillights winked. "I don't know."

CHAPTER FIVE

A suicide around Christmastime was especially rough for everyone Robbie left behind. Freeport did holidays in style. There didn't look to be a brick or half-timbered panel not covered in tinsel or bright red and green lights from the village square to the edge of the suburbs. Janet and Russell Milner contended with the lawn of the Morrison family closer to home. The Morrisons went way overboard every Christmas. Their lawn featured an inflatable snowman with a stovepipe hat and coal buttons on his chest, along with a nativity scene that looked to be due for a collision with that jovial plastic Santa putting the whip to all nine of his reindeer. The snowman was the size of a children's bouncy palace at an amusement park, and he hovered over the split-level house as if he intended to crush it.

Russell and his wife were in the kitchen hashing out the final details of the obituary they intended to submit to the *Freeport Lancer* for publication soon. This was the first death in the immediate Milner family, and neither knew the exact protocol. They thought it might be unusual to do an obituary after all of the other arrangements were made, but they put the task off specifically because it required so much coordination between the two of them. Each held a private grudge against their dead son for forcing them together again like this.

"Okay," Russell said, and stopped scribbling with his ballpoint on the yellow legal pad. "Let's try this on for size."

Janet stood up from the table and walked over to the percolating coffee pot on the counter. She turned the Mr. Coffee off and poured two cupsful into the Peanuts mugs.

"'Robert James Milner, born April 5th, 1972, died …'" He paused, sighed, and massaged the waxen folds in his forehead. Then he resumed. "'Died September 5th, 1994.'"

"So far, so terrible." His wife carried the two cups to the kitchen table and set them down on the cloth. She leaned around her husband and shouted through the entryway into the living room. "Can you turn that television down? Your father and I are trying to work in here." She added, "I would be eternally in your debt," before taking a sip of her hot coffee.

"'Robert served his country with distinction in both Operations Desert Shield and Desert Storm, selflessly volunteering for service to his nation. He won the Southwest Asia Service Medal, as well as the more prestigious Army Commendation Medal for Valorous Actions in direct contact with members of the enemy republican guard.'"

Both Charlie and Johnny heard that last bit even over the sound of the loud television. They hadn't turned it down, despite Mrs. Milner's request. Charlie wondered what Robbie would do if he could somehow reassemble himself from the pile of ashes he now was. He would probably get up and smack both his mother and father for trying to pass him off as a hero, even in something as *pro forma* as an obituary.

"Good," Mrs. Milner said. "You do this before in the War?"

"No, too many guys died for us to bother with that. If we managed to get your body back to the States, that was enough respect paid."

Mrs. Milner shuddered. She didn't like that her husband was so flippant about death. On the other hand, she couldn't blame him. He saw much more of death than she. Janet gave him credit at least for not pouring the torture of his soul into her ear during the course of their marriage. Russell never talked about the war unless asked, and then only reluctantly. Robbie told his parents nothing of his own experience with war, and only a little bit to Johnny and Charlie.

Elise returned back to her dorm at the University of Cincinnati, two days after Robbie took his life at the Days Inn. His method of suicide made an open casket impossible, and the idea of honoring his request for cremation that much easier.

Charlie watched her as she packed her things and he decided she was angrier at Robbie than the rest of them. She was angry not so much at the selfishness of the act. Charlie thought she was angry that Robbie forced her to be reminded of her love for him, and to take away the armor that her hatred gave her. If he was sensitive enough to take his life, then that meant he wasn't the war machine she wanted him to be. She was pissed. He was dead and there was no way to get even with him, which pissed her off even more.

"'He is survived by …'" Russell clenched his teeth together, and his wife looked away from him. She reached her hand across the table. She slid the yellow legal pad over to her side of the table and read what her husband wrote.

"'He is survived by his father, Russell Milner, his mother, Janet Milner, his brother Charles Milner, and sister Elise Milner. He had no children.'"

"That we know of," Russell said. "Craig said he sowed the hell out of his wild oats while they were with their Cav unit in *Deutschland*."

Russell relaxed a bit. His son was no longer a pile of sand for the moment. He was a virile young warrior crusading against barbarians and leaving a wake of offspring in each castle he stormed.

"Who's Craig?" Mrs. Milner asked, and then she remembered. "Oh, when's he going to be here?"

Russell glanced down at his Rolex. "Any time."

She looked over at the vulcanized kitchen range. "Think I should make something?"

"He said he just wants to get the ashes and go." Russell winced from his own words. He felt the family should keep Robbie there on the mantle where he was now or that his son should be respectfully interred at Arlington. Robbie left specific instructions in his final note. He said he wanted to be cremated, and he wanted Craig to have his ashes. The existence of the letter was kept secret between Mr. and Mrs. Milner, the only two who read it. They told Charlie Robbie spoke with them

before deploying to the Gulf about what he wanted
done in the event of his own death, and their
remaining son accepted their words without a further
question or comment. They were his parents after all
he thought, and wouldn't lie to him.

Russell gently took the legal pad back from
his wife and resumed reading. His nerves were
calmed and there was now less chance of him crying
for the first time in more than forty years.

"'Robbie specified that he did not want a
wake, funeral, vigil, or graveside service. Those who
wish to express condolences or want to make
charitable donations of either flowers or money are
requested to direct their generosity to the care of the
Milners. Their address is 1610 Lafayette Circle. The
Milners would also like to take this opportunity to

thank all of the members of the Freeport community for their help in aiding them through this bereavement process.'"

Russell sighed with relief. "Okay, we got through that." He lifted his coffee to his lips, sipped, and shook his head. "You know, that cheap prick Corbett didn't send so much as a card?" He shook his head at the audacity. "I practically sodded a PGA course in the cocksucker's backyard, and not so much as a word. You figure he has an army of secretaries who could do it, but he can't even be bothered."

"A priest called earlier," Janet said absently.

"What did he want?"

The Milners rarely, if ever, went to church themselves. "He wanted to know if we wanted him to say a prayer over Robbie's ashes." She finished her mug of Joe and walked back over to the percolator.

"His dog tags said 'No rel. pref.'"

Janet poured herself another cup, looked back to see what kind of headway her ex-husband made on his own Joe. His coffee was still sloshing around the fill line. "That means no religious preference," Russell said. "I don't blame him. The military's filled with people who are full of shit, but a chaplain's a bit more full of shit than anyone else."

"So no priest, then?"

"That's what the smart money says."

It was raining outside, and fog lights blasted against the window over the kitchen sink. "He's here," Janet said. "You got the trunk?" Mr. Milner sprang to his feet and walked into the entryway of the living room. He kicked the footlocker across the carpet and then slid it along the scuffed linoleum of the kitchen floor. It made a scraping sound as he shoved the tough box until it was flush with the mudroom.

"Charlie!" Russell shouted and walked back toward the living room. "You have to pay your last respects to your brother." The boys were on the couch, and Johnny quickly stashed the bottle of rum beneath one of the throw pillows on the sofa. They were already slightly tipsy, but Charlie's parents were too deep in their own fog to notice. Charlie thought one of the only benefits of his brother's death was that his parents were too crushed to ride his ass about grades or smoking weed, or pretty much anything else, ever again.

"Shit." Charlie stood and reached across the glass coffee table for the remote resting next to a recent issue of TV Guide. He finally turned the set down, as his mother asked him to do about ten minutes ago. The loud bleeps of cussing on *Jerry Springer* grew several octaves quieter. Security Guard Steve got between two identical twins trying to take a swing on each other. They fought over the objections of a white trash homewrecker, a peroxide blond married to the first of the two twins. She'd just confessed she slept with her husband's brother.

"Can I open it?" Charlie asked. "Just look at him?"

Russell massaged the tear ducts on the sides of his nose. "I don't think so. You're not supposed to open those things." Charlie walked over to the urn on the mantle. It was mahogany with a dark nutmeg stain and satin finish. His brother's awards were pinned to the outside of the little wooden vase. "I'm sure Craig will let you look at it later. Maybe, he'll even give it back to the family." Russell thought of adding, "When he comes to his senses." He fought the urge to offer the guy a few honeybees just to leave empty-handed. He was a combat-hardened veteran himself though, and knew what friends in foxholes meant. If someone offered him money to relinquish the remains of a friend, he might have to roll up his sleeves and dig back into his Golden Gloves repertoire to show the pisser what for.

Johnny wanted to stand with his friend to touch the urn one last time. He didn't want to get between Charlie and his dead brother, though. If he stood now, he also risked loosening the throw pillow beside him. Then Russell might see that bottle of rum they snuck from his condo to Mrs. Milner's place.

"Hello!" An unfamiliar male voice came from the kitchen. Charlie touched the edge of the urn one last time. Russell picked it up off the mantle and carried it into the kitchen.

The boys followed Russell. Craig Lowenthal had a bodybuilder's physique. There were just the traces of a paunch at his midsection, suggesting he was in the bulk phase of his cut and bulk cycle. His high and tight was much shorter than Robbie's was the last time they saw him alive. It was recon tapered, and looked like a Mohawk worn by a member of a warlike tribe. His right forearm featured a faded India ink depiction of an M-16 with bayonet fixed and staked into the ground. A K-pot with dangling chinstraps rested from the butt of the weapon.

He flexed and showed the tattoo to everyone, pointing out the scrollwork commemorating his friend's death with the month, day, and year he fell. "Just got it done on my way up from Columbus." He grinned. "They got their fair share of tattoo parlors in army towns." He laughed, and the reek of alcohol on him was stronger than on either boy or Mrs. Milner. She switched to stuff much heavier than her old carob liqueur awhile back.

"You know army towns." He coughed, and the smell of alcohol was even heavier. Mrs. Milner wondered if he might get into a car accident on his drive back to Benning, and then maybe reunite with his old friend in the hereafter. "What was it Mark Twain said? 'There is a saloon every ten feet and some talk of building a church' or something like that?"

Russell relaxed a bit, and fell into the easy camaraderie of one vet speaking to another. "Fayetteville was always the worst when I was stationed at Bragg. You could get a dose just driving through there."

"Fayettenam," Craig said.

Dose, Johnny thought. The boys loved to ride the old man for his arcane slang (especially

Robbie), but that wasn't actually half-bad. Mrs. Milner pretended she didn't hear the word. Craig sensed her discomfort, not just with this conversation, but with his presence here. Her expression softened, however, when she looked down at his tattoo.

"Thank you for doing that."

He held the arm aloft, and clenched his fist as if doing the black power salute. "The way I figure it, the war did it to him, so I'm treating it like a K.I.A." He shook his head. "He wasn't the only one either, and he won't be the last."

He glanced over at the table, saw the yellow legal pad there, and guessed correctly at its purpose. "You guys writing an obit?"

"Trying," Russell said, glancing back at the table. Charlie walked over to the pad and squinted at his father's cursive chicken scratch. His handwriting was about as legible as that of an M.D.

"You guys should make up some cool heroic deeds," Charlie said. "Like he took out a nest of republican guards or slit a sniper's throat, or something."

"Charlie," Mrs. Milner said.

The soldier's eyes hardened. "He didn't have to make anything up." Craig reached for the urn, and set it down next to the footlocker at his feet. "The Guard had some MELS." He turned to Mrs. Milner, and then looked over to Mr. Milner. He decided a fellow vet made a better audience for the shop talk. "That's a Mobile Erector Launcher for scuds. Aerial reconnaissance couldn't spot them, and they were causing a lot of trouble. Milner took them out with a couple of two-oh-three rounds. He did what candy-ass Schwarzkopf with his left hook couldn't do."

"Our son was a hero," Mrs. Milner said. She spoke more for her remaining son's benefit than for any other reason. She also spoke to stop Craig from going on to elucidate some details having to do with death, and the work of killing. She came of age during Vietnam War and was part of the protest movement, ostensibly for the good of world peace. She privately thought that war and soldiers were low class. She also noticed that most of the richer, more attractive kids on campus were antiwar.

Craig remembered his own prior oath to come quickly and leave with the same speed. He had the footlocker and the urn now, which was what he came for. He intended to do some more serious drinking and to maybe pick up another tattoo or two before signing back in with his battalion. He was not looking forward to policing up spent brass rounds on the range. There was yet to be a replacement assigned to the command in the wake of Robbie's death, and range cadre was short one hand. The weather was still ugly down in Georgia, which meant he and the remaining crew would be working in the goddamned rain and mud.

"Hey battle buddy," he said, stooping down to the urn. He touched one of the soft ribbons attached to it. "Your brother was modest." he said. Craig now looked at Charlie, perhaps because he was crouched down below the other two adults. "He used to call the Service Medal the 'Pulse and Respiration Ribbon' because everyone who went to Iraq got one whether they were chair borne or airborne."

Craig let go of the ribbon on the face of the urn and undid the clasps over the footlocker. Mrs. Milner shifted uneasily in place and glanced up at Russell, who turned away. Both of the boys looked at the young soldier, who rooted through the top layer of class b and a uniforms lain across the pile of Robbie's old effects.

"Could you ..." Mrs. Milner started, but Charlie interrupted her.

"What's that?" he asked.

Craig glanced up, holding a pamphlet covered in Arabic Naskh calligraphy. The cover artwork featured several Iraqi soldiers talking to one another, casting their little cartoon Kalashnikovs into the desert sand at their feet. "I haven't seen one of these things in a while." Craig smiled, as he remembered the good, or at least interesting, parts of the war. "These are PSYOP leaflets telling the *Hajjis* to abandon their equipment and turn themselves in to the Americans, who won't harm them."

"*Hajjis?*"

Craig shrugged. "Yeah, carpet kissers, camel humpers, whatever."

"Okay!" Mrs. Milner no longer squirmed, but lunged toward the footlocker. She took the pamphlets from Craig's hands, placed them back inside, and closed the lid. "We want to thank you for coming, driving all the way up from Georgia, and for ..." She glanced at the tattoo on his forearm. "For remembering our son in your own, special way."

"Did I do something wrong?" He looked over at Russell, who leaned down and whispered, "There are some photos in there Mrs. Milner and I don't want the boys to see." He looked up at his ex-wife. "She wanted to burn them, but I wasn't sure if we had the right."

Craig nodded, and looked over at the two boys. They heard the whole exchange, and would remember it, even though they were both already tipsy. The soldier locked the trunk without another word, placed the urn on top of it. Then he lifted everything he came for in his muscled arms. He grunted slightly, as if performing bicep curls.

A crucifix attached to a gold necklace dangled and spilled out from underneath his shirt, flopping over his chest. He grinned at the two boys. They looked up, not at him, or even at the urn, but at the black footlocker containing the forbidden photos. "You got to keep these things inside your shirt when you're in Saudi," Craig said. He motioned toward the crucifix with his chin, since his hands were full, and he couldn't point.

Charlie looked down at Craig's chest, at the electroplated Jesus swaying back and forth like a pendulum. Rich golden beads of blood leaked from the platinized crown of thorns, and the expression on

Christ's face mirrored the way he felt at this moment.

Charlie turned with Johnny following behind him. Neither of them bothered to say goodbye to the young man, who came to take Robbie's remains away to Georgia. Russell Milner was a bit more cordial, patting Craig on the back and walking with him out to his car. Janet only mustered a mild expression of disgust. She felt soiled by the whole affair, and slightly enraged. She and her husband were well on their way to cultivating a relatively tasteful aura of grieving. She found it therapeutic to edit and revise the obit, until it said exactly what they wanted it to say about their son, and left out everything they preferred to keep hidden about him, and themselves.

CHAPTER SIX

In the movies, the jocks didn't do any drugs. They just drank. At Freeport Junior High though, the lettermen liked to smoke an occasional joint or two. Maybe they did it to make a statement, to test the limits of what the faculty would let them get away with on campus, or to gamble on whether or not Vanhauser would schedule one of his random urinalyses. Maybe Crowes and Corbett wanted to prove the cannabis smoke did nothing to their lung capacity, and that they could still outsprint most of the track kids even after blazing a bit of Acapulco gold.

Charlie ran into them shortly after getting out of his father's car. He told his parents about the ongoing campaign of bullying he endured on the bus, and said he would never go to school again if they tried to make him ride the yellow Bluebird one more time. They could call the truant officer on him. They could homeschool or transfer him, but he and the cheese were done with each other.

The ultimatum worked, perhaps because it came in the wake of Robbie's death, when Mr. and Mrs. Milner were more willing to bend on their only remaining son's behalf. Russell didn't have to get to Freeport until 9 a.m. to check the morning's messages in the front office, so he drove Charlie to school.

Charlie wandered off the main sidewalk, over toward the gathering of trees to the side of the school's main building. This was the spot where the cigarette and pot smokers blazed before classes started. The smokers' pit consisted of an ancient plush couch from which dangerously sharp springs sprouted, as well as a couple of blue gym mats someone dragged out here after their foam innards sprouted out through their tears, and the custodian pitched them into the industrial trash bin.

Charlie wasn't exactly sure why the blue gym mats were here, but a bumper crop of used condoms, weighed with white goop at the reservoir tips, gave him some kind of idea. He was prepping to smoke a cigarette he stole from his mom when he heard Crowes' voice calling from a knot of trees a little farther back from the mouth of the smokers' pit.

"Hey, Charlie!" he whispered. There was a friendly tone to his voice, as if he was inviting him to partake in a conspiracy. Crowes called him Charlie, not Cat Piss, for the first time in what felt like forever. Charlie remained planted where he was. He looked over at Crowes, the collar on his jacket upturned and shielding the pimpled flesh of his strong jawline. "Come here, man."

Corbett appeared from the other side of the tree, coughing and pounding the chest of his varsity jacket with a clenched fist. "Good shit, man." He removed a glass bottle of Brut aftershave from the pocket of his cargo pants, doused a couple of splashes on his fingers, and then applied them to his neckline. Corbett was mostly hairless, Charlie noticed, like a swimmer. His smooth skin and aquiline nose gave him that perfect dash of the feminine that drove girls crazy. He wasn't vulnerable, but he could feign something poetic around females his own age or older. It was possible, Charlie thought, that he could cause a scandal by the time he got to high school. Most of the teacher-student sex crimes involved male teachers and female students. If anyone had the power and charm to pull off the rare inversion though, it was Alex Corbett.

Charlie lit his cigarette, and tentatively stepped toward the tree where Crowes and Corbett were smoking the resinous remains of their joint. The aroma of maple leaves comingling with marijuana smoke was a soothing tonic to his stomach, which was always most turbulent right before school.

"You want to get high?" Corbett held out the roach.

Charlie shrugged, puffed his cigarette double-time, and walked toward them and the tree they hid behind. He thought the smokers' pit was pretty well concealed by the gathering of trees adjacent to the school. None of the Chronics were ever busted out here by any teachers or the patrolling couple of "resource officers." Maybe Crowes and Corbett trudged deeper into the woods before blazing up because they had more to lose.

The image of Robbie danced before his mind's eye as he smoked his square down to a butt. He remembered his brother talking about the "choo-choo train," a program range cadre instituted for the basic training privates at Benning. After the raw recruits were done firing for the day, they were required to submit themselves to a pat down from the cadre. Robbie and the other soldiers would check their trainees for either spent brass rounds or live ammo after the recruits left their firing positions.

Both alcohol and tobacco were forbidden in basic training. Anyone found with cigarettes could be recycled. That meant they were forced to repeat the entire experience from day one. Robbie and the other cadre were merciful to the rule breakers they caught. They merely forced the soldier to smoke and jog until all of their cigarettes were gone, or the soldier collapsed in a heap in the hot Georgia mud.

Charlie threw his butt into the array of dead, snow-covered leaves at his feet. He reached for the joint with his nicotine-stained fingers. Corbett withdrew the offer as quickly as he presented it. Crowes grabbed Charlie around the throat with his strong right hand, flinging him into the tree, back first.

Charlie's spine felt like an icicle, more shock than pain at the moment. He knew it would smart when the fear wore off.

"Okay, Cat Piss. Breathe."

It was an odd command. Charlie didn't know how not to breathe. He figured Johnny was getting off the bus about now. Charlie breathed. Crowes slapped him. "Not like that, faggot. Breathe deep."

The task was difficult when he was scared and confused. Corbett pinched the little bit of remaining joint in the improvised roach clip he made of his fingernails, but it was no use. The resin was now mucilage thick as molasses. He tossed the roach into the dirt, wiping his hands off on the bark of a nearby tree.

Charlie inhaled deeply, hearing the sound of his own labored breathing in his ears, like the surf hitting the beach and releasing a salty ocean spray. He breathed, and both Crowes and Corbett crowded close to him. He saw nothing else besides them. He knew they were just going to make his life hell for the short term, whatever they had planned for him. He was certain for a terrified moment that these two faces would be the last thing he ever saw. It was a frozen image he would take with him to the other side after Crowes killed him. It was somehow fitting, one ugly and the other beautiful, as different from each other as the weeping and laughing drama masks representing Comedy and Tragedy.

Crowes folded his hands one over the other while Charlie breathed and his eyes widened in terror. He heard the distant chatter of the kids who just arrived at the smokers' pit, talking about videogames and ignoring what was going on over here. He didn't blame them. Crowes could kick all of their asses with one hand tied behind his back. Charlie looked down at those substantial meat hooks laid on his chest now. The knuckles were covered with a fine layer of downy black hair that looked pubic and reminded him of a troll. Those hands could grip a pigskin as easily as Charlie could hold an egg.

Charlie breathed, and Crowes pumped his hands vigorously into his chest. He performed some demented version of CPR, until Charlie's vision dwindled to a tunnel. There wasn't enough air in his

lungs or blood in his head for him to understand
what was happening or for him to think. An
explosion of fireworks crackled in his retinas. He
woke up with a bruise on his forehead from where
he passed out and his skull bumped against a hollow
log. He remained alone and in the woods for quite
some time, before walking back into the school.

He massaged his head now, looking up
toward the front of the room.

This class was kind of okay when Brackman
took them to the lab since there was cool stuff to
steal there. This class was tedious as hell though,
when the teacher was moored behind that pedestal
desk. He'd stand writing on that twelve-foot
blackboard, tapping his chalk against the map rail.

Brackman wore short sleeve shirts with clip-on ties, and something about that made the man look oily. Mrs. Milner met him during a parent-teacher conference to discuss Charlie's inattentiveness. She left the meeting, went directly back to her son, and said, "Never wear a short sleeve shirt and tie. You'll look like a vacuum cleaner salesman."

Right now Brackman was fumbling with the pull-down projector screen, getting ready to talk about the pituitary gland. The gland's image glowed on his overhead projector and splashed across the chalkboard, as the teacher thrashed and struggled. Mr. Young already covered this stuff in health class, but Charlie didn't want to raise his hand and point that out to Brackman. The science teacher was petty and held grudges against both other faculty and students. Many teachers quickly devolved into children themselves in the fever swamp of Freeport Junior High. Brackman might have started out as fresh-faced in the beginning, but Charlie thought he was sunk deep into the mire now. He was notorious for handing out detention arbitrarily on the pretext of finding trash underneath a student's desk. He was more liberal with his red slips of paper when they were in lab and not in the classroom for whatever reason.

"Hi, everybody!" Amy Porterhouse stuck her head into the classroom, smiled with a face full of orthodontia, and disappeared after briefly warming all of them. Even Brackman and Charlie were cheered by her presence.

"Hey, Amy Steak!" Someone in the front row said. Brackman let the outburst pass without comment. Charlie glanced up at the black schoolhouse clock. *Right on time*, he thought. She always ducked into the room at 11:33 a.m. on the dot.

Brackman finally got the pull-down projector's screen to stay in place, and a student in the desk nearest the room's door stood up and killed the lights. The pupils seated along the far wall stood and pulled the curtains shut, giving themselves a reprieve from the sun's heat. Luminescence from the projector spilled onto Brackman's pedestal desk, and Charlie looked at the contents glowing there. There was a piece of obsidian lava, the frozen scoria looking like the droppings of a prehistoric monster. Next to that was a mortared chunk from the Berlin Wall Brackman said he picked up with his own two hands as the barrier between East and West

Germany fell. It was a keepsake from his time as a Fulda Gap soldier, he said. Brackman wasn't Charlie's favorite person, but the teacher didn't strike him as a bullshitter either. The thing looked real enough, scarred with blue and pink graffiti, with umlauts and essets thrown in for good measure.

"Progesterone," Brackman said, as he slapped the canvas with his rubber-tipped pointer, "is triggered by the pituitary gland, which is about the size of a pea." Brackman scratched the fine black hairs running down the skin exposed along the length of his sleeveless right forearm. "Testosterone causes body hair to grow, your voice to deepen, and …"

Charlie thought Crowes must have a pituitary gland the size of that old rock from

Checkpoint Charlie, or maybe the size of that volcanic slab, since that was actually a little bit bigger.

Class wasn't so bad now, since it was darker and he could relax. He closed his eyes and thought about the conversation he and his father had on the ride in to school today. It was certainly a more pleasant experience than riding the bus.

"You tried ignoring them?" Russell asked in reference to the bullies. They were queued up in the carpool lane adjacent to the dedicated bus loop.

"Doesn't work," Charlie said. "Makes it worse." He sank deeper into the warm, heated leather of the Benz's passenger seat. "The more I ignore it, the more people join in on the game of 'let's all pick on Cat Piss'."

Russell snorted at that, and turned his head toward his son while keeping his hands on the steering wheel. "Jesus, you don't smell like cat piss. If anyone smells in this car, it's me." He took his right hand off the wheel and stabbed his chest with a thumb. "I'm the one who works with chemicals all day, and you only spend weekends at my place. You ain't picking up the smell from being around musty old me."

Charlie just shook his head. "It's been too long since you've been in school. You forget what it's like. If the Populars say the sky's purple, the sky's purple."

"Nah, I see what you're saying."

Charlie glanced out his window at that point, toward the row of cheeses spewing carbon monoxide from their tails. He searched among the shadowy figures in the berths of the yellow Bluebird busses for the faces of the kids who specifically taunted him. The inside of his cheek still hurt from the last day he rode the bus to school, when he bit the inside of his mouth with his molars and gnashed until the tissue tore slightly. A jet of blood leaked out onto his tongue. He tasted the metallic warmth, liking the tang of it. He wished it was the blood of either Crowes or Corbett. One question burnt in his mind on the final stretch of that car ride, as he and his father approached the haunted mansion where he spent his days. *Whose blood do I want more? Crowes is the body, Corbett the head. Kill the head and the body dies.*

"You want to know what's worse than being bullied?" Russell stopped his car in front of the school. Charlie gripped his door handle to get out, held his heavy backpack on his lap, and waited for his father to continue.

"Let me tell you a story about my time in the war that I've never told anyone, not even your mother."

Charlie didn't really think that was saying much. His parents rarely talked even when they were married. When they did talk, it was about insubstantial things, like *I need such-and-such bag of fertilizer for the backyard.*

"We were in the Ardennes, and we came across some American soldiers who'd been slaughtered by the Germans."

"Did they torture them before they killed them?" Charlie asked.

Russell shook his head. "No. Most of the Germans weren't your *Wolfenstein* supermen types, believe it or not." Charlie's eyes widened in surprise. His dad showed very little interest in the games his son played on the 486 computer in his father's study. His dad only used the computer for spreadsheet, taxes, and other boring stuff, but the old man at least paid enough attention to notice his son was obsessed with the shooter.

"The Russians were more likely to go the rape and pillage route than your average line unit kraut, just based on what I saw. I've told you before that we didn't run into the S.S. Sturmbahnführers.

We ran into plowboys." Someone honked in the car behind the Mercedes, but Russell ignored them.

Charlie glanced in the rearview and saw cheerleaders streaming out of a Land Rover. "We were going down the line, identifying bodies, checking dog tags, doing what we had to do. I stopped in front of this one corpse." Russell paused, looking at the glowing dash console, debating whether or not to continue. "I get to maybe the third or fourth kraut bait there on the line, and it hits me."

"What?"

Russell looked back at his son. "I don't need to see his dog tags. It's Kondriak."

"Who's Kondriak?"

The car behind them honked one more time before pulling around the Benz and driving out of the parking lot. "Kondriak was a kid who used to beat the Sakrete out of my ass on a daily basis when we lived in Hell's Kitchen. I didn't even know he was in the service until I ran across his body there. I checked the dog tags just to make sure. Wouldn't you know it, it was Kondriak."

"Holy shit."

"Yeah," his dad said. "There are worse things than getting bullied, son. Like seeing someone who controlled your childhood dead on the ground beneath you."

Charlie thought about that as he got out of his dad's car, and he thought about it now as he sat in the back of Brackman's class and listened to the man go on about glands. The lights suddenly went up in the room, and a student stuck his head into the class. Brackman turned from the projector, livid and brandishing the wooden pointer as if he intended to break it over the interrupter's head.

The teacher's expression softened, however, when he saw who it was. "It's the man whose name rings bells." Brackman's enthusiasm didn't sound authentic to Charlie's ears. He didn't think the man gave a shit about football. He just thought Brackman was too weak to express anything less than full-throated support for what the strongest among them worshipped.

People said, "His name rings bells" for a very specific reason. There was a miniature Liberty Bell in the adjacency between the red clay track and the home team's end zone, just below the expansive arms of the field goal posts. Each time Freeport scored a touchdown, one of the cheerleaders would spin off from the hands of the pyramid base below her, doing a logroll through the air and landing with an aerodynamic flourish. After that, she would dash toward the bell and ring it loud enough for it to sound like the carillons chiming for solstice down on the village square. This was also a tradition at the high school.

"You forgot this," Corbett said to Charlie. He basked in the stunned smiles of the students around him, who felt honored to be graced by his presence. "You left this out by the smokers' pit." Brackman's rare show of goodwill dissolved into disgust and anger as he looked down at the boy to whom Corbett handed the book. Charlie Milner did smell like smoke a lot of the time when he came to class, now that Brackman thought about it.

"Thanks," Charlie said. He accepted the book with a dumb expression on his face. His ears pricked with red hot needles, as he felt the eyes of all the kids in the class fasten on him.

Corbett left, and Brackman motioned to the kid seated in the desk nearest the door to stand and kill the lights again. Then the science teacher slapped that gland on the glowing canvas once more. Charlie used the little available light to look at the book the school's star quarterback quite literally just dropped in his lap.

The cover was softbound, smooth as cloth. It possessed the substantial dimensions of a coffee table book. Gold lettering on the front spelled out

"Slam Book" in engraved font. Charlie could run his fingers into the golden grooves and read what was written there just by tracing the outlines of the words impressed on the cloth.

He opened the book up. The lined pages were filled with scribbling and curlicue writing in various colors and inks. Some things were written in the perky glitter pen of a cheerleader with an artistic streak. Others were done in little magic marker flourishes or smudged colored pencil. Each page was covered in comments that reminded him of the kinds of "best wishes" doodled on plaster leg casts or inscribed into the yearbooks of the most popular kids.

Some of the comments were anonymous, and others were underscored with signatures that were easy to read. There was one that hurt more than the others, written by Bethany Dondolinger. She squiggled out in pen, "Charlie Milner should try to become a veterinarian when he grows up. That way when cats pee on him he won't have to take a shower since he already smells like cat piss." Below her words, she drew a small oval and crude smiley face inside the circular little head.

Charlie closed the book without reading anymore. He sat silently through the remainder of class at the position of attention with his hands down at his sides. He deposited the mockery of a yearbook into the nearest trashcan after class.

Johnny Cotter swore he smelled something burning while sitting in front of a computer monitor about an hour and a half later. The scent sort of reminded him of briquettes that soaked up the flavor from a dozen or so earlier barbecues with a hint of mesquite carrying on the wind.

The smell was only enticing for the shortest of times, however. The blaze picked up into a properly dancing conflagration in the trashcan a short time later. The sprinkler system was triggered, and panic set in. Kids ran for the exits. The lighted headlamps inside the signs fogged over in a steaming combination of hoary extinguisher foam and smoke rising from the smoldering trashcan. The master amplifier system sprang into action. The page signal beeped out several times before an automated voice announcement advised students where to go and how to proceed. The alarm tone wailed through the speakers and the fire alarm gongs howled.

Kids ran and teachers shepherded them toward the green lawns of the junior high school. Charlie Milner walked though. There was a faint smile resting on his lips. The bruise on his head was turning purple but hurting much less now.

***

Some volunteer firefighters under the supervision of the marshal were thankfully nearby when Charlie lit the trashcan on fire. They were hosing down one of several buildings in a Potemkin village endowed by Gentleman Jim Corbett, which was built for the express purpose of letting the volunteers get some practice.

The marshal got the call from Freeport Junior High on his Motorola and left with two engines to meet the other firemen arriving from the stationhouse. A quick walkthrough after securing the premises confirmed the blaze was confined to a single trashcan, and that it was quickly doused by the automatic sprinkler system. Damage was not extensive, consisting mainly of black stains on the quarry tiled floor near the trashcan.

Johnny was in the library when he smelled the fire, playing *Oregon Trail* on one of the computers in the lab. He unsuccessfully attempted to ford a river and paid the price for his hubris, losing two oxen and the homesteader riding shotgun in his canvas-covered wagon. He always made sure to name the members of the pioneer party after people he personally knew. That made the game more interesting, investing it with some personal appeal. It hurt more to discover Elise Milner contracted typhus or scarlet fever, rather than losing whatever female party member came with the preset names.

He laughed slightly at the headstone planted in the weeds. "Here Lies Charlie Milner." Then he looked over at the two girls pouring over an issue of *Teen* something or other, which they selected from the wooden case where magazines and newspapers sat. The magazines saw a hell of a lot more use than any of the books in the general circulation stacks, Johnny noticed.

"I've kissed," the one girl said to the other, "just not French."

"Oh my god," the other one said. "I *love* these."

"What?"

"The Embarrassing Moments column. My favorite was …"

Their voices trailed off, or at least Johnny tuned them out. He glanced around the library. It was peaceful here. Most of this wing was floored in looped carpet that made no sound as feet passed over it. Natural light spilled from the windows onto the walls where large cast iron letters spelled out the names of writers from Jane Austen to Mark Twain.

The floor near the front circulation desk, composed of red tiles, was the only part of the library not carpeted. Johnny thought it looked a lot like what he imagined the Roman atriums he learned about in history class would look like if he were to travel back in time and find out.

"The worst was when this girl lost her top after jumping off the diving board," the one girl said, bringing him back from his thoughts.

"No, this one girl peed in the pool and everyone …"

The students filed out of the library in an orderly fashion after the fire alarms went off. They mustered on the lawn and stood around in clusters, grateful for the disruption. It meant they could gossip and flit from group to group, missing classes that sucked especially for those kids doing presentations or who had pop quizzes.

Johnny didn't share the sentiments of the other students. He was having trouble controlling his anger toward his friend much later in the day, as he walked up the sloping floor of the auditorium toward the stage apron.

Alice melted some of the rage, as she popped her head up from where she hid among the fixed seating in the audience. "I'm looking for an earring," she said. Her brown eyes glowed behind her tortoise-shell glasses.

"I didn't know you wore glasses," he said.

"Oh." She pushed them up the bridge of her nose, and he noticed her hand tremble slightly. It was the smallest gesture, but for him it was a revelation. Girls could get nervous! It meant they were human, or at least that some of them were. Then again, the same could be said about boys, that some of them weren't necessarily human, and he was thinking specifically of the bullies.

"Yeah, I usually wear contacts because I never found a pair I liked before."

"I like them." He never really understood the bias against glasses. They just underlined the mix of intelligence and prettiness already in her face.

"Thanks." She smiled, and the brown warmth of her eyes contrasted with the bright white of her even teeth. He looked away from her, not counting on himself to get through any more interaction until his heart rate slowed. He thought about Robbie and his advice about girls. He knew Robbie was right. Then Johnny remembered he wasn't here to have awkward interactions with the prettiest girl in the school or maybe the world. He was here because he was pissed at Charlie.

Alice spoke to him as if she didn't expect him to be nervous, and that somehow made him even more nervous. He tried to calm himself with several deep breaths before pulling himself up onto the dusty stage apron.

The ceiling erupted with a discordant jangle. He reflexively jumped to the side at the same moment he looked up, as if he expected some counterweighted sandbag to plummet down and land on his head. It was already a screwed up day, and that would be the capstone.

"Relax," a voice came from beyond the acoustical dead space in the darkened theatre below. Johnny squinted. That ocean of seating was intimidating. He felt butterflies wrestle in his stomach, as if it were opening night and it was now incumbent upon him to knock them dead.

"Everything's done with automation these days." He saw the shadowy outlines of two forms standing in front of that planetarium console, the engineer's board glowing like the lambent array on a UFO mother ship.

"Yeah," the second shadow said. Johnny didn't see Alice, and he assumed she was still looking for her earring in the dark. He wondered why she didn't tell the two dummies to turn on the house lights and decided pride or the challenge of searching in the dark must be the reason.

"If we put on a production of *Peter Pan*, we can make him fly form one side of the stage to the other without batting an eyelash."

"Check out the curtain call's fastest tempo."

There was a mechanical whirring and the billowing folds behind Johnny rushed toward one another. They moved like the lips of a giant mouth pressing together for a sloppy kiss. He was tempted to pull an Indiana Jones and try to jump behind the stage before the burgundy jaws closed on him. The moment passed, and he was left still standing on the stage. The curtains crowded around him. If this was *Indiana Jones* and if those curtains were metal doors, he would now be severed in two neat halves.

"Why the hell did I even come today?" Alice shouted into the darkness. "It's just tech rehearsal, so I technically didn't have to be here. I'm an actress, after all." Her voice echoed through the room, which was both cavernous and intimate. That was the magic contradiction at the heart of this cave, and it offered a dark solace. It didn't offer enough for Charlie apparently, since he was now burning things at school.

Johnny pressed his hands together as if praying, turned toward the backstage, and split the two curtains with his folded palms. The techies hit a switch on their engineer's board a moment later and the curtains pulled open behind him. He turned toward the left wing where he knew his friend liked to hide out if he wasn't doing something up on the stage.

"You don't understand," Charlie said. His sketchpad was open in front of him. He applied a light layer of crosshatching with a charcoal pencil, to the scale drawing of the stage on the paper before him.

"Jesus, that's good." Johnny cocked his head to the side, and silently cursed himself for complimenting his friend. It would be harder now to go back to being pissed. Charlie glanced over his shoulder at his friend and then looked back at Luke Hansard. Hansard was a freshman from Freeport High, who came over here to supervise when the full tech rehearsals required someone a bit older and more mature to oversee the junior players.

Charlie pointed the dull tip of his charcoal pencil toward the stage apron. "If the play's been turned into a movie, like maybe *Grease* or something like that, you'll get more people to come. If you schedule a play for the night of a big football game, you'll get less people. Other than that, you only get the friends and relatives of the players, and that's about it."

"So the only way you're going to get more people is by having a bigger cast size. Is that what you're telling me?" Hansard's arms were crossed over his chest and his flexor muscles bulged like iron bars. Johnny suspected he must still do some manual rigging on the plays over there at the high school to have muscles like that.

Charlie held the charcoal sketch out at arm's length, inspected it one more time. Then he walked it over to the squirrel cage fan and pallet covered in the multicolored silks. He left the pad on top of the pallet in the corner of the room. Hansard nodded toward Prometheus' silken tendrils of flame without uncrossing his bulky forearms. "Did you see what your friend did?"

Johnny nodded. Charlie said, "It'll look better with the dry ice."

Hansard laughed, uncrossed his arms. "Not sure if the fire marshal will give you the okay on that one after what happened earlier today."

Charlie showed no surprise or fear, and it scared Johnny. "Yeah," Charlie said, "but I should thank whoever did it for getting me out of class." He didn't miss a beat, Johnny noticed.

Hansard looked from one boy to the other. He sensed something was up (though probably nothing related to the trashcan fire). Then he wordlessly excused himself.

After he was gone from the backstage area, Johnny looked at Charlie and said, "Why?"

The question bummed Charlie out. He sighed as if disappointed in his friend. Johnny thought he had quite a bit more reason to be put out with Charlie, and his friend's show of exasperation pissed him off.

"Why?" Charlie paced from one vanity mirror to the next. All were unilluminated except for one, on top of which sat a tackle box overstuffed with pancake makeup and spirit gum. "I'm in stagecraft, man. 'Why' is a question to ask an acting coach when you're an actor and you need motivation." He stopped in front of Johnny. He noticed his friend smelled, not like cat piss, but like a barbecue pit.

"Want to know how?" Charlie asked.

Johnny nodded. If he wasn't going to get the why, he would settle for the how. "I used some lint from the dryer at my mom's house for starters." Johnny felt slight twinges of guilt and panic. He realized, when his friend mentioned the laundry in the basement, that he had his own things to hide.

"If you do a load of nothing but one-hundred percent cotton shirts, you get a better yield of burnable lint." He grinned. "At least that's what I've found."

"I smelled briquettes," Johnny said.

"You smelled right. I cooked some cotton in a metal can, prodded the cloth with a Tenpenny nail until it roasted. I got me my char cloth. I know how to set a trashcan on fire without going through all of that trouble, but I didn't want to use fuel and risk the blaze getting out of control."

"That's good," Johnny said, adding, "I guess."

"I didn't want to hurt anybody."

"This time."

Charlie's eyes narrowed. "What the hell does that mean?"

Johnny stepped back two or three paces so quickly he feared for a moment he might trip and fall backwards. "Setting fires at your mom's, or at Freeport, was one thing. This is public property, man. You could get suspended." He lowered his voice. "Arrested."

"Yeah," Charlie said. His rage melted just as quickly as Johnny's when he saw Alice in her new glasses. "Look, man." He walked forward, and this time Johnny didn't back away. In fact, Johnny took a couple paces toward his friend, just as Charlie was walking toward him. They each placed a hand on the other's shoulder.

"I understand you're just looking out for me," Charlie said. "I just wanted to blow off some steam."

Johnny pointed at the purple bruise expanding over his friend's forehead like watercolors spreading over a thin sheet of paper. "I understand, but don't let those fuckers goad you into doing something that fucks up your future. Let them fuck up their own futures."

Charlie shook his head, and Johnny saw in his friend's eyes that his heart was plummeting to his feet. "Crowes, maybe. I can see that Cro-Magnon sitting around a dive bar with his Pabst, talking about that time in '97 when he made a block that let Freeport get to the state championships." He laughed at the image in his mind. Johnny laughed with him, seeing Crowes nursing his brew and reminiscing to the indifference of the few other bar patrons. The luster would be long since eroded from the class ring he'd be forced to pawn if he wanted another drink to drown his sorrows. Then he would head home to face his wife who was more lard than meat, and called soap operas "her stories."

The laughter stopped and Charlie's smile disappeared a moment later. The smile left Johnny's face as well. He knew what Charlie was thinking, and also what his friend was about to say. "Corbett's always going to be a winner."

Johnny looked down at the wooden floor beneath their feet. Charlie said, "He's going to bully me 'til we're out of junior high, and then he's going to bully me in high school."

"Nah, man," Johnny said, and shook his head. "Things will …"

"Then he's going to get into his first choice school. Or, if he has to go to his safety school, who gives a shit?" Johnny looked up from his feet and saw rage boiling in Charlie's eyes. "He'll still inherit his dad's company, and he'll be rich and fucking happy."

Johnny thought about that. He didn't want to lie to his friend or really argue with him. He didn't see the harm in at least challenging him though. "Rich, maybe. No," he said, shaking his head, "definitely. You only need two eyes in your head to see if somebody's rich, but how the fuck do you know he'll be happy?"

Johnny held both of his hands up toward the ceiling. "How do you even know he's happy right now? You don't know what's going on in his head."

"No," Charlie said. Resolve built in his voice. He gritted his teeth as he spoke, the words filtering through the enamel as he sanded it off and bit down. "I don't know what's in his head. I don't know whether or not he's happy. I do know this though." Air hissed through his teeth. "He's always

...*smiling*."

Freeport, Ohio 1998

CHAPTER ONE

Freeport High School was never really a high school for Johnny Cotter. He imagined the giant red brick building as a crematorium after his English class read *The Diary of Anne Frank* and *Night*. He saw the steam pouring from the cafeteria not as the mist from greasy tater tots, but as the vaporous souls of all the teens liquidated in the ovens rising up toward the suburban sky. The featureless cream brickwork made the place look like a general hospital at other times. He would gaze up at one of the rare windows in the face of the building and imagine himself as coming here to visit a terminally ill relative in the cancer ward. Then there was the idea that the building was just a medium security prison, and the quad and cafeteria were spaces where the general population mingled and bartered with each other.

His imagination didn't slow or give him any relief when he walked through the halls, either. It always felt, no matter in which direction he was travelling, that the vast majority of the students coursing down the halls were moving in the opposite direction. He saw himself at those times as a lone, infertile salmon pushing upstream against all of the Darwinian winners rushing past him in order to spawn faster.

Speaking of spawning, every moment inside the classroom was filled for him with the sense that everyone else already had sex. They knew secret lore about the act he was sure he would never take part in. He was certain each of the assured cheerleaders and poised lettermen were walking around with as much history behind them as the *Kama Sutra*. Meanwhile he was lucky if he managed to finish masturbating in his bedroom before either his mom or dad knocked on the door.

Johnny kept his thoughts to himself now. He didn't want to bother Charlie with his problems, since his friend had more than his fair share of his own. They'd have time to talk later, since after this stupid assembly they had gym class together.

Large rooms like the cafeteria or gymnasium were always echo chambers where a thousand different teenaged voices ricocheted around and made concentration impossible. The auditorium at Freeport High was especially conducive to trapping noise. The walls were covered in soundproofed padding. That deadened the noise before it reached other rooms, but also somehow made the acoustical wash worse inside the auditorium. The muffled voices sounded like a giant cult gathered around and preparing to make a sacrifice in the darkened theater.

It wasn't altogether unpleasant in here, though. It was dark, and dark was good.

"Kid's worse off than I am," Charlie suddenly said.

"Who?"

Charlie pointed up a few rows, where Clark Mercer was seated. "No doubt," Johnny said. Neither of them knew what his deal was. All they knew was that every day at school, around noon, he walked out to the pickup and drop-off area underneath the aluminum pole where an American flag billowed. Then a taxicab always picked him up there. Any kid who got picked up by a cab every day was pretty screwed up.

"I'm going to clap first," a voice to their direct left said. Johnny looked over, and Charlie leaned over as well to see who spoke. It was Greg Mason. He wore enough gel in his hair to make his head hard as uncooked bowtie pasta. Today two cowlick strands flared up from the sides of his head and gave the impression of devil's horns.

"You and your stupid clapping," Johnny said.

"It's not stupid," Greg replied, and he was serious. He always felt compelled to be the first person in the crowd to clap whenever the speaker on the stage said something that required applause.

"Oh, crap." Greg leaned forward to stare at a scene unfolding several rows ahead of them.

Johnny and Charlie briefly thought he was going to say something about Mercer the Taxicab Kid, but he said, "Looks like Whitney won her note fight with Darlene."

"No shit," Charlie said. He felt bad for Darlene, as she curled in the fetal position and cried. "I've been getting my ass kicked so regularly I forgot girls get bullied too." He wondered what kind of trump card Whitney Granger used in their Post-It note war that lasted from homeroom to home economics. *Slut? Dyke?*

Crowes and Corbett made Charlie cry last night. They called him at home from a party where they were getting drunk. They humiliated him in front of a roomful of people on their end of the line. The call was on speakerphone, but at least Charlie was alone in his bedroom crying onto his pillow. He wasn't in an auditorium full of kids who would drink his tears like fresh rainwater.

"May I have your attention!" It was Coach Vanhauser up at the podium. Mr. Largo was the head principal, but that was in name only. A roar like a war cry carried through the stadium seating and the ground rumbled after he spoke. Hundreds of boys beat their feet against the floor. The choral shell on stage trembled slightly. Johnny wasn't sure, but he thought he saw one or two of the crimson and gold balloons fixed to the risers pop.

Vanhauser was the head coach for "the Franchise," as the football team was called. He transferred from the junior high to the high school around the same time as Corbett and Crowes. His face was always red. Johnny didn't know whether it was the result of a drinking problem, constant exposure to the wind and snow during football season, or if it was more due to his crippling rage. He always looked ready to berate someone, and the ruddiness of his skin made his grey hair look even more silvery in contrast.

Jill Brentwood and a handful of the other top cheerleaders were onstage behind the coach along with Corbett and Crowes. Both wore their letterman jackets and basked in the adulation of the crowd. There were quite a few people who didn't like them, like Charlie and Johnny, but contempt didn't make as much noise as worship.

"I'm waiting for them to sacrifice a virgin," Johnny said.

"Good luck finding one here," Greg said, and then frowned. "Unless you count us."

Jill was still tanned from cheerleading camp, Johnny noticed, and one of her almighty thighs was wrapped with a tensor bandage. There wasn't enough room up on the stage for her to pull one of her insane moves, like the inverted pike or the layout full twist. Soon after Vanhauser spoke, the girls assembled themselves into a four-two-one pyramid. Jill took the "one" position, exposing her gold-spangled bloomers as she climbed onto her friends' backs.

The bronzed inner adductor muscles of her thighs flexed, just inches away from what all three of them gazed on as if it was the meaning of life. Greg looked at Charlie. "I know you have your problems with Alex, so don't take it personal when I say I'd suck Corbett's dick just to see what Jill Brentwood's pussy tastes like."

"No offense taken." Charlie was equally spellbound. *Maybe*, he thought, *I should become a male cheerleader*. The team needed them to perform certain moves and to assume certain shapes. A male cheerleader should be an easy object of ridicule in a climate where every and anything could get one labelled a "fag," but neither Corbett nor his minions ever bothered the male cheerleaders. The bullies probably left them alone because their one purpose in life was to make Corbett's girlfriend look better than she already looked, if such a thing was possible.

The great pyramid disassembled, and Jill was now being high-chaired by one of those male cheerleaders whose ranks Charlie briefly contemplated joining. She was in a high Statue of Liberty position with a poster held aloft. She waved it frantically, the same way she did when trying to lure people into the parking lot for a fundraising carwash.

"GO TEAM GO!" the sign said.

Johnny could barely make out Darlene's form a few rows ahead of him. She was using her Sephora camouflage applicator kit to cover the streaks her tears caused.

"Now listen," Vanhauser said. He paused to unbutton his burgundy windbreaker. He gripped the sides of the podium and spoke with authority. His voice had the dulcet charm of a man who was media savvy and gave press conference after both big wins and inexplicable losses. "You guys had a safe and productive winter vacation, I trust."

He looked back at the cheerleaders and the two star players behind him. "They don't want me to call it Christmas vacation anymore because that offends some people." There was some low snickering tapering off in murmurs and hisses. "If you ask my boys, I make sure they're lifting weights in the off-season." He looked out into the darkness of the rapt crowd.

"You've got to show some initiative. It makes it easier when summer drills begin, for one thing." Vanhauser looked to the left and right, as if there might be a secret audience in the wings offstage gauging his performance. "What does this have to do with you guys?" He stabbed the dark air in front of him. "Everything. If you got a B in Latin this fall, then maybe you should take an hour each day to study your conjugation charts, or your what have you." He waved away his words, his own high school experience too far receded in the misted rearview.

"Or," Vanhauser said, "maybe you got a D, or even an F." He held the last syllable and a little bit of spit flew into the darkness before him. "Well, the Dream and the Nightmare haven't always risen to the occasion, believe it or not. We've even been blown out in back to back games on occasion!"

Charlie leaned over to Greg and asked, "Hey, why does he always call them that, anyway?" Charlie knew better than to ask Johnny, since it was a sure thing he wouldn't know. Everything they knew about football came from *Joe Montana's Sports Talk Football* for the Sega Genesis.

Greg sighed, hating to dignify the coach's crap with even a cursory explanation. "Corbett's the dream because he's the star in Vanhorshit's unbeatable option. That bell gets rung at least twice a game when he hands it off, runs it, or does a pitch."

"I wouldn't know," Charlie said, "because I've never been to a game."

"My girlfriend drags me along," Greg said. "You're not missing much."

"What about Crowes?" Johnny asked, leaning in.

"Crowes is the nightmare because the defensive coordinator says he can break any option the other team has. He's like the anti-Corbett in that way."

"Oh," Charlie said, nodding. "I get it. Thanks for the explanation."

"Personally," Greg said, "I just call them Douche and Bag."

"Yeah, but not to their faces."

"The best thing to do," Vanhauser said, "is to put that F behind you the way we put our worst loss behind us. Well …" Vanhauser suppressed a giggle. "Not exactly like that. The fire marshal was there for that one."

Charlie smiled, and Johnny shot him a wary look. He remembered that outdoor assembly well. Vanhauser went over the tape as many times as he was going to, and finally resolved not to torture himself or his men anymore with replays. The loss to Anderson was so stunning that he and the rest of the faculty hit upon the ingenious idea to have a controlled blaze, in which they would burn the game tape. The memory of the loss would be exorcised by the flames, and put behind them forever.

Multiple fire trucks were standing by. The student body was far enough back from the conflagration for Mr. Largo's conscience to rest easy, regarding the potential for a lawsuit.

Gentleman Jim Corbett was dubbed honorary fire marshal for the day. He performed his duties quite well, squirting lighter fluid into the steel drum where the VHS tape of that rare loss smoldered and cremated. Corbett Senior prodded the ashes with a wooden two-by-four, once the fire was settled. Then he slapped his son on the back. Gentleman Jim went down the line, shaking the hands of the coaches and other players, each in their turn.

Johnny and Charlie were in that crowd with the rest of the students that day. Attendance at these stupid things was compulsory and neither boy usually enjoyed the dumb things at all. Johnny glanced over to his friend, worried at the expression of orgasmic satisfaction on Charlie's face as he watched that barrel burn. He wondered if Charlie was comparing the authorized blaze with the impromptu one he lit in the junior high hallway four years ago.

"Repetition," Vanhauser said, "is not the enemy. When you're not in school, use flashcards and drill, drill, drill. I make my boys practice 'til the cows come home. You've seen 'em out there, hustling in the twilight. Some of their parents call me crazy, but you can call me Coach."

***

The natatorium (as Tom insisted on calling the pool) was a tribulation for Charlie. He avoided the greatest humiliation so far, but time was not on his side, and he knew it. Tom Price was the gym teacher, an ex-Freeport High linebacker who looked like he hadn't felt anything since 1988. His eyes were colorless, foggy from the several pain meds he used to cope with old sports injuries. He only wore tracksuits, and Johnny hazarded he'd be buried in one as well. He was going bald, losing all of the hair on top of his head and none on the sides, so he achieved a kind of natural monk's tonsure.

Everyone liked him, if only because his indifference was a relief from the constant enthusiasm of the other teachers and the expectations of parents. "Let's go," he muttered, coming to the edge of the pool's choppy waters. "Finish up your last laps and then hit the showers."

Charlie and Johnny thrashed along, side by side in their twenty five by seven yard lanes. They swam through the lukewarm water that felt like soup stock on their naked skin. Johnny swam to the end of the lane, touching the cold tile. It smelled fungal and he wondered for a moment if it was possible to get Athlete's foot on your hand.

His best friend wasn't far behind him, turning on a dime and getting a splash of warm chlorinated water in the funnel of his ear. He hoped it didn't get infected. Charlie swam after Johnny, moving as if a shark was behind him. He had his reasons for rushing. Actually, there was just one reason.

There were two ways to shower after leaving Tom's prized natatorium. The first choice was the gang shower. It was a communal tiled room next to the changing room with the heavy gauge metal lockers that rattled as the boys threw their doors open and grabbed their towels, soap, and shampoo. Or, one could go into Tom's office and queue up with the other boys waiting their turn for the single-man showers.

Tom was generous enough to let the more timid boys use his own facility. He usually ignored them as they stood in line and he sat with his feet up on his desk, listening to classic rock and reminiscing about long-since drained kegs and the ghosts of touchdowns past. Sometimes, his students would beg him to turn the station on his little radio to the *Howard Stern Show*. He would only shake his monk's head and blink with those slate eyes, saying, "There's only so many times you can listen to two lesbians kissing on the radio, my friend. I like Skynyrd more."

Showering naked in a roomful of other boys was not something Charlie Milner relished. He was sure he would eventually catch up to his friend in terms of growth. They were bound to accidentally see each other, hanging out as often as they did. In addition to this, being hit with cold air upon leaving the warm pool made his already small penis shrivel, until it was the size of a martini olive and his fully retracted balls resembled peach pits.

Then, there was the most important factor to consider. Crowes was in this gym class with him, and his dick looked like a medium-sized kielbasa. He was uncircumcised. That might earn him some ridicule if he didn't have the physique of a Roman gladiator as well as all of that testosterone raging through his system.

The choice was a no-brainer for Charlie. He turned right to wait his turn in line for the one-man shower. He was determined to wash alone, even if it meant he was late for his next class. Tom stopped him with a hand as he went to go toward the room today, however. The door was closed, and the old gym teacher said, "Paint's drying. Use the other one." He pointed his class ring-bedecked finger toward the locker room. It was a jungle of metallic sounds and catcalls, off-key Sinatra impressions echoing off tile not cleaned in a solid decade.

Charlie sighed, and walked into the steaming room. The flush-mounted steel lockers gathered around him like coffins in which he yearned to crawl, hide, and die. He padded in his sandals toward his own locker, next to his buddy

Johnny's. His friend was nowhere in sight, probably already in the shower.

The air was spiced with body odor riding on a fine dust of talcum powder. He breathed, opened his locker, and grabbed his Dial soap. He also snagged his Head & Shoulders shampoo. It was cheap stuff, and it caused dandruff. He wasn't too worried about his appearance. He was Cat Piss no matter what products he used. Acne blossomed on his face in pitted, leprous craters, which gave him more reason to grow his hair long to cover the wounds of puberty.

He walked toward the shower, and decided to wash up while wearing his swimming suit. No one would notice, would they? *I mean*, he thought, *if someone looks over to make a comment about my dick, doesn't that indict them as much as me? I can just ask them why they're looking at my dick in the first place, unless of course Crowes is the one who asks.* If Crowes asked, his best and really only option was to curl up into a ball. He saw himself as one of those Pompeiians clutching their children to their chest, as Mount Vesuvius roared and lava poured through their pitiful Italian cities.

He walked toward the far right shower stall, queasy from the sight of pale, naked male asses. Some of the rears were hairless and others covered in hirsute black down. Something mildly intoxicating flitted through his stomach. He wondered for a brief moment, *Am I bi? Gay? No, I like girls. Yes, there is the slightest little twinge when I look at a man with a face like the actor Johnny Depp or something. I could never get down to the actual act, though.* He didn't think he could even fuck a girl in the ass, honestly. Even kissing a guy would be senseless, like slamming two male ends of an extension cord together to no good end. He didn't hate or even judge gay people though.

He turned on the shower faucet and let the warm nettles blast him in the face. The hot water always washed away that chlorine and mildewed scent of rotted decay the pool left on him when he emerged from its swampy waters. He ran his fingers in his ears as the water beaded over him and spilled down in rivulets.

He soaped and lathered, washing underneath his arms, hitting his privates with a sopping layer of bubbly white foam. It felt, as he finished, like he might actually get away with this. All he had to do was walk out of here and head to his locker, dry off, get changed, and go to his class. He bet the paint in Tom's office would be dry by this time tomorrow. Then he'd go back to waiting in line with the other timid, but decent boys with no desire to show off their junk to their fellow students. Tom would explain to them why David Lee Roth was a better front man than Hagar. They would pretend to listen, a courtesy they owed him for the one he extended them as they waited to shower alone, and in peace.

Charlie was back at his locker, running his terrycloth towel over his sopping body, when the voice came from behind him. "Is it that small?" The voice belonged to Crowes. Charlie turned and saw the naked body standing in front of him also unfortunately belonged to Crowes. The definition of the bully's shoulders and chest was one marbled slab. Charlie thought he looked like a Minotaur, a superman posing for a likeness to be sculpted and later displayed in the capital of some Fascist empire.

"What?" Charlie heard him clearly, but was too stunned to say anything else. His heart beat so hard in his chest it sounded like a sonic boom thundering in his ears. He tried to breathe, was sure that he couldn't. He decided he would be dead of suffocation in a few minutes, which was better than having to deal with Crowes any longer.

He shouldn't have said "What," he realized. Now Crowes would repeat himself, louder and slower, for the benefit of the crowd. Most of them were smiling, except for Johnny and a couple of the other boys who were forced to migrate here after

Tom gave them the boot from the single-man shower.

"Is … your …dick … so small that you have to wear a bathing suit in the shower?"

"Fuck you." He knew a punch was coming, but he preferred that to this humiliation.

Charlie held his hands over his head and Crowes' fists landed on his back. The shots made a sound like Ping-Pong paddles slapping against a leather sofa. There was one meaty thud after another. Most of the boys smiling a moment before turned back to their own lockers, after the fourth or fifth unanswered blow from Crowes landed on Charlie's naked back. Three boys were still watching. Two were smiling. The other one was Johnny, feeling like the biggest piece of shit in the universe.

He thought this was not the way a friend should behave. He would run to Charlie after the ass whipping was administered and apologize for not defending him. His friend would respond that it was all right, that he didn't expect Johnny to get involved.

Nothing would be improved if Johnny waded into the fray while Corbett or Crowes were bullying Charlie. If he did try to help Charlie, he might find himself targeted by Crowes as well. That was a fate he avoided so far.

Johnny watched Crowes picking shots on his friend, searching out weak areas on his victim's curled form. He delivered hooks to the liver and a tentative jab to the kidney. Johnny wondered what made Charlie a victim and not him.

He many times suspected he was weak and deserving of bullying. He sometimes believed the secret way he felt about girls like Elise made him weaker than other boys. Males were supposed to conquer, score touchdowns, get blowjobs and brag about them. He didn't want a blowjob from Elise or Alice, though. He wanted to go down on them and was afraid maybe that meant he wasn't as much of a man as the other guys.

"You done talking shit?" Crowes asked. He stopped punching, not as a show of mercy, but because he was out of breath.

The back of Charlie's neck was red from where a few punches landed, a blossoming Pangaea of pain radiating outward. He kept his head down, and his arms shielding what portions of his body he could hide. He said, "You've been hitting the smokers' spot too much. You're already winded."

"What!" Crowes was genuinely shocked, too surprised by this rare show of resistance to throw another punch for the moment. His fists unclenched and he leaned down to his victim. "You fucking faggot, I'll put my balls on your chest!"

A still-naked Crowes attempted to pull Charlie's hands free from where they covered his face while he trembled in a fetal ball. He looked a lot like that girl during the earlier assembly, curled up after losing her note war with her spiteful rival.

"Crowes, man," someone behind Johnny said. The bully turned to see who spoke. It was Marky Halpern, a fullback for the Spartans. "Tom's gonna come in here in a minute, and we need you for the team. This shit could get you suspended."

Crowes looked back toward his teammate. He was still heaving from the exertion, still naked. Charlie's voice came from behind the bully, defiant. "I realize this is probably not the appropriate time to contradict you, oh Overlord, but if you're threatening to put your balls on my chest, wouldn't that make you gay, not me? Not that I'm judging."

"You fucking faggot!"

Crowes lunged for Charlie and Johnny found himself involuntarily going for the gargoyle-like, scapular definition of the bully. Crowes' back muscles coiled and writhed sinuously as he prepared to drop more pain on his victim. Marky Halpern reached Crowes before Johnny could get there. That was a good thing, Johnny knew, even though the flames of adrenaline were burning his brain and heart now. There was no way he alone could pull Crowes off Charlie, and the bully was a lot less apt to beat up Marky Halpern for stopping his fun.

"It's prison rules," Crowes said, allowing Marky to lift and carry him back toward his own locker. The fullback set his friend down gently, and Crowes laces his fingers in the metal grated vents on the face of his locker. "If I'm pitching and you're catching, you're the fag, not me."

Charlie thought about arguing some more. He figured Marky would restrain Crowes if he tried to dart across the locker room. In the worst case scenario, maybe Crowes would beat Charlie into a coma and he could miss a lot of school and stay high on pain pills. The words that streamed in a torrent of novel bravery until this moment would no longer rise to his lips.

Prison rules, he thought. He wanted to say "This isn't prison," but he knew for once the dumb fucking caveman told the truth.

***

Life was bleak but at least the icepacks were improving. Charlie usually got one of the disposable, squeeze-activated jobs when he went to see the nurse. Johnny went to visit him in the auditorium after school. He found his friend backstage, sporting a large blue latex bag with a white polar bear imprinted on the pouch's fabric.

"Where'd you get that?"

Charlie looked up from his conversation with one of the other members of the technical crew. He held a blank CD in a jewel case with the hand not applying the blue icepack to his back. "I finagled it from the nurse." He shifted the bag slightly. "She took one look at the bruises and gave this to me. She said to bring it back tomorrow when I'm done with it."

"Cool beans."

Johnny sat down in one of the foldout, canvas-backed chairs in front of a vanity mirror whose glass was ringed with a collage of characters from *Beverly Hills: 90210*. All of the pictures of Brenda Walsh were mangled in some way. Shannon Dougherty's eyes were poked through with a pen in some of the pictures. She sported a Fu-Manchu, blacked out teeth, and arched eyebrows drawn on in black magic marker in other photos.

"The public address system is for the birds," Charlie said to the boy, who Johnny knew by sight but not name. He had corn blonde hair and wore a checkered pajama ensemble. One of the Populars took to wearing plaid pajama bottoms to school, and the trend caught on and filtered all the way down to the point where even Johnny sometimes sported them. This was the first time he saw someone wear both the top and bottom. He wondered how the Populars might react to that.

Charlie pointed in the direction of the proscenium arch. "Those speakers out there are made so Largo or Vanhorseshit can announce an assembly or a fire drill. They're not made for natural sounds like the sound of waves splashing as Hester, Dimmesdale, and Pearl set sail away from this intolerant, puritanical shithole of a village." He sighed.

"Well, then, what if we mess with the volume?" The blond boy asked. "I can tweak that."

Charlie shook his head. "No, because the speakers are placed all wrong. They're way up high." He raised his hands above his head. "If I want church bells ringing in Salem, that's cool. It doesn't work for sounds taking place below."

"So, portable speakers, then?"

"Yeah, but not too much bass in them. I don't want some clopping horse hooves to sound like a stampede of elephants." Charlie held up the jewel case. "I've already got some sounds here. I wrote the cues on the list I gave you in study hall. It's everything we'll need for the play that can't be done offstage like crowd noises and whatnot. Those will sound better done naturally."

"Cool." The boy took the case. "Where'd you get these sounds?"

"The same place I get my WAV files for my shooters."

Johnny previously saw the custom wads his friend made for his violent videogames. The levels he constructed were impossible to beat. Johnny quickly found himself overcome by zombie soldiers and demons, whenever he tried to play as the hapless space marine trapped on a forlorn Martian colony. They would rip his little character to shreds or shove him off a cliff into a sea of radioactive slop. Then he would quickly become a mutant corpse and dissolve screaming in agony.

The kid tapped the CD case against his leg and headed for the front of the stage, adding, "See you on the flipside."

"Peace," Charlie said, and he looked over at Johnny. "So what's up with you?"

Johnny shook his head. "*Nada*. I just wanted to see how you were after …" He didn't know how to finish and was sorry he started.

Charlie shook his head, uncomfortable, almost guilty from the force of the invisible waves of sympathy radiating from his friend. "That three-time, world-champion, Greco-Roman meat gazer's going to get his comeuppance, soon."

Johnny laughed but also felt a little uneasy. It was usually more abstract when Charlie talked about what might eventually happen to Crowes or Corbett. Now it was "soon." That still wasn't specific, but it was a hell of a lot closer than "someday."

"It's official, though. Word got around and now I'm no longer Cat Piss. I'm Tiny."

"It's shrinkage," Johnny said. "It was cold in the pool."

"I'm through with the girls," Charlie said, looking at the bulb-ringed vanity mirror before him.

"Not that I had a chance before, but I'm definitely, well and truly fucked now."

"I doubt they take those rumors seriously. Honestly, when some asshole says, 'Such and such girl is a slut,' all that really means is she wouldn't sleep with him. If Crowes is going around talking about your dick, there's something wrong with him, not you."

"Yeah, but he can play football." Charlie shifted the icepack on his back. "His ticket's punched. Mine's punched too." He held out his hands to the room full of props, makeup, and costumes. "Just in a different way."

Johnny wanted to wake his friend from his depression, and definitely not return to the subject of cocks. Charlie looked at him a bit sheepishly, and muttered, "You're lucky, man." His voice was a barely audible whisper, faint and secretive. "Not to be gay about it, but your dick is big, man, and not just for a teenager."

"It doesn't help," Johnny said.

"What?"

"Having a big dick. It doesn't help me."

Air hissed through Charlie's nostrils as he laughed. "What, pray tell, is your dick supposed to help you with? Your algebra homework?"

Johnny laughed with him and said, "No, I mean it doesn't help with the girls. It's supposed to give you like this," he paused, and then said, "This force field of confidence or whatever, when you talk to them." He shook his head. "I still get nervous."

"Yeah, me too." Charlie looked back in the mirror, and stared not as if he was looking at his reflection, but at a stranger who was going to tell him a secret soon. "Some of the Frosh Bitches started calling me 'Tiny' earlier today. That means it'll continue until I graduate."

"Fuck the Froshes," Johnny said. The Frosh Bitches were the freshmen athletes who availed themselves to the upperclassmen who hazed and enslaved them in any and every way they could imagine. They made them do things like duck walk in the locker rooms with peach pits gripped in their assholes. They also demanded more basic and menial tasks, like bussing their lunch trays to and from the tables where the Populars held court in the cafeteria. Corbett and Crowes were Frosh Bitches last year, and it was only a matter of time until they assumed control of the hazing program. Johnny shuddered as he thought about how much more obnoxious they would become when they were seniors, especially Crowes. Mike Crowes, despite his limited intelligence, was still probably at least dimly aware these four years would be the high point of his life. Then again, maybe Corbett would let him be some kind of hanger-on when he took over his dad's business.

"Come here!" Alice's clear voice came from the stage apron. Charlie and Johnny looked toward the sound.

"Who?" Johnny said. "I mean, which one of us?"

"Any one," she said. "Either!"

Johnny stood, walked toward her voice. He was grateful when Charlie remained seated. Johnny was alone on the stage with Alice now that the blond kid in pajamas was departed. She was in her red velvet costume, with a white bonnet pulled over her head. It was bridal white and laced like a doily, framing her heart-shaped face into an oval.

Alice held a plastic baby in her hands, and strands of honey brown hair fell from the bonnet. She wasn't wearing her glasses. The liquid warmth of her brown eyes was like an opiate, coursing through Johnny's nervous body when he made eye contact with her. The problem with the healing nature of her face though, was he couldn't get away with staring at her dumbly for the rest of his life. That was a shame, since it would solve all of his problems. He would eventually have to speak, or it would creep her out. He tried to muster whatever confidence came with being endowed. He realized he couldn't summon that confidence because he didn't want to fuck her. He wasn't even sure she could be fucked. Alice could be admired, maybe even kissed. There was also the potential to make love to her, though not for him. That honor was reserved for someone with the deportment of an Oscar Wilde and the bravery of a Winston Churchill.

Still, there was a part of him that thought he would have a chance with her if they compared notes. He wanted to show her his CD collection and his bookcase. He wanted to tell her the movies he enjoyed. She might return the favor, and then they would realize how similar and complex and sensitive they both were. Then they could melt together in a love where they wouldn't need words. He wanted to open her diary and read it. He wanted to open the drawers on the dressers in her bedroom, look through her closet for the relics of her childhood, and compare them to his own.

"Help me," Alice said. She walked over to Pearl's crib and grabbed the script. She handed him the open spiral-bound manuscript and Johnny read. It said, "Hester Tableau Three."

"Do you like *The Scarlet Letter*?" she asked.

He nodded, and thought, *That was dumb, literally, you dumbass. Maybe you should try communicating with words next time.* "Yes." *There, that's better but not much.* His voice sounded too exasperated, not like he just answered a question posed to him. He sounded too excited, as if on the verge of an orgasm. That wasn't entirely impossible, come to think of it. The unstoppable erection was growing, and that was stage one.

"Yeah," Johnny said. "I don't know much about the play, just the Hawthorne novel. He uses the word 'ignominy' too much, and I honestly wouldn't even know what the hell that meant if it wasn't on one of Mrs. Gardner's vocab quizzes a couple months back."

She laughed, not at him, but at what he said. Actually, he didn't give two shits if she laughed at him. If he heard that little clarion again and it exposed those white teeth, then he was willing to pratfall and vaudeville clown it up. He would slip on banana peels until he got a concussion, if she bit those bee-sting fat lips once more and it exposed that slightly thrilling gap in her teeth.

"The play presents problems that aren't necessarily inherent in the novel," she said. *Necessarily inherent*, he thought. If she and he had children together, one daughter and one son, they would place in all AP classes like Corbett. They wouldn't be douchebags like him though.

"Like what?" Johnny asked. He thought, *I'm asking questions, Robbie, just like you told me. I'm going to ignore the beating of my heart (and the pulse of this erection). I'm going to listen to the words coming out of Alice's mouth. I know your dog tags said 'no rel. pref.' but I hope there's a God, and I hope you have your face buried in her pussy at this very moment.*

"Well, it's hard for the players, especially for me," she said. "Don't get me wrong." She paced back toward the crib where the rubber doll lay. "I'm not self-absorbed. I'm the one who's going to have to deal with the most grief from this production."

"What kind of grief?" He complimented himself silently on posing a second, flirtation-free question.

"Those idiots can't separate reality from theater." She pointed toward the rest of the high school beyond the doors of the darkened auditorium. "My character's pregnant at the beginning of the show, and later she has a little child out of wedlock. The rumors are going to be Alice is pregnant, and she's about to have a baby. They'll say she doesn't know who the father is. The better my acting is, and the more believable my performance, the worse the rumors will be."

Alice came to stand before Johnny, less than a foot away from him. "The rumors are already starting."

"Screw them," Johnny said, meaning both the rumors and those spreading them.

"They wish," she said, and then looked at the script in his hands. "Okay, listen, and correct me if anything's wrong." She closed her eyes and concentrated on the lines stored in her memory. Johnny took this opportunity to look at her because her eyes were closed. He watched her supple lips flutter as she recited the words silently to herself, readying to say them to him. She was as unaware of her beauty as she was of the crush he nursed these last few years.

"Oh, glorious father on high." She placed the back of her hand to her forehead. "I speak now of the gift of the child you hath bestowed on me, and implore you to answer. What, prithee, shall I make of this child that thou hast given me?" She pointed toward the crib, which still rocked slightly from her previous touch.

Johnny stared down at the paper in his hands, reading along word for word as she recited. She made no mistakes, yet. "No other child hath such strange and peculiar whims as mine, Pearl. I love her, though she is bane and punishment for my sins."

Alice dropped to the ground and clutched the scarlet "A" sewn into the blushed dahlia material of the dress. Johnny suppressed a smile, not wanting

Alice to think he was laughing at her performance. He thought the letter on her dress bore an uncanny resemblance to the ones sewn onto the jackets of the Spartan lettermen.

"Prithee tell, will all her days be as cursed as those endured by her ignominious mother? She already knows thy name, and thy Good Book." Alice looked heavenward, more of her nectarous brown hair spilling from the bonnet. Her agonized pose reminded Johnny of her performance in the school production of *The Miracle Worker*. "I shall love my daughter with all my being, determined however, that she shall never know her earthly father's name. Only thine."

Johnny turned the page, expecting her to say more. She was finished, though. She opened her eyes, gathered the billowing folds of her dress that was the same color as the stage curtain, and stood. "How was that?"

"Perfect," he said.

"Oh." She blew a raspberry. "Quit kissing my ass."

He trembled slightly. She looked away, misinterpreting the effect of her words, thinking she was rude. "Sorry," she said.

Johnny shook his head, thinking he would trade his life at that moment for one peck on either of her ass cheeks. They could pillory him before the whole of the Puritan throng. They might put him in stocks, then gibbet him or set fire to him with the faggots whose etymology so amused Charlie, if only he could for one moment do what she bade him do in jest.

"No," he said. "It's fine. I just meant your performance was perfect in that you didn't mess up your lines. You got it right, word for word." Elation shot through him. He really did like *The Scarlet Letter*, even though he tended to dislike anything he was forced to read in school under duress. The list of books school ruined for him included *Fahrenheit: 451*, *The Great Gatsby*, and *The Catcher in the Rye*. He was sure he might thoroughly enjoy them if he picked them out on his own and wasn't forced to produce stupid essays, reports, or summaries of nightly readings for class the next day.

The Scarlet Letter thus far escaped the contempt he had for most of the other books he read for school for whatever reason. It finally occurred to him, standing there with Alice, why the book held the appeal that it did. The Midwest wasn't New England, but when he and Charlie walked through the woods, or he sauntered beneath the trees alone, he felt himself transported to another time and place. He felt himself transported not just to Hawthorne's New England, but also to Irving's Poughkeepsie. He saw himself traversing the darkened byways beneath a frosty moon where the colonists slept in their thatch and slate-roofed houses. He could even see, hear, and smell the livestock as they slumbered and he walked along the darkened paths. He wandered in ecstatic fear of the headless Hessian coming soon on his horse. The horseman would brandish an enflamed jack-o-lantern in one hand, and a sword in the other. There were no gas stations and SUVs here.

There were no McMansion cul-de-sacs in this world. There were only cabins and cottages built by the people who lived in them. There was no obnoxious, synthetic pop music, just jigs and reels played by the townspeople themselves.

There was a problem with these fantasies though, and with these feelings that gave him as much basic enjoyment when he used his imagination. The problem was, ultimately, that he couldn't hide totally from high school or Crowes or Corbett, even in his daydreams. The feelings and joy that sprang from his breast as a little kid when he thought of Halloween or Christmas were deadened now. The feelings weren't muted by time, but by what time did to the people around him. Time did something to the boys with whom he shared this high school. They might sense his private happiness, ferret it out, and call it weakness. He was afraid

they would see him happy and call him gay.

"What are you thinking about?" Alice asked.

He shook his head and said, "Nothing," as

he thought, *I'm thinking how I'm in love with you,*

how I've been in love with you for years. I'm

thinking, twenty years from now I'm going to marry

someone and have children with them, and I'm not

going to love them as much as I love you right now

on this stage.

I'm thinking I can probably never touch you.

At least let me have something that belongs to you.

I'll cherish it like a bushman with his little fetish.

The glasses! he thought. *Forget them somewhere on*

this stage before you go home, and I'll suck the

stems the way a cheerleader sucks a quarterback's

dick after he sails a game winning Hail Mary in the last thirty seconds of a gridiron contest. I'll lick the lenses until they fog so badly you'll need Windex to clean them. I'll-

Alice closed the distance between him and said, "Thanks for running lines with me." She kissed him on the cheek. The impression of her soft lips lingered there, but it wasn't enough. He turned and kissed the lips she just used to peck him. She kissed him back. Both of them were stunned. They closed their eyes, no longer in high school or even the world for one brief moment.

"You're right, though," she said, after they unlocked their lips from one-another's mouths.

He licked her cold spit from his lower lip and swallowed it, imagining her water traveling down his throat and into his stomach. He saw her spit glowing there, lighting him up like the flame burning inside the head of the Hessian horseman. "What?"

She smiled, those white even teeth killing him and making him live. "Hawthorne uses the word 'ignominy' too often."

CHAPTER TWO

Goose Creek was a condo community tenanted for the most part by divorcees and retirees. There were a few intact families residing there, but they were in the minority. Russell Milner's condominium was about as bachelor as bachelor pads came. There were a couple of framed photos hung on the walls. One was of Marilyn Monroe, with her nude breasts covered in a thin sheet of see-through material. The other was the famous one of a sailor and his girlfriend. They shared a deep kiss in front of cheering crowds and streaming tickertape in Times Square, at the close of the Second World War.

There were also a couple of Chagall reprints that made the place feel even sadder. At least it felt that way to Johnny on the nights when he stayed over. The walls, carpet, and leather furniture were white. The coffee and dining room tables were glass, and the place felt to him about as intimate as the waiting room in the dentist's office. The house Mrs. Milner got in the divorce was far cozier. Johnny thanked God Charlie spent five nights a week there, and only two here.

The boys were in the study, sitting in swivel chairs in front of the 486 computer. Charlie played one of his custom game wads while Johnny drank root beer from a frosted mug. He used a blue mouse pad as a coaster in between sips.

Charlie was spamming the "1" key. He sliced his chainsaw through a cacodemon that lunged for him with its jaws open, and the one

Cyclops eye in its head filled with rage. The chains whirred and gore flew from the monster. It crumpled in a heap before it could lob another fireball from its mouth into the marine's face.

"I don't understand you," Johnny said.

"What?"

"If you're going to make these hard as hell custom wads, why do you enable the cheat codes? Where's the fun in that?"

Johnny saw the marine get hit with several of the meteors from hell, and the soldier didn't lose a single digit from his one-hundred percent life bar. "Who cares if I enabled god mode?" Charlie said. He walked toward an imp with spikes growing from its back and razors for claws. "I like the feeling of being invincible."

Charlie strafed for the hell being with the "1" key depressed, the chainsaw shrieking for butchery. Splashes of red pixilated goop drenched the screen and wetted his hands as he wielded the weapon.

Johnny glanced back toward the bedroom. "Why's your bag packed? You planning on going back over to your mom's place?" He couldn't say he blamed him if he was.

An ambush of cacodemons and imps appeared, sprites spawning from a teleportation hub Charlie programmed into the level and then forgot. He fled from the exploding barrage of heat-seekers flooding his way. Johnny saw his friend activated more than just the god mode, as Charlie walked through a wall and stumbled into a secret ammo and armor cache. He apparently forgot about that. He shouted, "Kick ass!" before answering his friend's question about the backpack in the bedroom. "We're going on a little mission."

"A mission?" Johnny swiveled and took another sip of his root beer.

"Well," Charlie said. He slid back through the wall, confidence growing now that he found new supplies. *At least*, Johnny thought, *he didn't activate the unlimited ammo codes*. That would make things even more unfair.

"A party, too," Charlie added, a moment later.

"A party?" Johnny was dubious. They never went to a party before, mostly because they were never invited. If they were invited, they would stay home. They would think the invitation a trap, and would probably be proven right in their suspicions.

Charlie hit the "ESC" key, giving the marine a breather. He looked over at his friend. "Well, the party's on the way to the mission." He looked back toward the screen, closed the game out, and opened a folder labeled "Robbie War Pics."

"We'll kill two birds with one stone," Charlie said.

"I don't know." Johnny had misgivings about the party, the mission, and the folder of pics. Then there was the looming question about the backpack, and what was in it. Johnny guessed not school books.

Charlie looked over at his friend, and double-clicked the mouse on the folder. "I could never find his suicide note."

"He left one?" They rarely talked about Robbie, not even mentioning his name now as they brought him up. He was always on their minds, though.

"I heard my lying-ass parents talking about it one night."

Charlie pointed at the 486, whose monitor was filled with an image Johnny glanced at sidelong. "They've hidden it well, wherever it is. Or maybe they've thrown it away or burnt it."

He enlarged the image on the screen. "They didn't get all of his photos. His buddy whatshisname has most of them in the footlocker along with his ashes."

"Craig?"

Charlie nodded. Johnny let his curiosity get the best of him, staring at the screen with his friend. What looked like fifty mummies were lined up on the ground in some remote desert location. They were mostly featureless. The general outlines of their faces, as well as their hands and bodies, could be made out. They were identically entombed in some brown sort of plaster cast. Each face was frozen in a slightly different look of horror or agony. Johnny thought it would be some kind of expressionist masterpiece if it wasn't real and it wasn't war.

"What the hell happened to them?" He felt something stir in his chest. There was fear and disgust, which he expected, but also something he didn't want to admit was there. It was something he suspected most other people carried around inside them. The knowledge that everyone had the sickness didn't make him feel any less alone with it. Then there was the guilt that came with the near-sexual excitement of seeing someone dead, and realizing he enjoyed an exhilarating victory of sorts because he was still alive. He wanted to punch Charlie for showing him the photos, and hug him for the same reason.

"I got on a BBS," Charlie said, reaching for his friend's root beer with the hand not holding the mouse. "I mean, I uploaded the images and then showed them to some vets on the bulletin board."

"Just recently?"

Charlie snorted. "Yeah, right. I haven't been on a BBS in like two years. Those things are deader than disco."

"Someone tell you what this is?" Johnny pointed at the screen. "What happened to these guys?"

"Yes, indeedy."

"What?" Johnny had to know. He needed to know how these men became mummies more desperately than he needed to lose his virginity. He already kissed a girl, so he was getting closer to losing it.

"This one guy said some engineers used plows to clear lanes to the minefields and to wreck the berms and spider holes the republican guard used." Charlie set the root beer back down on the mouse pad. "They bulldozed some bunkers with some Iraqi soldiers still inside and *voila*. They buried the poor bastards alive."

Johnny pointed back at the screen. "On accident or on purpose?"

Charlie let loose with a carbonated burp and shrugged. "Doesn't matter. They're dead either way, right?"

"Yeah," Johnny said, faintly. "I guess so."

Charlie right-clicked the mouse, and things got worse. Johnny looked away. There was a man, or what once was a man. His flesh was stripped down to red sinew below the skin. He looked like one of those charts in the doctor's office, where each muscle group was highlighted on a male figure's skinless form. It looked to Johnny a lot like a picture Mr. Young showed them in health class. It was during one of those scare sessions, like the one in which the teacher tried to gross them out of having unprotected sex by showing an endless number of slides of horrible venereal diseases in the late stages.

This particular session concentrated on the perils of riding motorcycles without the proper protection. The hapless rider in question spun out of control and hydroplaned without a helmet or protective clothing. Several layers of his skin were sheared off, and sliced through and carved away by contact with the surface of the asphalt.

The man in this jpeg was even worse off, though. His ears were melted and the flesh around his eyes liquefied so it clogged the eye sockets and blinded him.

"What the fuck happened to him?" Johnny asked. The revulsion made him literally sick, and there wasn't that slight thrill that accompanied his horror when he gazed upon the mummies in the previous photo.

"I got conflicting reports on the BBS," Charlie said. "The best authority was this guy from a Cav unit in Germany who said he knew Robbie."

"You believed him?"

"Yeah," Charlie said. "He knew too many personal details about him for me not to."

"What did he say?"

"He said that Robbie's unit ran into this political prisoner who was tortured at…" He paused. "Fuck, I can't even pronounce it. I have it written down somewhere." Charlie glanced back in the direction of the bedroom as if the name of the torture chamber might be scribbled on a legal pad or piece of printer paper somewhere in there. Charlie's bedroom here was a lot cleaner than the one at his mom's house, probably because he didn't really live here. He just stayed here.

"Anyway, in English it's called the Palace of the End."

"What is?" Johnny asked.

"Where Saddam liked to torture people. He liked to make kids shoot their own parents when they weren't loyal to the *Ba'athist* regime. Apparently he also liked to dunk people in acid." Charlie laughed, but it wasn't a sadistic laugh. It was a laugh of disbelief. Johnny thought it was good that there were limits on the extent of the destruction he was willing to admire. It wasn't necessarily good that it took a cruel dictator to show him those limits, but it was better than a bottomless capacity for evil. Johnny sometimes feared that evil might someday be unleashed in Charlie. It wouldn't surface on its own, but it might be brought out by the bullies and Populars. Johnny was sure they didn't yet comprehend they might be fucking with the wrong kid.

"This guy got off easy." Charlie pointed at the man who looked like a hotdog left in the microwave for too long.

"Really?" Johnny pointed at the image. "You call that getting off easy?"

"Compared to some of the others," Charlie said. "Supposedly Hussein liked to dunk guys in the vats and not leave the palace until they completely dissolved."

"Who was he?" Johnny asked.

"The guy on the BBS said he was probably a political prisoner. The photo was probably taken by some other political prisoner who keystered a spy camera and made it out alive somehow with the pictures. Maybe he escaped or something."

Charlie closed the window out, also Xing out the folder. He stood and walked toward the bedroom. Johnny got up and carried the empty frosty mug to the kitchen sink. He deposited it on the side with the garbage disposal. "You better not let your dad find out you have those pictures." Johnny walked into the bedroom. His friend slid the straps of the black backpack over his shoulders.

"He only uses the computer to do his taxes, and some spreadsheet stuff for Freeport Fertilizer. You ready?"

"For what?"

"A mission."

"Depends," Johnny said. "What kind of mission?"

"Wars," Charlie said, "must retain popular support." He walked toward his friend. "I need you with me on this. Are you with me?"

Johnny inhaled slowly, and sighed deeply. "Sure." There was already regret in his voice.

"Von Clausewitz was a smart man." Charlie walked toward the landing and down the carpeted stairs. "He said no one should start a war without first being clear in his mind what he intends to achieve by that war and how he intends to achieve it." He killed the light. The lightswitch was another reminder that this was a bachelor's pad, for it was the penis of a merry old fellow whose gut draped over the phallic toggle.

"What do you intend to achieve," Johnny asked, "and how do you intend to achieve it?"

Charlie walked to the bottom of the stairs. Johnny trailed after him, and noticed his friend's backpack smelled like a pump beneath the canopy at a gas station. "You're about to find out." Charlie opened the door. He didn't step out, though. He waited for Johnny to exit the condo first. Then he closed the door and locked it. He hid his house key in the faux rock next to the mulched bed of ornamentals to the side of the house.

The identikit nature of the condos was muted by the gloaming hour. Each of the buildings was shadowed in the eventide. Spring was only a few weeks away. Winter gripped the Earth with a bitter determination, like a lover refusing to accept it was over. The pool was closed and covered. Frost was piled on top of the parasols on the sundeck, making them sag until they looked like they might cave.

They walked past the various Goose Creek amenities. A lone dryer was groaning in the laundry facility. They continued on past the clubhouse, and the tennis court where dead leaves were scattered across the clay. They headed beyond the seldom used horseshoe pits where the little metal rings shined in the moonlight.

"You ever see any ducks here?" Johnny asked, wondering if the place lived up to its name.

"I used to," Charlie said, and pointed to the manmade lake to their rear. "But DJ and the rest of the Lanes crew used to show up here and throw rocks at them and scare them away."

He shook his head. They left the condo community and waited for traffic to halt for a red light before running across the four lanes. They came to a grass island on the other side of which Corbett's most recent development began. Signs for various local elections for everything from sheriffs to judges were staked in the yards. There were also adverts for real estate. The male realtors in the photos on the signs wore blazers, and the females sported pantsuits. All of them wore million-dollar smiles. "That guy buys fertilizer from my dad." Charlie pointed at one realtor's mug plastered on a "For Sale" sign.

"Yeah, I think I've seen him before." Johnny was personally surprised there was room on the lawns for the signs, even as small as the signs were. The luxury houses were oversized for the parcels they were plotted on.

Christmas was over, but he could see more than one Douglas fir sprouting toward the cathedral ceilings of the monstrosities. The crest of the tree in one house touched the last crystalline bauble hung from the chandelier dangling in the entryway.

They were in the heart of Millionaire's Mile, or at least the *nouveau riche* version of it. Then again, some of the homeowners weren't even that. Mr. Milner called them, "a bunch of wannabes breaking their necks to make a monthly fifty-thousand dollar nut, up to their ears in debt, and underwater on their mortgages." He shook his head as he said it.

Johnny didn't need Mr. Milner to tell him a lot of these houses were empty. There was a creepy, wraithlike stillness as they walked past the empty giants. It was as if the bloated mansions were unsellable once word got out they were built on Indian burial grounds.

Johnny shivered. Someone told him the smallest houses here were three-thousand square feet. It looked to him like they started out that way, but maybe when it rained, the water caused them to grow. Then they slowly inflated outward, and their brick shells widened until the edges of the houses were virtually at the curb. That left just enough room for the owners to say who they wanted to elect sheriff or judge.

They were still building new houses here. Johnny saw the wooden skeletons and fiberglass outlines of new properties being constructed just beyond this development. Charlie walked toward that ghost town, and Johnny walked with him. Teenaged voices and music poured from the house directly in front of them. A number of SUVs, jeeps, and sedans were parked up and down the street, blocking their view of the partiers.

"Let's cut through here," Charlie said.

"Whose house is this?"

"Mark Tobler's."

"The track star?"

"Yep."

Johnny had nothing against Tobler. That showed that his hatred for Corbett had nothing to do with the wealth of his parents or his popularity, since Tobler's family was rich and he was popular. Mark Tobler had a cockscomb crown of beautiful hair that made him look more like a tortured romantic than a sprinter who cleared hurdles like a gazelle.

Any time a girl mentioned him, the very utterance of his name called for an aside. "You know Mark Tobler?" a girl would say. "He is *so cute*." After that, the rest of her point could be made.

Johnny had no problem with a shortcut through his property. Tobler was not likely to give them any grief even though they weren't popular. Johnny knew he and Charlie posed a serious liability to any party, that they could clear dancefloors with their arrival like the release of an audible fart.

Tobler probably wouldn't step in to save them if someone decided to humiliate them in some way. It wasn't that Tobler was indifferent to their suffering. It was just that the luck of the Tobler types gave them a kind of grace not to notice such ugliness in the world. Life was good to the Toblers, so why wouldn't the Toblers expect it to be good to others?

It was dark though, and the kids were drunk. That gave Johnny and Charlie a good chance to slink by without their unpopularity trailing them like a mist that got them noticed and then punished for brushing shoulders with their betters. Jocks reeking of cologne and cheerleaders smelling of perfume bumped past them and jostled them. Kids sang and yelled. Some shitfaced letterman shouted out audible cues, as if he might hike a football at any moment.

The blue of the backyard pool shone in the night light, and the craters of the moon reflected across the warm, rippling surface of the water. A few girls in bikinis and as many boys in swimsuits splashed or relaxed with cans of beer, while floating on rafts in the pool. A long white table stretched across the length of the backyard. There was a catered spread of punch and *hors d'oeuvre*, cold cuts and deviled eggs lain out on a white cloth. Johnny thought that meant parents were probably involved. Kids didn't give a shit about food unless maybe they had the munchies.

They left the party behind them: the girls in conch bikinis and neon thongs that made Johnny's erection press against the fabric of his boxers with the force of a dart nestling in a bull's-eye. The voices receded, and grew muffled. The tension that entered Johnny whenever he was in the presence of kids his own age melted, at least for the moment. They walked farther into the woods toward the skeletal outlines of the next Corbett construction project. The voices returned. This time though, the noise of male jocks wasn't counterpointed by the sounds of singing coming from speakers or the chirp of girls laughing.

"Fuck," the voice from the dark before them said. The moon threw white light over the three forms before Johnny and Charlie. It was two football players from the JV team. Both were huddled in their bombers, fidgeting with a keg before them that looked like was tapped and drained in short order. A girl slept soundly on the ground before them.

One of the two ballers kicked the keg, which resounded with a hollow echo reverberating through all twelve of its empty, imperial gallons. The keg's ribbed, stainless steel contours reminded Johnny of a giant hand grenade. Charlie once asked Russell, "Did you ever pull a grenade pin out with your teeth?" His father replied, "I never threw a grenade in combat. If you tried to pull a grenade pin out with your teeth, the only thing you'd end up pulling out is your teeth."

"That's it," one of the two ball players said. He fiddled with the faucet knob and coiled the plastic tubing of the beer line around his arm. He staggered and glanced around as if searching for an ideal place to vomit. He looked over at the other JV player. "What else we got?"

His friend leaned on him for support. Neither of them was aware of the two boys in their midst, nor did they take any notice of the girl passed out on the ground before them. "We got a Zima." He handed the alcopop to his friend and dug into the right pocket of his jacket. "And we also got a hog's leg." The player held up a joint, fatted with reefer so that it almost resembled a blunt wrapped in a broken-down cigar.

"Hog's leg?" The other one said, reaching one hand out toward a neighboring tree to balance himself for support. He placed the swollen joint in his mouth and spoke around it. "You fucking hick, why are you calling it that? Maybe you should join the Future Farmers of America with the rest of those rednecks at school!"

The jocks both erupted with laughter. They leaned their skulls together as if they might butt heads or even kiss. "I don't have a lighter," the one with the joint in his mouth said. He looked up at his friend with glassy, drunken eyes. "Do you have a lighter?"

His friend shook his head. "Then I guess we can't smoke this joint." He kept it in his mouth, however. Then he held up the Zima, his only remaining option to get more buzzed. "Zima's a pussy drink." He finally looked down at the girl spread out on the ground, and leaned down to her. "Pussy drinks go in the pussy."

He lifted her skirt, and exposed her cold legs. He pulled her cotton panties down, and both Johnny and Charlie looked away. This was the first time they saw a real vagina, in the flesh. They were dying to get a look at one outside of a magazine or a computer screen, but this was not the way they wanted it. Johnny feared the two drunken boys were ruining sex for him permanently with this little nightmare show. It was destroying him inside, but didn't look to bother either of them in the least. They thought it was funny.

"We're bad boys," one of them said. Johnny wasn't looking, so he couldn't be sure which player spoke. "We're the kind of kids who put our whole mouths on the drinking fountain at school."

Johnny looked back. The girl was standing, puzzled, awakened by the boy's prodding of her privates with the bottle. Johnny didn't think she knew where she was, who they were, or how she got here. She braced herself against the nearest tree and urinated, the cold stream spilling over the rustling bed of dead leaves beneath her. She fell back down into the pile where she just pissed, and quickly fell back asleep.

A figure streaked forward in the dark, and bludgeoned both of the boys with what looked like a spiked mace. The boy with the club sent first the one, and then the other, to the ground. The joint flew from the mouth of the one boy, and he was out cold from the first blow Charlie swung. The other one was only dazed, a slight concussive strike from the makeshift weapon that came from Charlie's backpack sending him against a hollow log. He attempted to stand, to get even, his rage making his buzz evaporate quickly. Charlie brought the club down as if preparing to knight the jock struggling to his knees, beating him unconscious with a final blow from the kerosene-smelling club.

The girl and the two boys slept before them. Charlie looked back at Johnny. "I wasn't planning on using this until we got there." He pointed the end of his unlit torch toward the construction site. "Sometimes plans change, though."

Johnny could guess what came next, so he didn't ask. The moon loomed over the frameworks and scaffolding of the uncompleted houses. Johnny thought the moon looked to be without dimensions, as powerful and bright as it was. He imagined somehow climbing up and reaching the moon, and then peeling it from the sky like a giant, very thin pancake. The houses glowed like the tombstones of giants, and the thin tracery of cloud cover strewn over the sky looked like a clothesline serving those selfsame monsters.

"They didn't kill all the trees," Johnny said. The land here was nowhere near as logged off as in some of the other developments. The tree cutting usually happened before, not after the frames went up. That meant there was a good chance the trees were here to stay. Maybe this place was intended to present a more countrified impression than the rest of the Corbett projects. A good number of trees certainly made it easier for Charlie to do what he came here to do. He was scraping bark from a nearby cedar with a bowie knife, whose handle was made of elk antler. Johnny noticed Charlie was now wearing black gloves, which he kept hidden in his backpack up until this moment. The torch was momentarily sheathed in his pant leg.

"Cedar bark makes good tinder bundles," Charlie said. "We're not going to need much tinder. I've got gas, and there's probably enough sawdust collected in those frames to build a sandcastle."

A carful of joyriders in a Denali streaked down a road well on the other side of the work-in-progress. The SUV was at least a quarter mile from here. The probing searchlights of their high beams barely reached the perimeter of the nearest wooden skeleton, but it still startled Johnny for the moment.

"Don't worry," Charlie said, pocketing the tinder he shaved from the tree. "Witnesses aren't going to be a problem." He glanced back over in the direction of Tobler's house. The cathedral roof was pitched above the trees where the two potential date rapists and their victim slept soundly.

Charlie reached down into his bag. "Just in case." Johnny heard a rattling, and he caught the can of red spray paint as Charlie sailed it to him. "Draw a swastika or maybe a pentagram on one of the frames over there. Maybe spray your tag on a pile of lumber, or on a tree."

"Why?"

"Throw the investigators off," Charlie said, and slung his backpack straps back over his shoulders. He removed the torch from where it was stashed against his leg, secreted there like a massive shiv. Johnny looked closer at the torch. Braided strands of kerosene-soaked cotton rope protruded from a metal sterno can. It was crowned by a wooden dowel very much like the one Robbie sliced into pieces with the jigsaw, when he made them their doubloons for that treasure chest all those years ago.

Charlie took out a long-stemmed lighter Johnny recognized as being the same one Janet Milner used to light candles on birthday cakes or for special dinner occasions. Charlie depressed the trigger, and a spurt of orange flame danced and writhed with the sensuous motion of a belly dancer. "I feel like the leader of the angry village mob searching for the monster hiding up in his keep or whatnot."

Johnny was glad he stopped the words from leaving his lips and that they were still stored up in his mind. His words, which he didn't say, went something to the effect of, *That must feel like a change, since you're usually on the receiving end of the mob's anger. You're usually treated like the monster at least in the particular movie that is our lives.*

Charlie let the flame from the long lighter erupt in the mouth of the torch. The fire made a rippling sound. The noise was abrupt and violent, as if summoning an ancient spirit that didn't want to be wakened and resented its thousand-year slumber was broken.

Johnny was no Nazi or Satanist. He didn't have much love for LaVey or Hitler. He got a lot further with *The Satanic Bible* than he did with *Mein Kampf* (both of which Charlie owned). He didn't want his friend or himself going to prison though, so he searched for an ideal spot to tag his swastika and pentagram.

"They say never to hold a torch at an angle," Charlie said, "since it'll drip kerosene that way." He walked over to the nearest outline of an uncompleted estate. "But I'll make an exception this time, since more kerosene means more flame."

Johnny was glad Charlie was so relaxed, so flippant about the whole affair. For his part, Johnny was on the verge of panic. *What to tag, what to tag?* Charlie gave him several options. He said to tag some plywood, or to paint one of the frames, or spray one of the trees. Johnny decided to hit a tree. The frames of the houses and the plywood were most likely to burn in the fire that already started to sway and whirl from the first touch of the torch.

Charlie's act might start a forest fire that could potentially spread and grow like a cancer consuming the entire suburban township, but the trees were more likely than either the frames or the stacks of plywood to survive the blazing inferno. The piney evergreens nearest to Johnny were still dark. The flame was not yet high enough to illumine their whorled forms. He thought they looked not so much like trees, but more like giant pinecones dancing in the dark.

The needles hanging from the branches were too strong an armor however, too great a shield for his graffiti to get noticed there. He didn't know much about arson inspectors. He figured though, that whoever eventually came to the scene might not be diligent enough to lift the branches and inspect for the calling card of some cult.

Some nearby honeysuckles, empty of fragrance in the cold, drew his eye in their direction. Not only were they odorless, but their showy flowers were nowhere in evidence. Whatever life there was in the plants now hibernated in the piths, until spring came, and winter and football season were over.

There were some white ashes, perfect for leaving his little symbols. Diamond-shaped ridges were arrayed on the bark of the trees. Johnny walked toward the ashes. He held the can out, depressed the nozzle, and sprayed a bloody pentangle that dripped across the trunk and leaked downward. This would be a better job for Charlie, if he wasn't currently occupied touching his torch to the little tinder piles and to the piles of sawdust that were catching even faster. Charlie was a better artist, after all. His draftsmanship got him noticed by the stage manager and director at Freeport High, who now kept him around for a much larger number of tasks than just his previous work on stagecraft.

Flames spurted and climbed, licking the wood as if propelled by unseen gas jets. Johnny moved on to the next tree. He squirted out the spray paint, depressing the nozzle until it hissed and a ruby jet blasted onto the bark. A hooked cross formed, although it was a fairly sloppy version of the ancient Aryan symbol.

He stood back to inspect his handiwork and Charlie tugged his sleeve. "We've got to book, man.

This whole place is going to go up soon." The torch was no longer in his hand, and Johnny wondered if he tossed it into the mouth of the growing blaze.

Charlie ran through some trees, not directly retracing their path back through the woods with the keg and the two JV players. He didn't head back toward the party, either. The party was still going strong, and Johnny and Charlie could still hear the sounds of voices and music. Johnny guessed they were taking a route his friend mapped out in advance of this little caper. Charlie was smart enough to realize he could blend in with the crowd at the party before the mayhem ensued, but not afterward. Being seen walking around wearing all black and sporting a backpack after a few acres already burnt was not the smartest idea.

"What did we just do?" Johnny asked. He realized he said, "we" and not "you."

"No one lived there," Charlie said. He was still running through the trees, into whose dark midst fog spread in a wintery lattice. "That makes it second-degree arson, if we get caught, which we're not gonna."

"You think they might think it's an accident?" Johnny ran to catch up with his friend. Charlie stopped running as they broke through the tree line and paused on the grass embankment across from Goose Creek's slumbering array of condos.

"Not if they don't have their heads up their asses," Charlie said. "If we're lucky, they might suspect Gentleman Jim of insurance fraud." He grinned, hustled across the street, and Johnny tagged after him. Charlie lightly touched the gate code into the keypad nestled on the security guard's untenanted pillbox outside of Goose Creek. Then he shed his gloves. They walked past what management called the "clothes care facility," where a load still tumbled in the dryer.

Johnny saw the balcony of Mr. Milner's place even from ground level. The view through the glass showed all of the lights in the living room to be out. The boys rushed in the enveloping darkness toward the front door of Russell's bachelor pad. Charlie leaned down, and kicked at the wicker "Welcome" mat featuring two green-headed mallards floating across a pond. He snatched up the little quartz rock resting in the mulch bed, opened the ersatz stone, and extracted the key.

"Shush …" he said, quietly. Johnny thought there was a good chance they might get away with it. There was no guilt in him now. There was only a bit of fear that he would get arrested and become a juvenile delinquent. Then his future would be ruined. He couldn't be angry at Charlie, though. His friend made him do nothing. Johnny wanted to do it. He didn't know that until it was done, but now there was no use in denying it.

He looked back in the direction of Tobler's house, and all of the other McMansions sprouting from the colonized pasturage. He could see bright red light, like the reflection from the yearly display of fireworks exploding in the village square. He'd just helped lay waste to that asshole's newest pet project.

Charlie opened the door, and slowly slipped inside. Johnny entered the condo after him. Both quietly shed their shoes. They made eye contact, and realized they were stifling laughter. They padded up the stairs. The sound of Russell's snoring increased in their ears, and it got harder to keep from laughing.

They gave up altogether once they were safely in Charlie's room, and the door was closed. They rushed for the bed and slammed their faces into the white pillows and laughed, kicking their feet against the mattress beneath them.

Johnny looked over at Charlie, resting his head on the pillow. Charlie looked back at him. "That was awesome," Johnny whispered.

"Goddamn right. Mission a success."

"Yeah," Johnny said. His mood soured as he thought about the party, and what was going on in the woods behind Tobler's house. He was glad he and Charlie decided to walk back there. It would be a lot uglier for that girl if they hadn't.

Charlie sprang up from the bed, reached onto the shelf beneath his nightstand where he kept the old *Calvin and Hobbes* comics he loved reading when he was younger. He came up holding his latest pet project in a precarious grip.

"You going to light it?" Johnny asked.

"Yes sir." Charlie walked his genie's lamp carefully over toward the windowsill, not wanting to spill any olive oil as he went. He fired and glazed the little bit of pottery in art class. He decorated its body with scribes, giving it little arabesque flourishes and making it look authentic enough for the lamp to be mistaken for the genuine article. It resembled something ancient that washed up on the sands and could be rubbed to grant its finder three wishes.

Johnny hopped up, taking his cue. He ran into the bathroom, and grabbed one of the heavier beach towels from the shower rod. He draped it over his shoulders, and closed the bathroom door. Then he cued the two light switches, making the room glow and circulating air through the ceiling vents.

A nervous piss streamed out of his body and into the toilet. *If I had three wishes*, he thought and then tried to think of what he might wish for. He finished peeing, flushed, and then started washing his hands in the sink. He thought it might be nice to have his own bathroom, like Charlie, with direct access from the bedroom. If nature called late at night and he had to get up, the Cotter residence was built so he had to tramp sleepily down the stairs and use the hallway bathroom. Maybe his first wish would be for his own bathroom.

That left only Alice and Elise to wish for once he had his new bathroom. These days he thought much more of Alice than Elise. Maybe that meant he was maturing. He wanted a girl his own age rather than someone who was unattainable. Elise wasn't even a college student anymore. She was now a full-grown woman with a career, and even worse, a fiancé.

He dried his hands on the beach towel draped over his neck, turned the bathroom lights off, and went back into the bedroom. He tiptoed to the door leading to the hallway and lay the beach towel down on the floor. That would help mask whatever odor the olive oil lamp didn't drown out. Charlie already sparked his celebratory joint. Johnny walked over toward the open window. The cool night air filtered into the room. Charlie passed the weed off to his accomplice.

The soft mandarin flame from the genie's lamp billowed, cast titian light over their smiling faces. Charlie's eyes were already red, and he was clearly stoned. Smoke travelled upward from the lamp. Dark soot lightly stained the stucco pattern spackled on the ceiling.

Johnny puffed on the joint and pointed up at the ceiling. "Won't that piss your dad off?"

Charlie shook his head and wiped his red, watery eyes. "He never comes in here, plus he's been busy with June."

June was his new girlfriend. She was a blue-rinsed matron with a thick Slavic accent who survived the Shoah. She saw some of the same European lands as Russell, and under equally ugly circumstances. His nightmare with Janet apparently chastened him, and he now only lusted after women his own age.

Charlie shook his head and took the joint back. "I don't think he's going to move out of here before he dies."

Johnny looked up, consulting the calculator in his head. His ability to do math was dampened by the clouds of weed smoke now roiling in his skull. It made his nose and chest burn. It also made his heart relax though, uncoiling from the pulsing knot it formed when they lit that skeleton of a neighborhood on fire.

"You're right," Johnny said, finally wrapping his stoned mind around the problem. Russell said he was born in something like 1922, and it was now '98. That made him 76, 28 years older than Johnny's own father. Russell would probably be dead of natural causes before he even contemplated moving out of here and the landlord spotted the stains on the ceiling.

Charlie ground the joint out and pocketed it. Johnny didn't protest, since he was already good and baked. He could feel nothing below his knees. A golden opiated numbness carried him away from his body, his pubescent problems, and awkwardness. He was happy, at least for the moment. He imagined sharing a joint with Alice, laying on her trundle bed and holding her, listening to music with her.

Charlie slid the window closed, and blew out the flame in his little genie's lamp. Then he set it back on the bottom shelf of the nightstand, above the stash of comic books that were the center of his life when he was twelve. He hadn't entirely shaken their grip and he was a little embarrassed in hanging onto the habit.

He sat down on the carpet and coughed up a bit of resin, reaching for the TV set, and turning on the power. Johnny got down on the carpet with him. They sat side by side, with their knees folded and their toes curling into the soft contours of the shag carpet. Charlie turned the N64 on and an animated version of Pierce Brosnan turned toward them. Agent Double O Seven shot at the two stoned boys, who laughed at their deaths as blood dripped down the screen.

CHAPTER THREE

There was something spiritually soothing about *Roseanne*, sort of like *The Simpsons* in that way. Most TV shows didn't work for Charlie or Johnny, but these surrogate families and their cozy little lower-middle class houses somehow worked for them the way a fireplace did for previous generations. The shows meant even more to Charlie, probably because his family was no longer intact. The remaining pieces weren't much to write home about.

Roseanne and Dan were standing in front of the Afghan-draped couch. Mr. Conner's belly bulged in his red flannel shirt, as he denied sleeping with his old high school flame earlier that afternoon. "It was just lunch!"

Crystal breezed through the living room and fled out the front door of the house. "Roseanne's lost some weight," Johnny said. He briefly wondered if he could screw her, and decided it was possible.

"Yeah, but Dan's getting bigger. How do I look?"

Johnny turned from the TV and glanced back at his friend. Charlie sat at his bedroom desk. A grinding stone was on the desk's surface and a sword lay on the floor before him. A box filled with makeup rested on his lap, and the nylon stocking cap on his head made him look as bald as he claimed it would.

"Not bad."

Charlie grinned. "It'll look even better when the wearer's on stage." He peeled it off, and a light dust of concealer clouded the air as he pulled. "Now, I know I'm going to be an FX man like Rick Baker."

"Who?"

"He turned Michael Jackson into a werewolf for the *Thriller* video. He also did *An American Werewolf in London*."

"That's a good one." Johnny turned back to *Roseanne*.

"Yeah, computer-generated images don't really work for me. I like the old bladder and hydraulic effects more."

The shop talk would be wearing for Johnny if he didn't know when to tune his friend out and when to listen. On screen Darlene had her hands wrapped around DJ's throat. "Darlene," Roseanne said, "What did I tell you about murdering your brother in the living room?"

The laughter didn't sound like that canned stuff they used on the crappy shows, like *Full House*. It sounded like real people.

"Who's hotter?" Charlie asked. "Darlene or Becky?"

"Shit," Johnny said, with little hesitation. "Darlene." He was about to say, "She's got dark hair like Elise," but stopped himself in time. She was home now for some reason, and he needed to play it carefully. She was in her bedroom for the time being, and that gave him some relief from his nerves. Eventually, he would run into her but probably not at dinner. Mrs. Milner cooked less and less these days. Johnny and Charlie spent more time eating those nasty Kid Cuisines with the skateboarding penguin on the box. The only halfway palatable meal was the macaroni and cheese one with the mini-franks buried in the congealed slop. Johnny was convinced prisoners probably ate a less starchy fare.

He looked back over at his friend, who was now grinding his wheel against the edge of the blade. He was dulling it for performance night. "Is there a sword fight?" Johnny didn't remember one in *The Scarlet Letter*. The play might be taking certain liberties, but probably not as many as the crappy movie he saw based on the book. The movie with Demi Moore and Gary Oldman was basically softcore porn. He remembered there was even a battle with Indians in there.

"Nah, this is for an upcoming play." The wheel made a granulating noise as it slid back and forth over the already dull blade's edge. "I probably don't even need to go through all of this trouble since a guard's going to have the thing in a damn scabbard the whole time. It doesn't hurt to practice for when the time comes where my services will be needed."

"What are you doing with the makeup?" Johnny nodded at the box sitting on Charlie's lap.

"I'm going to put it on you if you have no objections."

"Okay," Johnny said.

"Good," Charlie said. "I don't want to bother with the grease paint anymore, and I need to do some experimenting with this hypoallergenic stuff before the next dress rehearsal. This makeup is a lot easier to clean off than that other crud."

"Don't guys bitch about putting on makeup, you know, like it's gay or whatever?"

"They're already in the drama department, so they're used to that. We're all eighties babies, anyway. You remember Poison and Mötley Crüe? The more you looked like a chick, the more chicks you got."

"Yeah, but now you've …"

More live audience laughter came from the screen. Johnny turned back toward the TV, sorry to miss whatever just happened. "That other stuff will give you pimples, too," Charlie said, from behind him. This time Johnny didn't turn from the screen. "If there's one thing that might cause my teen thespians to quit the program, it's the likelihood of getting pimples."

There was a knock at the door. "*Mi casa su*," Charlie said. He set the blade down on the carpet, and the grinding wheel back on the desk.

Mrs. Milner stood there, her eyes more shocked than usual. She held a cigarette in her right hand. She came out of the closet with her habit six months or so ago. Johnny was pretty sure she knew they sometimes stole smokes from her, and he was also pretty sure she didn't care. Charlie thought there was a good chance that if he and Johnny lit up in front of her, she might not object. Neither of them as of yet worked up the balls to test out his theory.

"There's someone here to see you," she said.

Charlie looked over at Johnny. "Do me a favor and run the edge of that blade against the carpet. It'll make it a little duller." He pointed at the nightstand, where some braided nylon rope lay. "Running that over the edge won't hurt, either."

"Will do," Johnny said. He had no intentions of sitting cooped up in here without at least first figuring out who was out there waiting to see his friend. He wondered if Charlie would rat on him to save himself. *Would I rat on him*? Potential outcomes for the prisoner's dilemma stormed through his head. He bit his nails for a moment.

He briefly glanced over at the braided rope on the nightstand. It was the same kind that served as the wick of Charlie's torch. It was probably cut from the exact same length, too. Neither of them ever talked about what they did that night. They buried it in clouds of weed smoke, under the veil of sulfurous light wavering in tendrils from that little genie lamp Charlie made in art class. Stories about the blaze were on the local news several times. At first it was reported with "arson not ruled out as the cause." Later it was reported as fire with "an arsonist as the likely culprit, in what authorities are now saying is most likely a deliberately set fire."

Their prayers that suspicion would fall on Corbett Senior went unanswered. Gentleman Jim was above reproach. He was probably above the law, barring perhaps sacrificing his wife on the altar of the fountain in the center of the Freeport Village Square. Johnny thought that even then people might close their eyes to his actions.

What was worse was Johnny's swastika and pentagram went unnoticed, or at least unremarked upon. If the police suspected Satanists and Nazis, they had yet to go public with their hunches.

Johnny ran to the bedroom window, cracked the Venetian slats, and peered outside. It was the white Crown Vic of the SRO, Officer Sandburg. Johnny earlier saw him stalking the hallways of Freeport High, politicking with various administrators in their offices or in the faculty lounge. He had a former athlete's physique, and reminded Johnny a bit of Tom the Gym Teacher. He looked like was working for something besides a pension though, unlike Tom. His large paunch spilled like a sandbag from his midsection, and made his white Polo shirt bulge over his belt. His gut concealed his belt buckle and the top part of his khaki's fly. He wore his badge on a beaded chain, and his eyes were two ashen olive pits. The eyes were intense and beady. Sandburg's fixed gaze always made Johnny feel guilty, as if it was somehow possible to be truant while sitting in class at his desk and at the position of attention.

No one said anything about Johnny having to remain in the bedroom. Charlie merely requested he continue dulling the blade. Johnny stood and padded down the hall. His feet made no sound on the carpet, but Elise somehow heard him. She looked up from her place where she sat on the edge of her childhood bed. Several of her boxes from storage were sitting next to her, open and overflowing with old books and toys.

"Hey, Johnny." She looked at him and smiled faintly. It took effort, and her features settled quickly back into her perpetual scowl a moment later. There were sharply defined lines running around the corners of her mouth, and tracing down to her lips. The lines were always there, but they deepened with time. They gave her face the harsh quality of a mask. The crease in her hair was knife-perfect, and the whiteness of her scalp stood out against the shining black hair spilling from either end of the part.

She was still beautiful, even more beautiful than she was when she was younger. He wanted only Alice now though. Johnny was trying to work up the courage to ask Charlie for her telephone number. He kept the numbers of all the actors and crew from the Freeport Players Club in a leather-bound daily planner.

"Come hang out with me for a second." Elise pushed aside a box on the bed and patted the pink comforter with her soft hand. He noticed her nail polish was black, that it matched her pantsuit, stockings, and heels. He didn't know where she worked, but guessed men didn't spend much time bossing her around.

He walked toward Elise and sat on the bed next to her. The mattress shifted slightly. He felt her warmth there next to him radiating from her stocking-sheathed thighs and soft ass.

"We need to talk," she said.

"About what?"

Elise tittered, snorting a little. Her masculine laugh reminded him of how poor her table manners were, and how she always talked with her mouth full when she was younger. "No." She held up a waxy little paperback, the cover of which featured two parents standing over their adolescent daughter. The little girl held a teddy bear in one hand and rubbed her tear-filled eyes with the knuckles of her other hand.

We Need to Talk, the title said. The subtitle said, *Explaining Divorce to Children*. She threw the book back in the box. "They bought this for me when they were still together and not having problems. They must have known something was in the wind, even then."

She looked around the confines of the room. The walls once plastered with a collage of various teen heartthrobs were now bare. She wasn't in a whimsical, reminiscent mood when she glanced around. It was more like she was surveying what she was grateful to leave behind. She was happy to be rid of this house, this family, this town, and maybe even Johnny, though he didn't want to think that. He guessed the odds were that he was too small a presence in her life for her to feel one way or the other about him.

Elise shifted slightly on the bed, and the scent of her perfume made its way from her to him. He held his breath for a moment, wanting it to pass. He didn't want her smell to cloud his judgment right now. He didn't want to say something stupid or something he would regret. He guessed that would happen if they kept talking.

"I didn't realize how fucked up some of these toys we used to play with are."

"Yeah," he said. He heard very little of her sentence, only the buried word "Fuck." Johnny knew she meant it as an adjective in the sense that, "That's fucked." She said it with the force of a verb. He could use that later. He saw the Elise in his mind addressing the lucky Johnny he wished he was. *Let's fuck*, she said.

The real Elise brought him back to earth by saying, "I mean, I understand dolls, but they even sold preemies." She held up a hairless, tiny baby doll that was malformed. It smelled like talcum powder cloistered away in water-damaged cardboard for too long.

"Yeah, that's screwed up."

She tossed the doll back into the same box where the book about divorce now lay. "Speaking of screwed up," she said, and shook her head. "One brother's dead, and it looks like the other one might be going to jail."

"For what?" Johnny asked.

She scowled at him with her demoness eyes. He smiled slightly and nodded. It was his way of acknowledging he wouldn't incriminate himself or his best friend to her, but he also wouldn't try to bullshit her again. He would save that for the School

Resource Officer if and when he faced the guy for an interview or interrogation.

"Things aren't looking good for your whole gender," Elise said. He thought, *Gender is what people who've been to college call sex.*

"What do you mean?"

She brushed her raven hair away from her face. "It's been awhile since I've seen the stats, but I'm pretty sure females are out-earning men, and getting more college degrees. It might already be something like a ratio of three-to-one."

She clicked her heels together, like Dorothy trying to teleport home to Kansas. It was the opposite yearning in her case, a desire to get as far away from home as possible. He wondered why she was back here. He was about to ask when she said, "Hey, can I ask you a question?"

Panic went through him and he remained silent. Elise lowered her voice. "Did you steal a pair of my underthings a few years ago?"

Oh, shit. Underthings? He smiled, held up his hands as if to bargain. She shoved him slightly. "I knew it, you little fucking perv. Do you know how much those cost? They were a present from my boyfriend."

"The boyfriend you're engaged to now?"

The question erased what smile there was on her face. Her black polished fingers flickered out in front of her dark eyes, and the hair she just tucked behind her elven ears spilled back down over her face. She gazed at her engagement ring. "No, but I probably should have married that guy when I had the chance. It's too late now, though."

"Why?"

Elise stopped glancing at the engagement ring. "He's dead. Heroin overdose."

"Another man down."

"Your gender's headed for a cliff." She actually touched him, stroking his hair. He was surprised to feel absolutely nothing sexual, at least aside from the low level of need pounding in his brain twenty-four seven. He took a chance and laid his head on her chest. She didn't fight him and he listened to her heartbeat.

"I guess I'm fucked too, then."

Elise cradled him and said, "The way of all flesh."

"I'm sorry for stealing your panties."

He heard her breath leaving her chest as he kept his ear cupped to her sternum. "It's all right. It's a compliment in its own pervy way."

"Johnny."

Both of them jumped up on the bed, startled. Mrs. Milner was too consumed with her own problems to notice them conjoined there, surrounded by boxes. "Mr. Sandburg would like to see you."

Johnny braced himself, attempted to plant his hands in the comforter and push off. He accidentally latched his hand onto Elise's warm, black satin-sheathed thigh. There was nothing maternal about this touch, unlike the previous one. Alice Berryman briefly melted away from his mind. There was only Elise, as in the beginning. *She-Ra*.

"Coming." He left her bedroom convinced for some reason, he would never see Elise again. It made him sad. Charlie walked past him, going in the opposite direction back toward the bedroom. They made one brief moment of eye contact, Charlie winking before passing his friend and returning to his trove of stage props. The *Roseanne* harmonica theme wailed, signaling the beginning of another episode. Johnny cursed the stupid cop for making him miss a rare back-to-back block. Maybe it was a marathon.

"Hey, Johnny." The officer stuck out his hand, and Johnny accepted the bear paw in his comparatively dwarfish palm. He wanted to play tough, like in the movies, but he was scared. "Pleasure to meet you." The cop tried to smile, the lines in his face making the flesh look like unbaked, dry clay. "You want to walk with me out to my car?"

"Okay."

Officer Sandburg turned back toward the kitchen, and waved once toward Mrs. Milner. She stared through them both. "Thank you for the coffee and the hospitality." The officer opened the door and let Johnny precede him outside.

The cop reached for his keys in the pocket of his starched khakis, and they walked toward his Crown Vic parked next to Elise's old VW. Her bug had roughly the same number of stickers as all those years ago. The nature of the slogans was somewhat different now and less strident. Johnny decided a car in an office park needed to be less ostentatious than one in a student garage.

Sandburg hit his alarm, and the car chirped once. The officer stood by the driver's side door, and the soles of his hush puppies crunched the gravel underfoot. He shifted his stance from bowlegged to pigeon-toed.

"I don't want you to talk," he said. "I just want you to listen."

"Okay." Johnny wondered if even agreeing counted as talking.

"There's no maintenance program for pyros. Do you know what a maintenance program is?" Johnny shook his head. "When someone does heroin, they put him a heroin substitute like methadone. It helps him get clean. Do you understand?"

Johnny nodded. "Your friend's behavior is only going to get worse. All right, he set a construction site on fire. The blaze was contained, lucky for him. If someone was hurt, this little stunt could get the attention of some really important people. I'm talking about the kind of people who always, eventually get their man. Do you understand?"

This time Johnny didn't nod or shake his head. He felt they were veering into incriminating territory. The cop kept speaking, anyway. "Next time, he's going to hurt someone, not maybe, but definitely." Sandburg paused, looked deep into

Johnny's eyes. Johnny felt as if the man was probing into his brainstem with his gaze. "If he gets caught now, he'll go to a diversionary program, maybe get restitution and community service. There's a chance he could serve some time in a juvenile facility."

It shamed him to admit it, but Johnny was secretly relieved the cop didn't consider he might be involved as an accomplice. He hated the idea that his buddy Charlie could go to jail, but he hated the idea of himself getting into trouble even more.

"If someone gets hurt, it'll ruin Charlie's life." The cop finally opened the driver's side door of his car. "Does he have any goals for the future?"

Johnny nodded. "What?"

"He wants to be an FX man in Hollywood, I think."

"Well, hell," the officer said, and slid into his car. "Maybe I need to retract my previous statement. Maybe there is a diversionary program for pyros." He slid his seatbelt on and stuck his key in the ignition. "Maybe you can divert him that way."

Johnny didn't move, or speak. If he acknowledged Charlie needed diverting, then he was admitting his friend needed to be diverted from something like setting trashcans and neighborhoods on fire.

"Oh, one other thing," Officer Sandburg said. Johnny grew rigid when the man said that. Johnny was familiar with all the cop movies. A detective always said something along the lines of

"Oh, one other thing," before he tripped up the suspect and got him to admit his guilt.

"Yeah?"

"I'm not deaf, and I'm not blind. I'm not heartless, either." Sandburg slammed his car door shut, but rolled the window down so he could keep speaking. "I know your friend isn't the most popular kid in school, and I'm sure he had his reasons for doing what he did. Hell, every criminologist and profiler knows there's a kernel of a legitimate grievance in every act of terror. Do you understand?"

Johnny didn't, so he shook his head. Officer Sandburg leaned on his car door, the sleeve of his shirt getting wet from the rainwater collected on the

Crown Vic's body. "You take Timothy McVeigh. You know who that was?"

"Yeah, he blew up a building."

"He blew up the Murray Federal Building in Oklahoma City. Now, he was pissed because the government didn't necessarily handle a couple of high profile incidents with the greatest of tact. A lot people agreed with him, actually." Those colorless eyes bored through Johnny's brain again. "Then he blew up a building with a bunch of kids in it."

Charlie would never hurt children, Johnny wanted to say, or animals. He was glad he remained silent, though. Charlie would be proud of him when he returned from this interview and debriefed. At least he hoped his friend would be proud, and that he wouldn't suspect Johnny of ratting.

"If Charlie, say, hurt Alex Corbett or Michael Crowes, things would only get worse. Sympathy cards would pour in, and the boys would be nominated for sainthood. Do you want to see Alex Corbett's mug up on a mural, like Saint Francis of Assisi? Do you think that's what Charlie wants?"

The man grinned, and Johnny suppressed a smile. A teenager should never laugh at something an authority figure said. That was lame. At least, one wasn't supposed to laugh when the grownup was trying to get laughs. This man caught him a little off-guard, though. "Terrorism almost always backfires."

"When doesn't it?" Johnny asked.

"Terrorism worked out pretty well for the IRA in the end if I'm to be honest." Officer Sandburg removed his sunglasses from the visor and put them on. "Charlie doesn't have their deep

pockets, and I don't think he has much of a

network." Sandburg smiled until his eyeteeth

flashed. "All he's got is you."

CHAPTER FOUR

There was a time when it looked like Charlie might have a real chance to escape. His father seriously contemplated a buyout offer and would often talk at length about leaving Ohio. He spoke of returning to New York, and living with June somewhere up in the Catskills. Charlie nursed the idea, cherished it, and talked about it a lot with Johnny. He didn't want to make a public announcement at school and risk it backfiring if the deal fell through, but that didn't stop him from fantasizing quite a bit about that last day at Freeport High. He saw himself throwing his middle finger to the wind, brandishing the digit in the faces of the counsellors, teachers, and especially students who made his life hell every day.

That guidance counselor, Mr. Sears, was full of shit, he was convinced. Charlie told the man about Crowes and Corbett harassing him, and said that if he was female they wouldn't have a problem categorizing what they did to him in the natatorium as sexual assault. Mr. Sears fidgeted with the links of his ill-fitting Timex, pushed his moist glasses up the bridge of his pimply nose, and said, "Do you know Eleanor Roosevelt?"

"Not personally." Sears was either too stupid or indifferent to realize he was being mocked.

"Mrs. Roosevelt," Sears said, "once quipped that 'no one can make you feel inferior without your consent.'" Charlie replied, "No, but they can punch you without your consent. That's the problem."

Mr. Sears told him to leave after that and to never come back.

Today was a Monday. Charlie spent Sunday nights at his father's, so Mr. Milner drove him to school. Russell dropped a bombshell on his son as he tooled his Mercedes around the carpool loop. "You know that offer Steinmetz tendered?"

"Yeah," Charlie said, and he found it impossible to conceal the hope in his voice.

"It's been withdrawn." There was disappointment in his father's eyes, but it didn't compare to what Charlie felt at the moment. There was no escape, and high school would never end, he was convinced. High school was forever.

If he couldn't literally escape, then he contemplated hopping into the bodies of those people around him. Adults were beyond the sadistic clutches of Crowes and Corbett. Many times he eyed the bus driver with envy, wishing he could be planted behind the wheel of that yellow Bluebird. He wouldn't mind making minimum wage, nor would he complain about sedentary days spent driving ungrateful, loud kids around. It would be a pathetic life, about as anonymous and fulfilling as that of a tollbooth operator. If Charlie was a bus driver, he wouldn't feel the terror that made him quake all day and long into the evening. The fear followed him home after school. He spent each night lying in bed and thinking of how bad the last day was, and how horrible the next one would be.

He also fantasized about becoming the janitor, who preferred to be called a custodian. The man probably only had a high school education, if that. The high point of his day came when he went down to the basement, unlocked the boiler room, and sat in a metal foldout chair eating a banana. He walked outside after that, unzipped his one-piece chino jumpsuit, and smoked a menthol cigarette. He was a loser, maybe, but he was an invisible loser. He melted into the background when it came time for the bullies to select their prey for the day.

Charlie watched the old seniors power-walking on the red clay track sometimes. It was open to the community for exercise as a courtesy from Freeport High, provided there were no scrimmages, games, or practices going on at the time. He thought it would be worth it, if maybe a little too Faustian, to trade the next forty-five years of his life away and become a senior citizen right now. He could spend his days scarfing down early bird specials, power-walking in the afternoons, and bedding down at twilight after an episode or two of *Matlock* and a handful of pills from an orange pharmaceutical bottle.

There was no hope now though, either of moving to upstate New York or of some kind of *Freaky Friday* hypothetical body switcheroo. He already faked sick for about as many days as he could get away with at this point. He now found himself at school, at lunch with Johnny, and eating a little plastic package of Dunkaroos. He selected one of the little graham kangaroos and dunked him in a miniature vat of icing, coating the cracker and then throwing it in his mouth.

He did an impression of an old-timey gangster when he next spoke to Johnny. "What'd you tell the fuzz yesterday, see?"

It was kind of a joke, Johnny knew, but also kind of not. He suspected maybe Charlie thought he told the School Resource Officer a bit too much. "That Edwin G. Robinson?" Johnny asked.

Charlie shook his head and submerged another of his Dunkaroos in a sugary swirl of icing. "Nope."

"Who?"

"Guess."

The cafeteria was louder than usual today. The racket caused by the voices was joined by some kind of drywall construction project going on. The hoplite warrior with his horsehair helmet was sandblasted off the wall, and the surface of the wall was now down to the gypsum board. The workers wore little white masks, and Johnny could see why. He coughed and wondered if it was possible for newer buildings to have asbestos in them. He turned back to Charlie. "Um, James Cagney?"

"Nope, but a little closer."

Johnny looked back over toward the workers. He had no idea what the hell they were doing. He only hoped they tore up the rest of this ugly-ass cafeteria after they finished over there. The walls here were made of vandal-resistant ceramic tile wainscot not fit for a bus station bathroom, and it made the competing voices of the kids sound like dogs baying out in the pound.

"I give up," Johnny said. He noticed Crowes flanked by what looked like every offensive lineman from the varsity team walking behind him. They had to be linemen because they were too bulky to be skilled position players.

"Paul Muni," Charlie said, only now Johnny wasn't listening. "From *Scarface*."

Johnny spoke absently to his friend, his eyes never leaving Crowes and his migrating formation of football players. "You watch all those old movies. I can't really get into them."

Crowes was forced to lay off Charlie in the natatorium shortly after the paint in Tom's office dried. He could still stare him down and intimidate him. He threw his voice when he saw Charlie in the halls shouting, "Tiny!" The word echoed off the cinderblock and found Charlie's ears. The last time Charlie did his beeline for the one-man bathroom in Tom's office, Crowes stood naked in the doorway of the locker room and shouted, "Warriors, come out to play-ay!" The laughter from the other boys draped in towels ricocheted behind the bully.

The Neanderthal shifted most of his fire to female victims of late, for whatever reason. Two girls in particular, Becky Wood and Martha Corbly, took up a lot of the time he used to spend on Charlie. The girls were close friends, and each ignored the flirtation coming from the pimpled strongman. Their close friendship and lack of sexual interest in Crowes were enough to get them classified as lesbians in the bully's book.

Johnny watched as Crowes literally walked right past Charlie Milner last Friday at lunch. The bully sidled up to the girls where they were busy applying jeweled constellations to one another's arms with body glitter. He splayed his pointer and middle finger, sticking his tongue between the split and lapping the webbing of his hand. It was the universal sign for cunnilingus. The dart of his tongue quickly retracted back into his mouth as if he were more asp than man. Then he said, "Something smells like fish," before walking off with his varsity crew in tow.

Johnny was embarrassed to admit it, but he hoped the girls continued to take the brunt of what Crowes dished out. At least Crowes stopped short of getting physical when he tormented girls. An icepack or two was required in the wake of his cruelty when he focused on a male victim.

Charlie was done with his Dunkaroos. He threw the plastic pack back into his brown paper bag, rolling that up into a little ball. He saw Johnny staring at something down the hall and looked with him. Then he saw Crowes. He stifled his own reaction as best he could, but Johnny still heard a gulp.

"You believe that old horror story about the boy who sat on the drain in the showers and got kicked out of school?"

"It's possible," Johnny said. That urban legend was floating around since freshman year. Some kid in the gym's communal showers supposedly wigged out one day and waltzed naked to the drain in the center of the room where all of the brown water and detritus filtered toward the grates. The drainage grating was already clogged with large clumps of ratty hair resembling seaweed. The boy in this tall tale promptly sat down and folded his legs under his body. He then shamelessly bathed in the dirty murk of his own private Ganges River.

"I heard they kicked him out of school," Charlie said. "Like a section eight in wartime or something." He thought about that. "Maybe I should shoot myself in the foot and get rotated back to the world."

He was joking but he couldn't laugh, because Crowes was getting closer. Hands gently slapped against both of their backs. Johnny felt the rustle of a piece of paper, on which he assumed someone wrote "Kick Me." They weren't being subtle though, if he actually felt the touch of their hand.

"Hey guys!" They turned. It was Jill Brentwood. Charlie smiled faintly. "Hey, Jill."

"I thought I'd give you guys some fuzzies." She grinned.

"What's a fuzzy?" Johnny tried to reach for the little Post-It stuck in the small of his back, but he couldn't get it. He felt his rotator cuff smart from the effort of trying to grab it off his back. Charlie grabbed onto his friend's back and handed Johnny the piece of paper. Johnny looked at it. It said, "You are awesome!"

"Fuzzies are little notes you leave on people to make them feel warm and fuzzy inside."

"Thanks, Jill," Johnny said. He wasn't sure what to do with the fuzzy now that he had it. He reached over to Charlie's back and pulled the piece of paper off him.

"What's it say?" Charlie asked. He sounded a bit serious as if it was SAT results and not a Post-It with a platitude written on it.

"Looks like we're both awesome."

"You are," Jill said. "Don't forget it."

"Good luck today," Johnny said, not looking in her eyes.

"Thanks!" She beamed once more and walked away from them. They turned to watch her go down the hall. She moved in the direction of the trophy case, underneath an outstretched white banner urging students to make Paul Bugler Class Treasurer. Jill adjusted the straps of her sports bra beneath her cheerleading shell, and furtively corrected a wedgie riding beneath the skirt of her outfit. Her hips were just wide enough for her expanding waist to balloon out a shade beyond hourglass form. Her figure made her skirt billow like the head of an umbrella beneath her, as she walked. Johnny thought her too much woman for Corbett, even though she was only a sixteen year-old girl.

Johnny contemplated crumpling up the fuzzy once she was out of sight but decided to pocket it instead. Charlie followed suit and asked, "Good luck with what?"

"Some kind of varsity competition going on or something. Everyone's talking about it."

"Yeah, I saw they folded the basketball hoops up into the ceiling in the gym."

Johnny shared homeroom with Jill. She was in an intense, heated conversation with another cheerleader this morning. She said that if those kids from Anderson tried to do a two and one-half high pyramid, she would pull out her regulation book and show the judges *exactly* where it was written in black and white that such formations were not approved by the bylaws. Those pyramids were legal for university-level teams, but not high school.

"Oh, shit on whole wheat toast." Charlie said. Johnny looked up, but it was too late. Crowes was right there flanked by his posse. Johnny and

Charlie were still sitting, and since Crowes stood, their eyes were level with his crotch. His cock bulged from his pants like a pair of rolled up tube socks.

"Nice going, faggot," Crowes said.

Charlie looked straight ahead with the determination of a Buckingham Palace guard. Crowes said, "I'm not even going to have to bother with bullying you anymore. This whole fucking school, no, this *whole fucking town*, is going to hate your faggoty ass pretty soon."

"'Faggoty' is not a word," Charlie said, still not looking over. "Type it into Microsoft Word and I'll bet the little red squiggly lines show up underneath it."

"You've got jokes, but I've got a little riddle for you. Want to hear it?"

Charlie didn't answer him. "What happens when a kid sets a fire that causes the adults to decide all minors need a ten p.m. curfew on weekdays, and a midnight curfew on weekends? Want to guess?" Charlie was still silent, still staring forward. He looked at the far wall of gypsum board from which clouds of dust continued to waft.

Crowes leaned onto the table, reaching across Johnny as if he wasn't there. He put his face in Charlie's face. "Everybody knows you lit that fire, faggot. If you think you're not popular now, just wait until next week, when the curfew goes into effect."

Charlie turned now, and they were close enough for the cilia in their nostrils to intertwine. "I've already bottomed out in terms of popularity. I can't go down any further." He looked away from Crowes whose breath was intensely fetid. "I may be in the gutter, but I'm looking up at the stars."

Crowes removed his body from the table and stood back up. His goons were watching him for a reaction. Their eyes darted nervously. They couldn't exactly follow the thread of the conversation but they somehow feared their leader was losing. If he kept up the verbal sparring, it might only get worse. He would need to switch to fisticuffs soon if he wanted to turn this damn franchise around.

"Who said that?" Crowes asked, of the quote Charlie just reeled off. "Some faggot like you?"

"Actually, I think Oscar Wilde was a homosexual, so …"

Crowes banged the table with the anvils he made of his hairy fists. The food of all the kids nearby danced and rattled on the Formica tabletop. "I got news for you, Charlie. Your faggotry didn't hurt Gentleman Jim one bit. He got a big insurance payout."

Charlie looked over at his friend who was enjoying his relative invisibility up until this moment. "I told you Corbett torched that place for the insurance money."

The whole formation of football players stirred as if goosed by a cattle prod. Most of the jocks thought Gentleman Jim was the best thing to ever happen to this town. Here was Charlie, not only badmouthing him, but accusing him of a crime.

"What about you rump ranger?" one of Crowes' crew asked. Johnny turned and realized the guy was talking to him. "You two take turns going from tight ends to wide receivers?"

Laughter rippled through their ranks. Crowes glanced down at Johnny with a revelatory twinkle in his eye. Johnny escaped his sadism all of these years for no good reason that he could think of now. He now had a new target, thanks to the intercession of the jock behind him. Charlie was used to the abuse, and maybe Crowes with his double-digit IQ realized he was getting diminishing returns on that front.

"Who pitches and who catches in this relationship?" Crowes asked Johnny, who now struck the same eyes-forward profile as his friend. "I mean, who's packing whose fudge. Who is exploring whose Hershey highway?"

Johnny wondered how many euphemisms there were for sodomy. He also wondered who came up with them, and why. *Probably not gay guys*, he decided. "Fuck you," Johnny said, "You ugly piece of shit."

"What?" Crowes looked genuinely confused.

Charlie stood up. "He said, 'Fuck you, you ugly piece of shit.' I heard him perfectly."

Crowes looked at Charlie, smiled so that the vulgaris scars on his face shimmied, and grew luminescent as fish scales. "You know, man, maybe you should do like your older brother and blow your brains out."

Johnny glanced at Charlie, who inhaled deeply and then spoke. "I'm going to kill you." He walked forward, so they were nose to nose again. Neither of them moved once they were within kissing distance. "I don't mean that figuratively, like 'Man, we killed Anderson in that game last night.'" Charlie took another deep breath. "No, I mean I'm going to take your life, even if it costs me mine, or if I have to spend the rest of my life in jail. I'm going to make sure you die." He paused. "How does that make you feel?"

The nostrils of the bully's nose expanded and contracted, like those on a snorting bull, readying to charge a matador. Johnny felt a punch materializing in Crowes' arms, gathering shape like a storm and hovering. He thought this feeling must be similar to the sixth sense an infantryman developed after several traumatizing mortar attacks. He doesn't even need to hear the whistle or watch the tracer of some flaming projectile striating through the air. He just knows a mortar is coming.

Johnny felt that punch. He even saw the biceps, those fontanels crowning on Crowes' arms, quaking as the bully bunched his fists. He imagined Crowes was thinking about cracking the smartass hard enough in the face for him to need wires in his mouth, and a liquid diet for the next few months.

Johnny and Charlie felt it as Crowes allowed his steroid-infested muscles to slacken, as he calmed and a plot formed in his own head.

Charlie just threatened his life really and truly. Crowes felt it just as much as they sensed his phantom punch. Now he needed to retreat and regroup. He definitely needed to talk to Alex, and maybe even Mr. Corbett himself. They needed to discuss this crazy-ass freak, this psycho. They would have to do something about this loser who set a neighborhood on fire and was now walking around threatening peoples' lives.

Crowes nodded at a question no one asked. He glanced once at Johnny and made a bit of far more intense eye-contact with Charlie. He stared at the boy who just crossed some kind of line, went from victim to potential threat. "I'll see you later."

"Your mother sucks dick like Van Camp's makes pork & beans."

That punch grew inside Crowes again, and then receded like the tide under the force of the full moon. He turned from the table and walked away with his soldiers trailing behind him. Their lettermen bombers bunched around their muscled bodies as they hunched over and nursed the wounded pride of their leader.

Charlie looked over at Johnny, smiled, and said, "That went well."

***

The latest scandal came from the unlikeliest of places. At least, it was one of the unlikeliest quarters, since word of misdeeds from the Asians or the Jew Crew would be even more unbelievable. Bandies tended not to get in much trouble either.

"Yep," one of the AV kids said. "They got caught performing oral sex out by that big forty-foot trailer they have over there in the parking lot."

Someone fiddled with the dimmer board. The forest drop on the stage behind them darkened, shrouding the painted elms in shadow. "Quit that," the AV kid said to whomever was playing with the board. "Do the light cues as they're written."

"Do they know who it was?" Johnny asked. Charlie was less interested. He held a torn and strange smelling T-shirt in his hands for reasons he didn't disclose to his friend or anyone else.

"They might know," the AV kid said. "I don't. I just got the general scuttlebutt on my way over to the theater here." He shrugged. "I know about as much as you two."

"Well, it couldn't be that big a deal," Johnny said. "They still had practice."

"Yeah, they've got some kind of big show coming up."

Johnny saw the spectacle on the football field on his walk over here after the last period of school ended for the day. The Bandies arrayed themselves into some kind of snaking formation while the drum major waved his wand from the elevated podium. There was a golf cart covered in foam trailing crimson and gold streamers in its wake beside the platform on which the drum major stood. The cart looked ready for the Macy's Thanksgiving Day Parade.

The major himself was dressed a little more ostentatiously than usual, wearing what looked like a hussar's pelisse instead of his regular vest. He was also crowned in something that looked like a pope's miter.

"Where's Mr. Grooms?" Alice asked. She appeared in their midst without Johnny noticing, and he tried to suppress the anxiety that rose in him when she showed up with no warning. He liked to prepare himself before seeing her.

"Probably grading papers," Charlie said. He twisted the T-shirt in his hands as if it was a towel with which he was preparing to whack someone on the buttocks. "'I have one-hundred and fifty students. That means if I only give out one writing assignment per week, and I'm only spending ten minutes grading each paper, that's …'"

"'Twenty-five hours a week,'" Alice said. She laughed as she interrupted his impression and finished it. "You do a better Grooms than I do."

"I'm not just stagecraft. I'm a topflight mimic too."

Johnny glanced down at the latex baby she cradled to the red velour of her Hester Prynne costume. The doll had the dimensions of a small wooden log. She noticed him looking and said,

"Yeah, they wouldn't let us use a real rug rat, even though I had the perfect one for them."

"You had a baby?" The AV kid asked.

She groaned and rolled her eyes. "Oh, great, the rumor mill churns yet again." She sighed and a lock of hair not imprisoned in her bonnet fluttered free. It turned gold in the light.

"No," Alice said. "My sister just had a kid, and he doesn't even cry. At least, I've never heard him whining."

"Too bad Hester doesn't have any pregnant scenes," Charlie said. "The FX book has a lot of different ways to do baby bumps I want to try out. They also work for potbellies, too."

"Yeah," Johnny said. "If you wore a bump around school, you wouldn't have to worry about guys hitting on you all the time."

"I don't know." She rocked the fake baby in her arms, some sort of maternal instinct startled to life by her playacting. "My sister said guys hit on her all the time when she was pregnant, more than usual."

Charlie walked to the forest backdrop and touched it lightly. The soft canvas rippled a bit. "What do you think?" he asked Johnny.

"It's cool, but I like the big, old-fashioned moveable scenery."

"Those are a bigger hassle," Charlie said. "A lot of the best shows didn't even use backgrounds or sets in times past. Shakespeare didn't use any scenery for his plays."

"Bull."

"No bull." Charlie touched the forest drop behind him one last time so that it billowed like a sail under a light wind. He walked back over to Johnny, and unwound the shirt he was ringing. "You know Bram Stoker?"

"Yeah, he wrote *Dracula*."

"He spent most of his life in the theater, working with this English stage actor Henry Irving." Charlie crouched down and laid the T-shirt on the wooden apron of the stage. He spread the damp shirt out before him, and that musty oregano odor increased in intensity. "There was a scene painter he worked with named Harker."

"That's where Jonathan Harker came from?" Alice asked.

"Right." Charlie reached in his pocket. "Stoker buried all kinds of Easter eggs like that in his writing."

He removed the long-stem lighter from his pocket, and they all stood back. Alice shielded her ersatz baby from whatever Charlie was about to do.

"Hey man," the AV kid said. Johnny wasn't sure, but he thought the lighter Charlie held was the same one he used to set those house frames on fire. His friend didn't tell him what he did with the evidence, whether he burned or buried it. Maybe it was languishing at the bottom of a pile of clothes in the closet of his bedroom. He personally thought it best to remain in the dark, and that the less he knew, the better.

"You're not allowed to set things on fire," the AV kid said.

"I'm not setting the shirt on fire." Charlie waved the wand of flame over the shirt. "I'm proving the shirt's fire-retardant, virtually *fireproof* at this point."

The kid shook his head. "You're not even allowed to bring lighters to school, man."

"I'm stagecraft," Charlie said, as if that meant anything.

Johnny thought this was stupid. If even a mongoloid like Crowes suspected him of setting that fire, then the word was out everywhere. Pulling a stupid stunt like this would only reinforce the idea that he was the firebug.

Charlie didn't care. His face glowed in the reflection of the fire spurting from the head of the lighter as he waved it over the shirt, which still didn't do so much as smoke. That myrrh scent became more powerful, with an earthy smell of dunnage and straw.

"What's that smell?" Alice asked. She was apparently less protective of the baby now and dangled it in her right hand.

"Alum," Charlie said. "I got it from my mom's spice rack."

"It smells strange," she said. "Not bad, just weird."

"It has its uses. It decomposes in heat. When it does that, it lets go of these gases that dilute the more volatile ones, which …"

"That's it!"

Mr. Grooms' high-trebled voice shrieked from behind them. He had perfect diction and was a Royal Academy of Dramatic Arts graduate Freeport High went out of their way to acquire. He always spoke as if there was more than a slight chance every word he said might be recorded for posterity. He spoke to Charlie now. "You have been of much assistance to this program, but I'm afraid your services are no longer needed."

Grooms gathered the soft end of his Attenborough beard in his right hand. He pointed with the fingers of his left hand toward the theater doors. "Go!"

Charlie removed his finger from the lever of the long-stem lighter. He placed it back in his pocket, and then wadded the shirt up with his other hand. He stood, and looked around at the AV kid and Alice for some support. The AV kid looked at his shoes, and Alice's eyes were downcast, focused on the docile face of the plastic infant in her arms.

"Convenient," Charlie said, gritting his teeth. He stood a full head taller than the diminutive drama teacher. "Getting rid of me after I did all of this work."

Mr. Grooms took a step back and nodded. Johnny felt sorry for him. He wasn't a bad guy. "I want to reiterate that you have been a great boon to this troupe, and I will make sure that the playbill reflects your contribution to the utmost." Grooms pointed toward the illumined "Exit" sign again. "I am giving you an ultimatum. Either you leave peacefully now, or you leave me no recourse but to get the SRO. I'll have to tell them you brought a lighter to school and were using it on stage."

Charlie jumped off the stage, his feet planting on the cold, hard tile of the auditorium's floor. He stormed off without looking back once. Johnny followed him, leaping from the apron and running past the rows of darkened seats.

"Charlie!" Johnny's voice echoed in the dark canyon formed by the high walls of the auditorium. "Wait, man!"

Johnny was sure that theater was pretty much all Charlie had left. If he lost that, then he lost everything. That would make it that much easier for him to make good on his threat to kill Crowes, or to hurt himself or otherwise get into some serious trouble. Johnny ran, but his friend ran even faster. Johnny walked out into the sunshine that always hit him like a flickering aurora after being in the theatre for any length of time. Charlie was nowhere in sight.

He wasn't at school the next day either.

CHAPTER FIVE

He walked to his friend's house after school on Tuesday. He usually took the bus home since he never faced the same harassment as Charlie. He suspected Crowes and his crew might lavish a bit of attention on him here soon after that lunchroom incident. *What will they make fun of me for? I'm not fat, or effeminate so they'll have to try a little harder than usual.* They could no doubt get creative when the situation called for it.

This part of town looked different since the last time he came through here on foot. The sidewalks were still lined with shade trees, gathered clusters of lindens and elms. He fantasized about a guileless afternoon spent here with Alice. He saw himself holding her hand and walking underneath the warm green trees. They'd talk about their future together and the children they might have.

She would make a good mother. She had her own ambitions and goals for the future too. They would hold off until after they both got through college and grad school before having their first kid. Maybe he would be a stay-at-home dad.

He looked down from the trees, which were the same and as beautiful as ever. He glanced at the houses around him, or the plots where the little houses were the last time he hoofed it through here. Some of those houses were no larger than dogtrots, but apparently they were still in the way and were torn down for that reason.

The teardown ran the entire length of the street he walked on. A sign planted in one of the yards confirmed his fears that the Corbett leviathan was spreading farther toward the historic center of Freeport.

There were a bit of wetlands, a reedy marsh serving as a barrier between the development of estate homes on the other side of the border, and this portion of Freeport. This part of town developed largely thanks to the VA home loans offered in the wake of the Second World War.

Johnny suddenly remembered what was being planned for these streets. There was some wrangling in town hall meetings and some flesh pressing at the Chamber of Commerce building. A rezoning took place after that, and Gentleman Jim got a sweetheart deal and permission to drain the everglades. Then he was to dredge the runoff from the mire to create a manmade lake. The Corbett crews would then construct roads and footbridges, linking his Garage Mahal properties to land where he intended to build what he called cottage models and townhomes.

Mrs. Milner's Volvo was parked in the gravel driveway. Johnny could see some of the lights on in the house, through the bay window. There were very few signs of activity other than the soft glow.

The garage door was open, and he walked inside. The cement floor was stained with a thousand drips of spilled motor oil. The garage was cold as a grotto, and he wondered why Charlie's mom left the door open this late in winter. He quickly wiped his feet on the straw mat, depositing a little mud from the treads of his Nikes. Then he opened the door to the house.

"Hello?" He looked around for Bowser. He listened for the jangle of his tags, before remembering the dog was long-since dead. "Charlie? Mrs. Milner?"

"He's out back." Mrs. Milner was in the living room, standing before a candy dish on an end table and ashing her Pall Mall into it. She didn't look over at Johnny, but rather kept her eyes on the mantle. It was empty except for a fine coat of dust on its wooden surface.

"Out back?" It didn't make sense. They were too old to spend much time in the backyard.

She turned around. She looked at him now, or at least looked over his right shoulder at the terrifying apparition she saw in the corner of every room she haunted. Her careworn features made it look like she was aging in time-elapse. The agony in her eyes gave the impression she was eighteen years-old less than an hour ago, and was now forced to wither away as punishment for some vain notion she cherished. She was a princess in a fairytale whose comeuppance was due.

"He's in the treehouse," she said as she let out some smoke.

Johnny turned from her, and ran across the linoleum of the kitchen floor past the mudroom. He headed through the door to the garage, and out toward the gathered trees looming above him and below the gray sky. It was some time since he was last in the backyard. It would make more sense for everything to strike him as smaller now, since he was older, but the impression he got produced quite the opposite effect on him. The trees looked bigger and taller. He didn't need to split them and gaze on the rings to know they would yield true heartwood if they were ever logged off. It might come to that if Corbett's developments encroached any farther.

He walked on a few more paces and was reminded of why they stopped playing here, besides the obvious reason that they got older and the videogames kept getting better.

That stream smelled like shit. It had always been malodorous, but it was now even more fetid than he remembered it. The usual sulfurous smell comingled with a putrid musk of decay that made him gag as he walked back toward the treehouse.

He looked up toward the canopy over him. The branches formed spirals reminding him of the tunnels the Spartan cheerleaders made with their arms and spirit fingers, through which the players would run onto the field one at a time. The names of the players would be called as they jogged through the underpass formed by the tanned arms of Jill Brentwood and her teammates. The roar of the crowd always grew loudest when Alex Corbett, the star quarterback, took his place in the center of the huddle. The incessant cheers were usually counterpointed by the ringing of the bell that sounded whenever Freeport scored a touchdown.

The treehouse was in damn good repair, considering it hadn't been maintained in many years. The shiplap siding and cedar shingles survived termite infestation altogether. The thatching and bamboo didn't fare quite so well. The roof of the hut was frayed, looking like a bird's nest raided by a predator swooping down to steal eggs in its talons.

Johnny scaled the wooden ladder to the Tiki fortress. He wondered what the hell he was going to find. He knew after he happened on Mrs. Milner smoking and ashing into that candy dish, that whatever he found, it would not be good.

He halted on the final step of the ladder, and looked at Charlie's body. The Luger pistol was in his friend's right hand, and several pieces of paper were clutched in his open left palm. The hole in the front of his head was small, no bigger than the little wax and putty gunshot wounds Charlie used to create with his tackle box full of stagecraft gear. A light dribble of blood trickled down his forehead and into his open mouth.

Johnny coughed. Something in here was searing his lungs worse than his first experimental puff on a cigarette in junior high school. He remembered that day well, standing with Charlie out back behind the Lanes. They shared a square and watched the SUVs blur past the gas stations and fast food restaurants.

He climbed the final step of the ladder into the treehouse and sat beside his friend's body.

"You asshole." He lowered his head and then shook it. He thought of those days back at

Freeport Kindergarten in Ms. Seever's class. The children had mailboxes made from half-gallon milk cartons sliced in two and hung over the door in a shoe caddy serving as their mail center. They left each other handwritten notes and crayon-smudged drawings something like two or three times per day.

Johnny didn't cry now. He was too angry for that. He thought about Robbie for a moment and the trouble he went through on their behalf one Halloween. He thought of how Robbie carefully climbed the ladder with his hands full, depositing a plastic cauldron on the floor of the treehouse.

"Close your eyes, or this won't work."

Charlie and Johnny obeyed, turned off the policeman's Maglite they previously brandished like a light saber, or held under their chins to turn their faces into fleshy jack-o-lanterns.

"Here are the eyes of the dead man." They ran their fingers through the plastic witch's kettle filled with squishy peeled grapes, squirming with disgusted delight as they passed their hands over them. "Here is an ear."

Johnny thought he smelled one of Mrs. Milner's dried apricots as the supposed severed ear fumbled through his fingers, but he still smiled and loved Charlie's older brother for doing this for them.

He looked around the room now, no longer able to ignore the smell. The place was a virtual mad scientist's laboratory of beakers and separatory funnels dusty with powders and chemical residues.

What the hell, he wondered, *has my friend been up to, and why didn't I have any inkling about it?*

It was natural for Mr. Milner to be in the dark about whatever Charlie was doing here. Russell lived over on the other side of town. It also made a certain amount of sense for Charlie to be able to deceive his mother, as she walked around in an impenetrable fog these days. Johnny felt embarrassment and a little surge of anger when he thought of how Charlie played him like this. He'd played him up until this very moment. Since he killed himself, the fucker got the last word. Even worse was that Johnny was now alone in the world and friendless because Charlie was his only one true friend.

There was a group of kids at school dubbed the "Floaters." They were friendly with multiple cliques and could pass from table to table in the lunchroom. They'd find themselves given a warm reception, but they could never remain comfortably at any one table for long. The regulars would always spend a good amount of time talking about what they did last weekend or what they were doing this upcoming Friday when the floater in question would be absent.

Maybe now that his best friend was dead he might have no choice but to float. He would float through high school and maybe float through the remainder of his life. He stared at the gun in his friend's hand and briefly thought about blowing his own brains out. He wondered if maybe that would be a good way to get revenge on Charlie. *Revenge for what?* There was no answer to the question he asked himself.

He looked at the gun, contemplated picking it up and taking it to school tomorrow. He would find Crowes and blow the bully's head off and then maybe turn the gun on himself. That would be a bit more dramatic than pulling a double suicide up here in the treehouse.

His eyes left the gun and Johnny returned his gaze to the whole of the room. There were quite a few cooking apparatuses stolen from Mrs. Milner's kitchen: a Teflon-coated cookie sheet, a turkey baster, as well as some nichrome wire. The heating element from the toaster was unraveled on the floor of the treehouse. That explained why Charlie stopped eating toasted Pop Tarts awhile back.

There was a college-level organic chemistry textbook, some generic antifreeze and potato starch, as well as a condenser and hotplate. It also looked like Mr. Milner and Freeport Fertilizer made their unintended contribution to Charlie's clandestine science project as well. There was some glass wool and some Green Thumb, in addition to a hefty sack of Rigo's Best stump remover.

A moleskin diary with a soft paisley cover caught Johnny's eye. The pages were filled to the margins with frantic ballpoint scribbling, as if Charlie was a Romantic poet composing sonnets and not someone working out the details of some combustible and deadly work. Johnny walked over to the notebook and read.

*11-3-97- Multiple batches can be run,
provided one is going through purification and
another is in the reaction vessel. Oh, the word online
I got from the ex- EOD guy from Robbie's unit says
you can get good quality Nitromethane from hobby
shops. It's used in model airplane fuel. The
glycerin's easy as marching down to the local
pharmacy.*

Johnny set the notebook down, and looked
around the room. The letter in his friend's hand was
the next thing he needed to look at, but he didn't
want to read it. He moved away from the notebook
and toward the letter, kicking over a tube of bathtub
caulk lying next to an opened package of baby
laxative. Glass shards from a Mr. Coffee pot
crunched under his feet. He kicked the glass, as well
as a vacuum hose attachment, from his path. He

leaned down and picked up the lined paper torn from a college-ruled notebook.

The letter said: *Hey, man. I hope you find me first, Johnny, and not that fucking dime store detective. You know, I don't know what he talked with you about-I'm sure you didn't rat, thank man!- but he gave me a lot of Freudian psychobabble about how I jerked off at the scene of the fire .He even tried the old scared straight routine on me, showed me a picture of some Future Farmers of America-looking kid who decided to have his first cigarette in his daddy's barn. The poor hick ended up toasting himself and burning the barn down. Then he showed me that one picture of the thumbless kid who held on to the M-80 for too long. If he was trying to scare me, he probably should have showed me those photos before I saw those pics that Robbie brought back from the sandbox.*

Anyway, to make a long story short, I decided to blow my brains out, but I told Crowes I'd kill him. I didn't want to make a complete liar out of myself, so I snuck into school and planted a bomb. I did it around 6 p.m. on Monday night. I programmed the stopwatch to blow her up around noon on Wednesday. That gives you some time to find the bomb and get it safely away from the school, assuming you find me in time and I did my homework right and it doesn't detonate early, late, or not at all. Maybe you want to try to defuse that bitch by yourself.

He flipped the letter over to the backside of the loose-leaf sheet. It was now Tuesday afternoon.

That left him a little bit less than twenty-four hours to act. That was plenty of time to call the cops. He would tell them to close the school, and the bomb squad would sweep through and find the explosive. Did Charlie really think he was going to play his stupid game? There was no way he would take Charlie up on his stupid invitation in life, let alone after he passed through to the other side and wasn't able to come back to force his friend to do jack shit.

He read on: *You might be inclined to call the cops rather than find the bomb yourself. I understand that. You need to understand this, though. You've been my sidekick, my sidecar even, for the last few years. Honestly, we've never compared standardized tests, but I bet I've got you beat by a standard deviation or two. I think it's time for you to prove yourself. I think you need to prove yourself my equal, as much for your sake as for my own. To do otherwise, would be, in the words of the estimable Mike Crowes, an act of sheer faggotry.*

I think you owe me that. I've been generous with you. I've shared everything with you. I shared my toys when we were little, my videogames when we got older. I shared my house, my little fertilizer fortress where my dad sells sod to the golfers. I shared my brother with you, and my sister- That's right, I always knew you had a thing for her!

Johnny jumped back, startled, as if Charlie was right behind him. It was as if Charlie got the drop on him and was about to apply a chokehold to the back of his neck. He looked over at the body just to reassure himself his friend was still dead. The body was where it was a moment before. It was as lifeless as ever, but Johnny still shivered. He felt Charlie come alive in the letter, his fingers trembling as his friend's spirit wafted in one window and then out the other one of the treehouse.

Anyway, I've left you a map that tells you exactly where the bomb is if you're smart enough and ballsy enough to figure it out. 'X' marks the spot, landlubber.

Johnny flipped to the last page, turning to the last bit of writing his friend left him. He wondered if this message from beyond the grave counted as a suicide note. It was more like instructions, or a last will and testament. Only it was the teenaged version, since Charlie didn't have much of an estate to bequeath. Charlie didn't even live long enough to lose his virginity or get his first car.

There would be no college for him, Johnny realized, no future as a topflight FX man. He would never carry on the work of Rick Baker, using his bladders and hydraulics and shunning CGI.

P.S. Careful with that mother! That plastique has a detonation rate of eighty-eight hundred meters per second. It's more powerful than C-4. Poor mama didn't know what Charlie was keeping in her freezer. Also, if you start seeing red gas leaking from the bomb, try to get downwind and fast!

Oh, P.P.S. Good luck with Alice. Yeah, I noticed that too!

That was the end of the letter. He set it down, looked once more at his friend's body. He felt rage rising in him, growing into a boiling ball of hate in his chest. He scaled down the ladder, taking the wooden logs two at a time and jumping to the leafy ground when he was halfway down.

He was going to do it. Charlie was not only manipulating him from beyond the grave, but he was piloting him like one of his little fighters in an arcade game. No, he was also forcing Johnny to choose, to make him accept his pride was worth risking the lives of the several hundred children at that school. He would accept the challenge just to prove his friend wrong, to beat him at this game.

That was what the kids at school were, he thought, children. Charlie finally crossed a line. He was willing to kill children. It would be better, even justifiable, for him to waltz into school with his dad's Luger and plant a slug in Crowes' pimple-covered mug. He didn't do that though. Instead he conscripted everyone else into his nightmare, even the silly cheerleader who wrote a fuzzy and patted it onto his awesome back.

The smell of the bilious creek filled his nostrils again. He took a cigarette from his pocket and lit up if only to drown out the stink and to fill the air with the richer aroma of tobacco.

Johnny looked back toward the house and the open garage. He saw Mrs. Milner watching him through the bay window, smoking as she stared. She would be no help. He looked back toward the water's edge and the spinous cluster of devil's walkingstick reaching toward him with its briery points bared and ready to stab.

Maybe it was the smell that provided the clue but he suddenly he knew where the map was. *Landlubber, 'X' marks the spot.* Charlie may be able to beat him on standardized tests, but he underrated his friend's intelligence if he thought those clues weren't enough for Johnny to unriddle the mystery.

Mrs. Milner watched him as he streaked toward the garage and ran over to the rack where the power tools sat. He picked up the shovel and jogged with it back in the direction of the treehouse. Janet Milner walked outside, the ash on her Pall Mall as long as the shed skin of a small garden snake.

"What are you going to do? Bury him in the backyard?" There was an amused lilt in her cigarette-scarred voice.

"Go back in the house."

He walked to the creek's edge with the shovel, and there he saw with his own eyes what his nostrils told him. The runoff from Charlie's little experiments was floating there. Discarded cherry-toned antifreeze fluid swam in the water along with chunks of pumice and paraffin his friend stole from the custodian at school. The detritus and slime swirled through the stagnant, brackish water in which several fish were belly-up. They stank as they rotted and decomposed.

Johnny stabbed the cold earth with the point of the spade, started digging. He knew he was in the right place, in the spot where Robbie buried the chest. Some of the features of this backyard changed, but that boulder upholstered in spongy lichen was where he remembered it being. It was planted directly in front of the spot where the treasure chest was buried all those years ago.

"Ahoy there, matey," he said, and his cold breath fogged the air in front of him. "Here there be doubloons."

He dug and threw clumps of dirt over his shoulder as he lifted them in the shovel, working his way closer to the antique walnut chest Mrs. Milner hated to part with so much back then. *Antiques Roadshow* didn't exist at the time. If it had though, he thought their chances of getting the chest away from the matriarch would be far slimmer.

The point of the trowel speared through the hardboard Masonite of the chest, slicing through a coat of glue that still smelled new and made him question the chest's status as an antique. The damage was done and it was truly too late for the appraisers, whether it was an antique or not.

He brought the shovel down again with the deliberate force of a gravedigger. The hardboard yielded and the walnut splintered. Chunks of wood flew in every direction, a little bit flecking his cornea and blinding him for the moment. He blinked rapidly and didn't care.

Smashing the chest open wasn't the most subtle approach, but it was the fastest and simplest way to undo the Gordian Knot Charlie tied for him. His brutal technique also made sense for the simple reason that he forgot, after all these years, whether or not they locked the treasure chest before burying it. He didn't want to waste time finding out. He reached his hand inside the chest, scattering the coins Robbie made with the jigsaw by slicing bits of dowel and spray painting them to give the illusion of gold.

Robbie, he said to what remained of Charlie in his mind, *committed suicide in style. He had as much reason, if not more, to hate the world, its governments, its leaders, and its lies. As selfish as his act arguably was, he didn't try take several hundred people down with him, or make a game of his suicide, you sack of Sakrete.*

He breathed, physically and mentally exhausted by everything that already happened today. His hands touched a piece of rustling paper, which he knew to be the map Elise made them from a brown paper grocery bag. He discarded that onto the bed of leaves behind him, and rummaged some more with his claws. His hands next latched onto a smoother piece of paper. This sheet was glossy, as planate as the sides of a diamond. It felt strange to his touch.

Johnny pulled it out, saw it was a schematic map of Freeport High School. He wondered where Charlie got it. He might have acquired it under some innocuous pretext, like a request on behalf of the drama department or something like that. Then again, maybe he just outright stole it.

Johnny unfolded the pleated sheet and stared. It was a black and white diagram, byzantine, complex, and intimidating. It was filled with ductwork and cross-sections, but the rooms were at least labeled. There was a circle done in yellow highlighter near the bottom of the sheet. There was also a crude arrow pointing to the boiler room and some words beneath that. *Bomb goes here*, Charlie wrote.

"Fucker." Johnny folded the map. He wasn't positive in his recollection, as he never had a reason to go near the basement. He thought he saw a lock on the boiler room door on his few trips to the basement. That would prove no obstacle to someone like Charlie, but it would take some doing for Johnny to get in there.

He needed to get in there to prove his friend wrong. It was his duty to save the lives of people who didn't like him all that much, were indifferent, or at best, allowed him to float toward their tables at lunchtime. He folded the map into squares, and looked back toward the water where the dead fish buoyed. Johnny finished his cigarette, field-stripped the paper, and threw the smoldering cherry into the murky water. Then he walked back in the direction of his home.

He had a couple of assignments to do tonight. There were some vocab exercises and a chapter of *A Separate Peace* to read, but that stuff would wait. There were more pressing matters weighing on his mind. He wondered whether or not everyone would die tomorrow. He also wondered whether or not there was a heaven and a hell, and if so, which one he would go to when he died.

CHAPTER SIX

The yellow Bluebird got stranded behind a car piloted by what Johnny's mother liked to call a "Taxi mom." Johnny invented a schedule for the hausfrau in the minivan. She drove Kyle to band practice once a week and took Kayla to soccer scrimmages three nights per week. Then later that same day, she chaperoned Skylar to guitar practice clear on the other side of town, blowing her whole evening and half a tank of gas in the process.

The minivan continued its snail crawl toward Freeport High. It switched lanes after the driver glanced in the rearview once and saw the Bluebird bearing down on its rear. Johnny looked out the window, dazed by the carbon monoxide exhaust and nervous because of the work to be done today. If he screwed up, at the very least his remains would be a finely scattered pile, fit for mulching. At worst, a hell of a lot of other people would die too.

He glanced through the smog-clouded window of the cheese. He saw that some of the quaint shops had been bought up, starting with the old pharmacy that once used a genuine zinc soda fountain. Now it was a coffee bar, where baristas jerked lattes whose smallest size cost more than a hot lunch at school.

The bus passed a few Corbett-constructed starter castles, and then made for the dedicated loop at school. It drifted slowly behind another bus and stopped in the drop-off area. The door hissed, and the students stood. They heaved their backpacks and moved like pack mules under their burdens.

Some of the Chronics wandered over from their recent smoke session by the gym mats in the woodland. The smokers' pit here was just as grungy as the one at the junior high. The potheads smiled, ensorcelled in sensimilla smoke and staggering red-eyed toward the brick entrance of the high school. "I'm high as tits," one of them said, to which his girlfriend replied, "Hey, my tits aren't that high, buster."

Johnny would join them on many a normal day, but he needed to be crisp and lucid to pull this off. There was no way in hell he could defuse that bomb, and he didn't want to try.

Priority one was to lay hands on a set of bolt cutters, and stash them in his pants. They were too large to fit in his backpack, and it would be dumb for him to try to walk through the halls holding them in his hands. When a student forgot the combination to their padlock, they were obligated to track down the custodian or go to the main office and have him paged. Then he would show up with the tool in hand.

Johnny veered right on the cement walkway, taking the path past the wooden gazebo and toward the gym. It was cold outside, and going through the athletic facility would warm him up. It also gave him a straighter route to the toolshed, saving him another thirty seconds or so in walking time. He still had plenty of time to get rid of the bomb, assuming Charlie knew what the hell he was doing with that stopwatch of his.

That bomb was just an experiment, he was convinced. He doubted Charlie ever built a time bomb before this one or fashioned a brick of homemade explosive. This was a tentative last bit of trial and error on Charlie's part before departing this world. Now Johnny was to be his guinea pig.

Largo's dull voice came over the PA system as Johnny opened the door to the gym. The principal sounded worse than Ben Stein in *Ferris Bueller's Day Off*, only Largo wasn't acting. "It has been brought to the attention of faculty and staff that the newest trend among students is to leave the price tags on items of clothing in order to show off how expensive said purchases are."

He paused, cleared his throat with a grunt that made Johnny think for a moment maybe he was choking. If he died, Vanhorseshit would take his spot, no doubt about it. The kids would eat it up, especially the jocks. He'd turn them all into bloodthirsty hoplite demigods before his tenure at Freeport High was done.

"If you can't behave like mature adults, maybe we'll put the kibosh on Abercrombie & Fitch, and American Apparel. Then we can all wear uniforms. Act like adults and be treated like adults, act like …"

Johnny ignored the principal, and looked up toward the high ceiling of the gym with his mouth open and his eyes wide. For a surreal moment it felt as if maybe God was hiding up there among the scaffolding and transoms. The wire mesh was draped like fishermen's nets over the scoreboards, ready perhaps to catch a miraculously multiplied school of trout.

It looked like cheerleading tryouts were over. The large folding wall that slid on runners was pushed back into its stowage space, the retractable curtain bunched up like a squeezebox. The basketball hoops and backboards were also lowered back down to their default heights.

Johnny walked through the weight room, whose far door led out toward the track. Weight plates were stacked on a metal tree. Someone on the wrestling team left their foamy ear guard and competition singlet draped across the bench, where two-hundred and fifty pounds' worth of plates were stacked on the bar of the decline press.

A framed poster of Coach Vanhauser hung on the wall, draped slightly askew on a panel of brick accents. Johnny pushed the double doors to the outside open. He was grateful it was still dark in the early morning and that he wouldn't attract attention. The sickly sodium lamps poured their light over the parking lot, which was slowly filling up with the used cars of the teachers and the late models piloted by the richer, more fortunate students.

For a second, it looked like there was a gang of dwarves assembled on the field, maybe the little evil druids who lived beneath the sodded greens. They could be the monsters who summoned bullies from the bowels of Hell to torment a carefully chosen few for a four year inquisition with no right answers. They were only dummies though. They were the stuffed bags used for punters to train their toes. Additionally, there were also pads for the tackles, and fixed manikins arrayed like scarecrows on carbon fiber sleds. There were orange cones laid out for Carioca drills, which were the little practice exercises done to increase flexibility and foot movement. Crowes called the Cariocas "karaokes," and no one had the balls to correct him. Some of the other players laughed at him behind his back though, especially the skilled position ballers.

A wheelbarrow sat in front of the toolshed. Two bags of salt were stacked one on top of the other, held in reserve to melt whatever ice the remaining winter might unleash on them in the next month or so. Johnny walked inside the shed, and found the cutters on the shelf sitting next to several cans of DuPont paint. He picked the tool up, slid it down the inside of his pant leg, and draped his shirt over the exposed metal shears protruding up from his hipbone. He gripped the bolt cutters through the material of his shirt with his left hand and waddled back in the direction of the school.

He knew his gait looked strange. If anyone asked, he would tell them he just really had to take a shit badly as was his early morning wont. Johnny shivered as he walked back through the gym using the same route he took to get over here. He got a hefty whiff of salty sweat in his nostrils as he returned to the weight room, where the perspiration of a thousand workout sessions kneaded its way into the fabric of everything. The whole chamber smelled like a giant armpit.

He walked back through the gymnasium and turned into the main corridor of the high school. The pandemonium of a hundred teenaged voices blasted from the cinderblock walls and reverberated across the floors. The students spoke as if they would never be able to talk again. It was as if they might go permanently mute when that first bell rang, instead of just having to just shut up for fifty minutes or so.

Certain voices reached his ear better than other ones, and he could even pick up bits of conversation here and there. "Maybe I should join the band," someone said. "Get a blowjob." So the fallout from the Bandies episode the other day was yet to completely blow over. It hadn't lost priority to that rumor about two girls being lesbians. There was also some grapevine gossip about a certain ninth-grade boy believed to be a little too light in his loafers. This was according to some Frosh Bitches, who were sure enough of his gayness to get a betting pool started.

"Jill, you look awesome today!"

Jill Brentwood acknowledged the praise with a faint nod to the ass-kisser. The girl didn't understand that trying too hard was the fastest way not to become a Popular. The only worse way for a girl to fail her popularity test was to bolo in her cheerleading tryouts. The girl who gave Jill the compliment turned to watch the star cheerleader walk on down the hall between the banks of lockers. Johnny watched as the girl looked after Jill. She stared at Jill as if she were a saint dispatching miracles to a flock of the afflicted, rather than just an acrobat who could do a mean logroll off a handstand.

He walked on down the hall. The floor went from tile to carpet beneath his feet as he got closer to the door leading to the basement. Alice headed toward him decked out in her Hester Prynne costume. Her empire waist pushed her bust upward in the manner of a corset. Alice Berryman didn't have large breasts, but that was another way in which Johnny thought he was not a normal or healthy, young red-blooded American. He didn't like breasts nearly as much as legs. He loved watching Alice's legs in the springtime, when her limbs were visible and she wore shorts. He loved the way the tan color of her legs matched her amber hair. He marveled at how her thigh muscles contracted and became defined and changed shape as she crossed her calves, one over the other. Her feet dangled and jittered while she turned the pages of her book and didn't even realize he stole glances. He sometimes grew brave enough to outright watch her, as intently as if this were her performance in a play and it was opening night. He wondered how the hell she remained so casual about being her.

"Are you trying to break the costume in or something?" Johnny stopped to talk to her, knowing the bomb could only wait so long. The vice-like jaws of the bolt cutters came open against his side, and the notched metal teeth were stinging the cold flesh.

"No," she said, and patted the pillow underneath her costume. "I just got tired of people talking crap behind my back."

"The rumor about you being pregnant?"

"Yeah, that one." She smiled and adjusted her cat-eye glasses. The black vintage specs made the blood rush to his heart again. They gave him that old feeling of memories before he was alive. He imagined that if he and Alice were to rush back to her house and make love in her bedroom, while listening to records from the time when their parents were young, then they might somehow literally time travel back a few decades and spend the rest of their lives there together.

Johnny patted the bump on her belly, soft as eiderdown and light as webbed gossamer. "Not bad."

"It's all right," she said. "Charlie could do better though."

Her mention of Charlie made him squirm. He hotfooted it for a moment, afraid she would read the fear in his eyes. He was afraid she would see it all. Alice would see Charlie dead in the treehouse, and see him heading to the basement with the bolt cutters. He looked into her luminous eyes and they were still twinkling, complimenting the smile she wore. He thought she didn't see his fear. Maybe girls couldn't read guys any better than guys could read them.

"Have you seen him?" Alice asked. "He hasn't been to school since Monday. At least, I haven't run into him."

"I got to go." Johnny dropped his eyes, sidestepped her, and walked down the hall. He came to the door leading to the basement. He pushed the door open, and glanced once back toward Alice. Then he walked down the cold steps into the basement. Sloped handicapped ramps ran along the corridor. They were his only company aside from the fluorescent fixtures crackling like bug zappers above his head.

He walked until he came to the door he recognized as being the one circled in highlighter on the map. This was the spot where Charlie planted the bomb before killing himself. Johnny dug the tool from his pants after a quick glance up and down the corridor. He gripped the handle of the bolt cutters, placed the teeth to the lock whose key only the custodian possessed, and he clamped down.

The metal of the lock bent and responded with give like melting taffy. He was almost all the way through when he felt a hand on his shoulder, accompanied by a voice that asked, "What the hell do you think you're doing?"

He eased his grip on the cutters and turned with them still in his hands, inadvertently backing the custodian up with the tool he held. He didn't intend to threaten anyone with the bolt cutters, but that was the way the janitor took it.

"You little shit! You stay right here! I'm going to go get the resource officer!" The custodian turned. Johnny adjusted his grip on the wooden handle of the bolt cutters so that he brandished the tool like a baseball bat in his clutches. He swung without thinking. A hollow sound rang out as the metal shears caught the janitor on the tip of his occipital lobe. Adrenaline did everything for Johnny he couldn't do on his own. He floated outside of his body and watched himself dole the prostrate janitor two more blows. The bolt cutters rained down on the poor man's head like illegal rabbit punches landing on the skull of a hapless boxer.

"Holy shit!" He reached down, and heard himself apologize to the unconscious custodian. He touched two fingers to the man's throat, felt a pulse there, and then turned back to the lock. It hung precariously by a last bit of metal, dangling there. Johnny looked up and down the sea of hallway around him one last time. Then he placed the slightly bloody teeth of the bolt cutters onto what remained of the lock. He clamped down and it relented easily as Swiss cheese. He opened the door.

The room rumbled with the sounds of multiple competing engines, a rotor whirring here and a motor groaning on the other side of some HVAC ductwork leading upward. Johnny knew jack about the school's heating system, whether or not it used central air or how its power was generated. He shared some creative joy in his friend's theater work, but the technical and pyrotechnical stuff was always Greek to him.

His eyes followed the boiler breeching, and then he glanced back toward the open door. He could see the hallway, and the feet of the sleeping custodian. He walked deeper into the boiler room. A blinking light, like that on a smoke detector, caught his eye. There was a tightly-packed Saran-wrapped package of what looked like flour taped there. The white powder was hardened and caked. On top of it was the blinking flashlight filament that first drew

his eye here. A nine-volt battery with wires attached

to it ran from the package down to the face of a

ticking stopwatch.

"Fucking A." Johnny walked toward the

length of pipe where the bomb was duct-taped. He

approached it carefully. His pace slowed even more

when he saw a little pouch of BBs hanging from the

side of the brick of improvised C4. The little metal

balls swung in a translucent sack that looked like

cheesecloth or sheer pantyhose. The pellets looked

to be the same kind Charlie used in his air rifle. The

sonofabitch rigged up an improvised claymore.

Johnny dropped the bolt cutters.

He peeled the duct tape from around the

bomb. He created his own baby bump as a little

show of solidarity with Alice, stuffing the plastique underneath his shirt. He walked back out into the hall. Johnny looked down at the floor where the janitor was a moment before. There were now only light flecks of blood on the tile leading away in a trail toward the nearest staircase.

Best, he thought, *to take the stairs on the opposite end of the hall*. He was aware as he ran that he might turn the thing into a proper bouncing Betty, if he kept banging it around. It banged up against his sternum, underneath his shirt, as he cradled it through the fabric with his hands.

There were few good options of which he could avail himself now. The plan was to climb these steps, making his way toward the front door of the building. Then he would waltz the bomb deep into the woods. The tree line began over by the smokers' spot. He'd carry the bomb to where gym mats were laid out and the Chronics recently enjoyed their traditional morning wake-and-bake session.

He reached the landing leading out onto the first floor. He started down the hall. The principal's office was the first room on his left. Largo's headquarters was a fishbowl of sorts. It was a glass structure built from demountable walls. The design allowed the head principal to watch students pass him in the halls, and for them to look on his mighty bank of monitors and PA equipment and quake with fright.

He spoke to his head secretary now, a homely woman with an ultramarine dragonfly stickpin affixed to the right breast of her double-knit

Cardigan. There was a phalanx of troll dolls arranged on her desk with lime green and bright pink hair and little gems for bellybuttons. Johnny was in that office several times. One time he went there to complain to the principal himself about the abuse Charlie was taking, and a lot of good it did. He saw on that occasion that the secretary's troll motif carried over into her choice of school supplies. She had a cupful of troll pencil toppers with rainbow hair, sitting below a couple of hideous Thomas Kinkade posters. One featured a babbling brook, and the other was of a glowing church.

The principal looked up at Johnny just as he passed the glass cage. Johnny ducked his head, and stroked the contours of the box held to his chest. He imagined the bomb glowing where it rested. He envisioned sunbeams shooting out of it in every direction, like from the heart of Christ in an Orthodox icon.

A detonation made him quake and he closed his eyes. He shivered and waited for the bright concussive flash, but it didn't come. A moment later he realized the rumbling he heard was not the sound of the bomb going off. It was rather several timpani players doing paradiddles on the loose skins of their drumheads with those furry mallets of theirs. Johnny briefly glanced into the band room, wondering whether the shame of the blowjob in the parking lot incident was already passed. Things looked returned to normal, at least for these Bandies.

The icy chime of someone doing scales on a xylophone barely carried from the top of the tiered floor in the room. The player made brief eye contact with Johnny before turning his attention back to a blackboard on which sheet music was arranged.

"Watch where the fuck you're going!"

Crowes was strong-arming a freshman, pushing him hard up against one in a series of lockers. Beyond the last of the lockers lay the door to the outside world, and freedom. Johnny recognized the bully's victim by sight, but not by name. He wore an eyebrow ring shaped like a dice. The trinket so far escaped Largo's gaze, and that of the various resource officers on the lookout for such contraband jewelry.

"I fucking hate when freshmen don't know where to walk. Have you ever driven on a road?"

"I'm too young to drive."

Crowes smacked him, and his protruding knuckles caught the boy on the unpierced eyebrow. His dice accessory struck Johnny as a good choice. He saw the boy in the cafeteria almost every day. He and several other role players spent their lunch period hovering over a Dungeons & Dragons core rulebook and tossing out a twenty-sided polyurethane dice.

"You ever *been* in a car when someone else was driving?"

The kid nodded, and Crowes squeezed his grip on the boy tighter. "It's just like that in the hallways here. You walk on the right. Got it?"

Crowes saw Johnny as he walked past. The bully looked at him, and away from the freshman. He grinned. His teeth were gritted the entire time he spoke. Johnny thought that if bullying ever got boring, Crowes could always try his hand at ventriloquism. "Tell Charlie he's fucking dead."

"I'm pretty sure he already knows that, but I'll tell him if I ever see him again."

A likely possibility, he thought, pushing the school door open. *I might be seeing him and Robbie, and Elvis for that matter, pretty soon if this thing happens to prematurely detonate before I can get it out into those woods.*

The cold air was liberating. It braced and invigorated him, and he drank it in. It made him dizzy. He felt as if he were high up in the Rockies and not living far below in among the low hills of southeastern Ohio. Coppery black oaks guarded the outer perimeter of the pothead retreat. Johnny walked into the secret refuge the trees provided, each of them standing like giant wooden watchmen. He imagined this was what it must feel like to steal away into the woods and lay with a woman who was not your wife, all those hundreds of years ago, to live in sin and bask in it. His mind left Hester Prynne and *The Scarlet Letter*. His thoughts wandered to what he considered to be a better and shorter Hawthorne work, *Young Goodman Brown*. The puritan must have passed through trees very much like these before leaving his wife and going to meet the devil on the road late one night.

Scaly acorns crunched underfoot. He was prepared to walk deeper into the woods. Johnny would find a sylvan pocket nestled in a meadow, and plant the bomb there beneath a heavy stump or within the shadowed recess of a hollow. A voice came from behind him. He knew it to be Officer Sandburg, the head SRO.

"All right, Johnny. You can set it down now."

He wondered if the janitor got to the man. Johnny expected to see a gun in the cop's hand when he turned. He was surprised to see Sandburg holding only his two-way Motorola.

"I …"

"I know you didn't plant it. We know Charlie did it."

We? Who the hell were we? Sandburg spoke into the radio. "Be advised, the explosive has been removed from the building. Do not, repeat, do not evacuate the school. Initiate lockdown protocol. The bomb squad will be here in five mikes."

"Copy that," a voice said through the static crackle.

Sandburg looked back at Johnny, who was beyond puzzled. "You did the right thing." He pointed at the bomb. "You did what you thought was right." Sandburg walked over to Johnny. He gently took the bomb from the boy's hands, and set it on the nearest semen-soaked gym mat.

The officer slung his arm around Johnny's shoulder and led him out of the woods. They headed back toward the parking lot, where SUVs and yellow Bluebirds basked in the sunlight under a cloudless winter sky.

"The right thing to do," Sandburg said, "would be to just tell us about the bomb from the beginning."

Johnny thought odds were good he hadn't seen the janitor yet. He figured he would at least face charges of assault when the smoke finally cleared and this mad day settled down.

Johnny stopped walking and shrugged the man's arm off his shoulder. "What are you doing?" Sandburg asked. "You need to get inside the school with the rest of the students. Then you need to remain under your desk until the bomb has either been defused or safely detonated. This is no time …"

"I planted that bomb."

"Johnny …" A cold edge snuck into Sandburg's voice, and his eyes smoldered with warning. "I know you probably get a lot of locker room lawyer advice from the other kids here at school. They tell you the law goes easier on juveniles, so commit crime while you're young, right? Get it out of your system?"

That hammy arm of his found its way to Johnny's shoulder again, only this time the grip was much tighter. "That's true, up to a point. You egg a house, maybe throw toilet paper over your neighbor's rose bushes on Halloween, and you'll get a slap on the wrist. This is different."

Officer Sandburg looked back toward the trees, and the bomb laying there. "This is the kind of thing that will affect your ability to get into your first choice college. You savvy?"

"I did it."

The officer squared himself to Johnny. He placed his right hand on the boy's right shoulder, and squeezed until Johnny's rotator cuff smarted from the force of the man's grip. "It's one thing to take the hit for your friend when he's facing time himself. Prison isn't in Charlie's future, though. He's dead."

Best now, Johnny thought, *to play dumb*. He tried to act surprised. "Dead? How?"

"He set himself on fire last night."

Now it wasn't necessary to pretend. He was surprised, as hell. "Fire?"

"I warned him," Sandburg said. Johnny thought he sounded a little smug. He broadcasted an "I told you so," with his eyes, a barely suppressed smile working its way across his face. Johnny wanted to punch him, but he knew that even a former athlete gone to pot was still more than athlete enough to beat his ass.

"He lit a cigarette, threw it in that bath of chemical runoff he dumped in the creek after he built the bomb. He set himself on fire, burned his treehouse down, and …"

"His mom?"

"She didn't get hurt since the firemen put the fire out before it got to the house. Janet Milner's a fifty-one fifty, right now." The man's radio crackled to life again, and he turned the volume down a little to speak with Johnny.

Several police cruisers appeared in the lot, along with a large bomb squad vehicle resembling an oversized ice cream truck. It lumbered along and stopped. A hydraulic-operated ramp distended from its side, flapping out onto the asphalt like a giant metal tongue.

"She's being held for observation. She was deemed a threat to herself or others. The firemen found her with a stomach full of three-hundred and fifty milligram Percocet when they came to put out that blaze."

"Jesus."

"She's all right. They pumped her full of charcoal emetic. She came through with flying colors, no worse for wear."

Something that looked like an alien rover rolled on its treads down the length of the ramp of the bomb squad truck. Two men in unwieldy suits and armored pads shuffled in their direction. The men were faceless underneath their ballistic helmets.

"Make or break time," Sandburg said. He released his hold on Johnny, trusting the boy would move toward the school of his own accord. If Johnny was smart, he would hide underneath his desk and forget about the bomb, forget about Charlie. "You've got nothing to gain by telling me you planted that bomb. And everything to lose." The SRO's eyes were overcast, lowering, waiting.

Johnny glanced over toward the red school building, then over at the bomb technicians and their robot plodding toward the spot where he stood. He looked at Officer Reggie Sandburg and said, "I planted that bomb."

"That's the way you want it."

It happened with the speed of a car accident. He heard a metallic clank and then the echo of the cuffs ringing in his ears. His hands were pinned behind his back and his shoulders were crying out from the force of the cop's sudden move. "You should know," Sandburg said, "There's no such thing as a zealous defense with minors." He walked Johnny in the direction of his white Crown Vic parked in a faculty spot next to a handicap space. "Your lawyer's job will not be to get you off, but to do what's in your best interest. They should try you

as an adult, since you wanted it this way."

"I just confessed, Jackass. Why would I care

about a zealous defense?" Sandburg pushed

Johnny's conjoined arms upward, and his shoulders

shrieked again. "Ow, you fucker!"

He felt good and numb now, like he might

never feel anything ever again. He was even with

Charlie now. Charlie thought Johnny would only

defuse the bomb, not take credit for his work. It was

stubborn and stupid to throw his life away like this.

Sometime between freshman orientation and today

though, it occurred to him that if life and the real

world were going to be anything like high school,

then life was not worth living, and the real world not

worth inhabiting.

He was certain now this good, numb feeling would last forever. He found himself proven wrong a moment later. This wonderful sensation of being totally detached didn't last as long as it took for him to make it to the backseat of the Crown Vic.

Hester Prynne defied the public address system, several teachers, and a resource officer or two, just to run outside and stand here. She ran so frantically across the lawn of the school that the pillow giving her the illusion of pregnancy fell from her midsection. It slid down her dress onto the lawn of the school.

She cried as she watched him being arrested, and that spoiled this whole suicidal act for him. If he was still human enough to make a girl cry on his behalf, then he was still far more human than he wanted to be.

The End